PARTY AT THE END OF THE RAINBOW

RONALD SCHULZ

Tumbleweed Books

Tumble through the pages of our books

PARTY AT THE END OF THE RAINBOW
RONALD J SCHULZ

Tumbleweed Books
Tumble through the pages of our books

Tumbleweed Books
HTTP://TUMBLEWEEDBOOKS.CA
An imprint of DAOwen Publications

Party at the End of the Rainbow / Ronald J Schulz
ISBN 978-1-998029-17-4
EISBN 978-1-998029-18-1

This is a memoir. Names, characters, places, and incidents are the product of the author's memory and recorded to the best of his ability to be actual persons, living or dead, businesses, companies, events, or locales recreated to the best of his ability. Permission to use legal names were obtained when possible. If permission was not received, the individual(s) name was changed.

Cover art by MMT Productions
Edited by Douglas Owen

10 9 8 7 6 5 4 3 2 1

EDITORS NOTE

This work contains descriptions of events that happened in the late 1960's and early 1970's, and are accurate from the viewpoint of the author. Due to this, some events may not fully coincide with recorded history of those events. This work also contains depictions of adult intimacy which may not be suitable for younger readers.

Throughout this memoir, there are excepts from news articles and pamphlets. In these cases, to maintain historical accuracy, no spelling or grammatical changes have been made to such articles.

This is for those too young to know,
those too old to remember,
and everyone in between.
You must live your dream,
not sleepwalk through life,
so get back up and do it.

1

REVOLUTION FOR THE HELL OF IT

Judge Saul Epstein cut me some slack, sentencing me to three years' probation to be served in Illinois, but I almost blew it when I asked for permission to leave the State to search for my missing girlfriend.

He reared back on his high throne. "Leave the State! No, young man, your sentence is to be served in the State of Illinois, and if I ever see you in my court again, you will regret it!"

Karen, an underage vagabond like me, was the love of my life. She had stuck by me on our epic journey through hitchhiker's hell from New York to Chicago, but we were homeless drifters, and she would be difficult to track down after so much time had elapsed. I could only hope that the fate that brought us together would reunite us again.

My arrest in the Weatherman rampage of October 1969 netted me a string of felony charges. Besides the usual mob action and resisting arrest, I had assault and battery and aiding an escape, which carried a higher bail than most of my fellow prisoners, however I was under eighteen with no priors, and after ten days in Cook County jail and four months in a mental hospital, my dad's lawyer convinced the court to reduce my charges to misdemeanors.

But why, you may ask, did I and so many of my peers join the Revolution? We were idealistic and believed in the promise of equality for all. Hypocrisy mired America and we, her privileged, runaway children, were born to set it right. Marches and sit-ins became desperate battles. Our cry for peace and love had become a fight for justice, an end to the neocolonial wars fought in our name against popular struggles for liberation around the world.

The news in 1970 was like a drum roll calling me to action. Throughout February and March riots erupted in Manila, targeting the US Embassy and the US backed Marcos regime. On February 26, five US Marines found themselves arrested for massacring Vietnamese women and children. On March 10, the military laid charges on Captain Medina and four others for the murder of hundreds of women and children at My Lai and other incidental rapes.

Whistleblowers who reported these crimes faced harassment and had their allegations denied by higher authorities, but it wasn't only hippies and leftists anymore. Middle-class straights and even soldiers revolted. *Vietnam Veterans Against the War* became ever more vocal about their experiences with war crimes.

Our post World War Two generation grew up squatting under our desks to prepare for a nuclear war that seemed inevitable, if not survivable. The World was in turmoil, and the Atomic Age put our species on the edge of extinction. We had to live with that, so gallows humor came naturally to us. Abbie Hoffman, founder of the Yippies, cried *Revolution for the hell of it*. That resonated with me and my like-minded friends. We were idealists, but we wanted some fun too before we died, whether in far off jungles, or on the hot streets of America. Keeping it light was a better recruiting tactic than the dry rhetoric of old school revolutionaries. We may as well have enjoyed the ride to the last stop and Skip Williamson captured the mood when he penned these immortal words into the mouth of his cartoon character, Phineas Freak.

"An' when yer smashin' th' State, kids... Don't ferget t' keep a smile on yer lips an' a song in yer heart!"

There was *hope in dope*, as the saying went. Dope, that is psychedelics, not the *death trip* of downers like heroin, appeared along with Eastern meditation as our generation's guide into the cosmic mysteries. Psychedelics became an important initiation into the growing hip counterculture, providing insights that helped us question those in authority over us.

Conservatives spread falsehoods about chromosomal damage and bad trips, or *freakouts,* which were frightening emotional reactions some of us experienced under the psychedelic influence. The journey could be a scary ride and required mental preparation. But those of us who confronted our interior demons head on opened the doors of our perception to a deeper understanding of our connectedness to each other and the cosmos. Cultural prejudices, the false presuppositions we had grown up with, needed to be reexamined for our spiritual progress in confronting the negative psychic baggage in our minds.

The CIA had opened Pandora's Box by their mind control experiments with LSD, introducing the magic mind medicine to Timothy Leary, thus becoming the unwitting agent that fueled the psychedelic counterculture, as if it was a cosmic plan. At least one CIA agent, researching psilocybin mushrooms in Mexico, dropped out to join the Indian tribe he was studying and became an early hippie.

In the new age of television, we watched the arrogant and shameless racism of our elders enforce an inhuman *establishment*, to uphold segregation, both legal and de facto in all parts of the country. We witnessed beatings and murders of Black students, idealists like us, fighting for the simple right to sit at a lunch counter or ride in the front of a bus, as if their color might rub off on some lily-white citizen who enjoyed the right to do as he pleased. We recognized people of all races as our brothers and sisters, the more so as we mingled and got to know each other.

Infused with the self-righteous idealism of youth, we hippie-freaks set about trying to create a better society, a counterculture, where peace and love reigned. We rejected the norms of mainstream society as a betrayal of our nation's founding myth: *all men are created equal.*

Inspired by the non-violent Civil Rights struggle, pacifist hippies advocated Flower Power. While it softened the hearts of those with a conscience, the Vietnam War machine continued to expand. The Establishment waged war against our counterculture and the change we represented. We had to stand up and fight back or be crushed.

In 1968, with the murder of Martin Luther King and Bobbie Kennedy, outstanding leaders who became dead martyrs, Mao's observation that political power grows out of the barrel of a gun was all too obvious. The passive, non-violent approach had not moved fast enough. *Power to the People* overtook *We shall overcome* as the main slogan of Antiwar and Civil Rights activists.

Then, in December 1969, the Chicago police murdered Fred Hampton, whose effective diplomacy had bonded his Black Panthers, white Appalachians, Puerto Ricans, and American Indians into the Rainbow Coalition. As he lay in bed unconscious after an undercover agent drugged his drink, a fusillade of bullets ended his life, making him one more murdered leader, a martyr to the cause. Win or lose, continuing the Revolution was our moral duty.

A group of stoned hippies in Ann Arbor echoed Abbie Hoffman's call for Revolution for the hell of it and called themselves White Panthers. They stood in alliance with the Black Panther Party and progressive movements worldwide. With nothing to lose, they shouted a new battle cry that some of us took literally.

Dope, Rock 'n' Roll, And Fucking in the Streets!
Right on!

2

FRIEND OF FOE

My roommate Chris bounced into our shared bedroom with a big grin on his face.

"Hey, Ron, come with me to meet the Doan brothers. They're inviting us to a meeting with some guy who wants to start the Revolution."

"The hell you say?"

"I'm not kidding. Come on."

After my discharge from Riveredge mental hospital in February 1970, I'd moved into Chris' bedroom until I found a job and earned some cash. Chris and I were both Aries; born one day apart, and we became subject to the military draft when we turned eighteen in March.

I grabbed my coat and followed Chris to hop in the backseat of Bob G's rusty, dented, backfiring wreck of a Ford Falcon station wagon that he called The Beast. Bob, a year and a half younger than Chris and I was our wheelman, the only one of us with a car.

"Let's roll," he shouted, scattering gravel as he tore away from the shoulder.

Bob pulled over at a brand-new house about a block east of highway 83 in north Elmhurst. Our neighborhood was changing fast.

Only two years before, a vast cornfield had filled that land south of Lake Street to the college town of Elmhurst. We felt like unwelcome aliens amid the maze of housing tracts and industrial parks that had taken over our beloved rural landscape.

"I'm kind of busy," Bob said, breaking into my reverie. "I'm cooking things up with my new chick, so I'll just drop you guys. Okay?"

Chris nodded. "That's cool. The Doan boys should be here soon."

A trim, dark-haired woman answered our knock. In tight jeans and a blouse that hugged her assets, she purred. "Hi guys. I'm Marvin's wife. He'll be ready for you soon."

Bedazzled by her charms, Chris and I followed her swinging hips downstairs to the basement, where a row of metal folding chairs faced a small podium and a chalkboard. A few children's toys lay scattered at the edge of the carpeted room.

"I'll be right back with some refreshments." The iced cokes and cookies she brought took the edge off our empty bellies, but our main treat was basking in her sexy vibe and catching a whiff of her perfumed scent as she come and went.

Another knock at the door and she led down two guys with medium long hair in jean jackets. Chris turned to me. "These are the guys I've been telling you about."

The older one clasped my hand, our thumbs interlaced in a *brother's* handshake. "I'm Don. This is my brother Tom. Chris told me about you being in the Weatherman *Days of Rage*. You did a stint in jail, huh?" I nodded, and he narrowed his eyes at me. "The Weathermen went underground to wage guerilla war, but I think we can do a lot more for the cause by staying public and organizing."

"Yeah," Tom said. "This guy, Marvin, seems like a right-on dude, and we'll hear him out. We're forming a chapter of RYM Two right here in Elmhurst."

The Revolutionary Youth Movement II was a surviving splinter of Students for a Democrat Society after SDS fractured into factions. As if on cue, a beefy, stubble-faced guy in his late twenties clomped downstairs.

"Thanks for coming, men. I'm Marvin and I'm looking to get some real shit started that'll blow the fucking lid off this country! Can you dig it?" He launched into a condemnation of "straight" society in an avalanche of words that didn't give us a chance to respond. His monolog was sprinkled with curse words like *Goddamn this* and *motherfucker that* as he spoke of sabotaging government buildings and roads to disrupt the local infrastructure. Then he grabbed his lectern and bellowed upstairs.

"Goddamn it, Lisa! Get your fat ass in gear and bring us some more grub. Chop-chop!" He turned back to us with a sneer. "Good help is so hard to come by."

Our pretty hostess came down bearing fresh snacks and soda without a murmur. Then a man's voice shouted from the floor above.

"Marvin, you son-of-a-bitch! Don't you talk to my daughter that way. You're walking on thin ice around here and I'm ready to kick you out."

Chris and I looked at each other, speechless. Marvin seemed more of a pig than a *right-on* dude, and I hoped her bellowing father would march down and smack him. Lisa deserved better than this loudmouth abuse. The unreal scene left me wondering if they'd staged this bizarre drama for some reason.

The rambling, relentless monolog adjourned with Marvin's insistence on further meetings to plan his revolutionary mayhem. Still dizzy from the shouting, we nodded our apprehensive acceptance before stumbling out into the darkness of a dark and chilly late afternoon and trudged to the corner of Route 83 where Chris and I would part ways with the Doan brothers.

"Who is this guy? I mean really?" I said.

Don shook his head, as if to clear it. "I don't think we should include him in our plans. He's too much of a wild card."

"*Well*," Brother Tom said in a drawl. "He shared some dynamite weed with us when we first met. Would a cop do that?"

Chris nodded. "Sure he would, if he was a Fed deep undercover. They can use some of the dope they get from police evidence lockers to gain our confidence."

Marvin hadn't earned my trust, and I never returned to his house, but he kept popping up in radical groups I became involved with. For the sake of his high-quality drugs, movement people too often dropped their guard and let him hang around despite my warnings.

Bob G told me he and Tom had gotten a ride with Marvin, who drove like a madman, running stoplights and doing donuts on suburban front lawns, tearing them up in a way calculated to get the attention of the police.

He looked at me wide-eyed. "Shit, Ron, Tom had a huge plug of hash jammed into his pants pocket! The last thing we needed was to get pulled over and, sure enough, we were. Marvin jumped out, fuming at the cop as he walked over to the squad car, too far for us to hear what they said, and I couldn't believe it when the cop drove off and let us go."

"You mean Marvin chased the cop away?"

"Sure, that's something I've never seen." Bob threw up his hands. "He's got to be a narc, FBI, or Red Squad."

The Red Squad was the anti-radical department of Chicago PD that shadowed and harassed movement people. I'd soon have my own run-ins with them.

Bob glanced over his shoulder as if afraid someone was listening. "We could have gotten serious jail time. I asked Tom if it seemed strange. What would he have done with his pocket full of hashish if the cop frisked him?"

Bob shook his head. "Tom told me that Marvin bragged about torturing cats, tying them on a shower rod and punching them into scalding water, like he was a boxer in training. Then he tossed them into the kitchen freezer. Their whimpers died away as they stiffened up into furry ice cubes. I'd steer clear of the sick bastard. Marvin is the *Man!*"

Chris agreed. "He's got to be an agent trying to penetrate and destroy the movement."

Everyone knew that the Feds were running agents among us. "Police Set Up at Elmhurst College" was the headline on page one of Elm Bark, the Elmhurst College newspaper on Oct. 23, 1969. Two men wearing storm trooper uniforms and claiming to be members of "Unicorn," an organization no one had heard of, tried to sell a course on guerilla war to the student chapter of RYM II, but they were suspicious and rejected them as provocateurs. We had to be careful who we trusted. Another stint in jail was the last thing I needed.

Whoever he was, Marvin stood for the ugly side of America, not the Peace and Love brotherhood of the counterculture. Marvin's real name is lost to time, but throughout 1970, he kept popping up in my life.

Earth Day Jailbreak

WEDNESDAY, April 22, 1970, was the very first Earth Day. Chris and I hopped on the school bus bound for Addison Trail High School. School began with a cheery assembly and pep rally. It was his alma mater before he dropped out, but his younger brothers were students who helped us blend in, but we were outside agitators, on a mission to disrupt it.

Early that morning, Chris had stormed into the bedroom from his night job waving a newspaper. "Listen to this Ron, *ahem*. 'The pollution crisis provides a much-needed point of agreement to bridge the generation gap. One day of emphasis on the environment will not save the earth.'"

A sly grin spread across Chris's face as he looked at me. "They're planning a garbage clean-up on school grounds and parks. Let's ramp things up and make their little pep rally a more radical experience for students."

"Hell yeah!" I sat up on the top bunk bed. "Let's stage a school walk out to build some political consciousness in them."

The administration's Luke-warm response to the Ecology movement wasn't enough. Long a fringe issue, dominated by a few far-seeing scientists and tree hugging hippies like us; we feared it was in danger of being co-opted by corporate values as it went mainstream.

We got off the bus and fanned through the halls. Addison Trail, with a lax dress code, seemed mellower than Fenton high where I'd gone before dropping out the year before. With our long hair, Chris and I would never have made it past Fenton's vigilant teachers who'd ram you up against the lockers if your shirt wasn't tucked in. Yet, the all too familiar scene chilled me, as if I'd awoken from my dream of adult freedom to find myself back in dreaded high school.

We whispered to the students, "Walk out after the assembly! Pass it on!"

"Where should we go?" they said.

"Elmhurst College, they've got some cool stuff going on and are showing a film, *Alone in the Midst of the Land*."

Elmhurst College was five miles away, and I hoped that contact with the hipper college students would radicalize these kids.

The five-minute bell rang, and the band blared out the school's fight song as if it was a pep rally. We were swept into the gym by the tide of bodies where we conspirators huddled in the bleachers. When the music stopped, the principal stood at the podium and called us to order, but it took his fierce glare before a few high-spirited catcalls subsided. He introduced several teachers who addressed us on the meaning of environmentalism. It was a good message. I was impressed, yet the advice didn't go far enough, and we craved stronger action.

The root cause of Earth's eco-disaster was capitalism and our selfish way of life. We humans had become aliens, spiritually disconnected from our dear mother Earth. To change our poisoned world for the better, we needed to rock our consumer culture to the ground. My resolve strengthened after we watched a silly skit performed by peppy and preppy students that got a few laughs.

The bell rang again, and the herd of students poured off the bleachers and through the halls as we continued spreading the word to walk out. To our gratification, a mass of students went straight out the double doors and scattered into the neighborhood, overwhelming teachers who attempted to stem the stampede, exceeding my wildest expectations. More than half of the student body made a break for it, the largest mass walkout of students ever reported for Addison Trail.

I was on probation and needed to avoid roving police officers on the lookout for truant students, so I took a circuitous route through side streets on my way to the college. Arriving from my cross-country jog, I found expressionist art on display in the Student Lounge, but most of it didn't impress me. I sought long haired Freaks, Movement People like myself in the Student Union, where, as the College paper put it, a "massive Teach-In on the Environment" went on all day.

I found a host of speakers and discussion groups from all shades of political persuasion mingled together. Members passed out leaflets around the campus and sometimes confronted each other in debate. There was Planned Parenthood, and S.T.O.P: Students to Terminate Over-population and Pollution, the Elmhurst Geography Club, Illinois Electric Company, even Commonwealth Edison sent a rep, who argued with someone from the *Campaign Against Pollution Committee* in the Science Auditorium. I decided to stay longer in that stimulating environment.

Amidst the social whirl in the Union, I approached a cheerful brunette whose wavy hair, parted in the middle, cascaded to her shoulders.

"Hello, I'm Ron, an ex-Weatherman who just got out of jail and looking for a place to crash a few days."

She took my proffered hand and smiled. "I'm Barbara. You can crash at our women's dorm for a couple of days. It should be cool so long as you are. Things are pretty much co-ed nowadays, even here in Elmhurst."

She explained that there were no bed checks and boyfriends sometimes spent the night with their room-mates consent. I wasn't sure how official that was and decided to keep a low profile. She introduced me to her activist roommate, Jill, who said, "Maybe you can help us print some posters and flyers."

"Sure, I'd love to."

Barbra said she would take off for a concert in Wisconsin the next evening, leaving me with Jill, who made it clear that she needed alone time to study. No hint of anything beyond Platonic friendship was offered, and I didn't press it, being grateful for a place to crash with nothing more than a blanket to sleep under on the floor. I drifted to sleep, wondering what Elmhurst College held in store for me.

THE NEXT MORNING Barb took me over to the Art shop. "Have you done any ink screening, Ron?"

"No, but I'd like to give it a try."

Students were cutting letters out of heavy paper and using a squeegee, smeared ink through a screen onto poster boards that advertised an anti-pollution rally and march against the war on Saturday the 25th. I soon had my hands stained as green and red as they did. We joked around and had fun.

Late in the day, Barb called out, "See you when I get back in a couple of days!"

She left me with Jill, poor company, as she sequestered herself to study in the library. The next morning, I awoke to an empty campus. It was an eerie experience wandering through the campus ghost town until I found a harried looking student hunched over his textbook on a park bench.

"Where is everyone, man?" I said.

"They've gone to that concert up in Wisconsin."

"Why did you stay behind?" That must have hit a nerve.

"Mind your own damn business and leave me alone. I've got studying to do."

I was bored after wandering the empty campus, so I walked back to the West End to find Chris gone too. "I'm not sure where he went," his mother said, shaking her head. "He said something about a concert."

It was a much bigger deal than I realized. A local version of

Woodstock, which I'd also missed. Wisconsin's first outdoor rock festival, officially called Sound Storm, lasted from April 24 to the 26, on the bucolic hillside farm of Irene York outside the village of Poynette.

Chris had taken off hitchhiking right after our Earth Day walkout and Bob, convinced that Officer Gore would pin the student walk-out on him, decided the concert was as good an excuse as any to split town until things cooled off. He drove off for Wisconsin in his white Ford station wagon, which, as I well-remembered, had no heater.

Back in February, freezing in the back seat, I tried to warm up by lighting small newspaper fires, holding the flaming pages to warm my stiffening fingers for the few moments before I dropped the smoking embers onto the bare metal floor. The April weather was warmer, although still cold at night, and Bob gathered a full load for the concert.

He took our friend John's sister Sue, who he was trying to claim as his own, as well as our friends Craig, Thumper, and a girl he didn't know named Wendy, but they all vanished into the crowd on arrival. Back in the neighborhood a few days later, Bob regaled me with his version of events.

"The Chicago Outlaws motorcycle gang guarded the concert. Walking around, I bumped into a minor riot behind a food truck. They were yelling, 'Power to the People!' Getting closer, I saw boxes of frozen chicken flying out of the back of the truck into the eager hands of the cheering crowd."

Bob winked. "Who do you suppose was throwing it?" Without waiting for an answer, he continued. "Chris stood at the tailgate pitching the chicken to an adoring crowd."

True to his Robin Hood character, when Chris found the food truck unguarded, he liberated those resources for *the people*. Even some of the Outlaw bikers joined in, grabbing their share before other bikers, more conscious of their duty to guard the food, arrived to spoil the fun. Chris slipped away to mingle in the backslapping crowd before Bob got close enough to congratulate him.

The Festival lasted four days and nights of wild partying, but all things end, and Bob's lady luck changed too. He found his would-be girlfriend making wild love under an India print tent with another guy. Nursing his broken heart, Bob got behind the wheel of his stalwart beater. The engine's uneven rumbling sounded like a lullaby as he drove back alone through the Wisconsin pines to Illinois. Dog-tired later in the day, he spotted a billboard south of Joliet and read the message of conservative America posted there.

"Beautify America, get a haircut."

Bob bared his teeth in grim defiance as he told me, "Fuck it, Ron. I was beat, and this seemed the perfect spot to camp for the shitty mood I was in. I parked right below the billboard, rolled out my sleeping bag, and slept like a baby. What a wild trip it was!"

"That's a hell of a tale, Bob," I said. "Despite crashing in the women's dorm, I was just as alone and lonely in Elmhurst."

I drifted back and forth between the West End neighborhood in Bensenville and the student scene in Elmhurst, where I helped collate handouts, making myself useful or at least not a bother to my hosts. In my free time, I meditated and expounded to whoever listened on the yogic path as well as the Marxism I'd been reading. Hard-liners criticized me for mixing mysticism with radical politics, but I insisted that revolutionaries need spirituality too, just as we need two legs to walk on.

3

THE ELMHURST MARCH

On Saturday April 25th I left the dorm before 9 a.m., and headed to Wilder Park, where a crowd was gathering for an Anti-pollution rally, organized by ACE, Action for a Cleaner Environment. It was a moderate group trying to work within the system. This was no angry protest, but an event sponsored by the Mayor with the Kiwanis, Lions and Jaycees, businesspeople. Searching the crowd, I found the Doan brothers with a couple of recent converts to their RYM group. It would be up to us to radicalize the crowd.

Don's long stringy hair hung to the shoulders of his well-worn denim jacket. Stitched on the back was the bold red and blue Viet Cong flag, with the eye-catching big yellow star in the middle. We were defiant, proud to call the National Liberation Front of Vietnam our heroes. Tom was more withdrawn. I had to strain to catch his whispered words.

At the park and all along the route, boxes were set up for participants to drop cards registering themselves for clean-up and beatification projects like litter pick up, landscaping and fence painting. Some of the marchers even carried rakes and hoes over their shoulders like soldiers off to war. Dr. Boyd Keenan, a member of the Presidential committee on pollution, spoke about the urgency of this. We had to act fast to prevent the further deterioration of our environment and life's resources, but he insisted WE could make a difference.

Radical students like us wore buttons proclaiming *POWER to the PEOPLE* and *Seize the Time!* We feared that by working within the system, the Establishment would co-opt and divert our agenda, transforming it into a cute, but non-threatening teddy bear of a movement and therefore impotent and irrelevant.

The crowd grew to four hundred, including pre-teens with their parents. I overheard a spacey hippie mumble to trust no one over thirty. I called out. "Such crap destroys our unity. We need everyone, young and old, in the movement."

We linked arms and shoved off, marching along Arthur Street to take a left on York, then north into the heart of Elmhurst. Big shots like the mayor rode along, waving from their convertibles to the adoring spectators along the parade route. Our small group of radicals in the middle of the march seemed dwarfed and out of place as we chanted: STOP THE WAR and other slogans. ACE marshals wearing armbands ordered us to stop.

"This is not the appropriate time and place to inject your peacenik rhetoric. Stick to the environmental agenda. You'll have to leave the march if you don't comply."

We toned it down. Only our stern presence, reinforced by a few hurriedly scrawled signs, proclaimed our stand for real change.

Snap-snap-snap. I turned to see a man wearing a gray suit and fedora, who sneered as he took our pictures. Similar angry looking men with cameras leaned out of the windows of cars cruising alongside the march, trying to get our faces close-up.

"Cover your faces," Don said.

Tom looked bewildered. "Are they with the press?"

"No," Don said. "They look more like FBI agents, or maybe they're Legion of Justice."

The Legion was a Right-wing vigilante group that sabotaged leftist activities. Whoever the cameramen were, I never saw our pictures posted in the local papers, but I learned that Chicago's Red Squad had updated photo files on all of us.

At Third Street we turned west to Addison Ave., which became Cottage Hill as we crossed the railroad tracks and finally arrived back at the park. We ten or so radicals stood before the speaker's platform in two ranks, proudly erect, in contrast to the hippie students slouched around us. We were committed Revolutionaries not wimpy hippies that could be pushed around without fighting back.

Republican State Senator Jack Knuepfer climbed up on the dais before us and spoke.

"The older generation needs to participate in this activity, which is so vital to us all. This generation of young people will move the older generation to a commitment for cleaner air and water by organized action of this sort. I am happy to see them concerned with the problems facing us."

He paused, shaking his head with approval over the admiring faces in the large middle class crowd until his gaze focused on us. He gulped and continued, addressing us, the angry youth.

"It is your generation that will improve the environment or that will pave the way for others to take bigger steps to do so..." He droned on, saying nothing about reigning in industry, nothing about the environmental damage caused by the war in Viet Nam, nothing about the defoliation caused by our mushrooming cities, nothing about the shift in cultural values we needed, like de-institutionalizing racism. Instead, he leveled slams at the *vocal minority* of disruptive youth. *We* were less helpful, tearing things down instead of building up society, so unlike the quiet, orderly, well-groomed youth who would make a true difference in the world.

Don whispered, "Fuck this guy." Then he called out louder, "Now is the time. Bull shit!" The rest of us joined in, chorusing, "Bullshit! Bullshit! Bullshit!"

The Senator yelled something that I couldn't make out, which gave us an excuse to fire back. "Bullshit! Bullshit! Bullshit!" I wasn't sure if pissing him off served our purpose, but it felt good to shout and stir things up.

ACE march organizers surrounded us, along with men carrying walkie-talkies, obviously plain clothed police. "You'd better shut up or we'll arrest you!" Tom didn't care, but I was on probation. For the rest of the speech, we just stood, ramrod stiff in silent rebuttal.

The official speeches ended on an upbeat note, advising everyone to join in the park cleanup that was to follow immediately after. Don called it a useless gesture and stalked off with his brother to keep his hands clean for the revolution. I drifted off to find Barb's friends picking up trash. With nothing better to do, I helped them.

Events marched on. Seven students had been shot during rioting at Ohio State with 73 more injured and 100 arrested on April 29. President Nixon announced that he was sending troops to invade Cambodia on Thursday April 30. The war was widening, and college campuses across the Nation began to erupt in protest. On Mayday, a Black Panther rally of 12,000 in New Haven, Connecticut, was dispersed with tear gas.

The Elmhurst campus was also in an uproar of less newsworthy student meetings, with talk of student strikes. Some worried about their grades, while others said that we bore a moral responsibility to disrupt the system even if kicked out of school. A few professors supported the strike, which got off to a late, rocky start in Elmhurst. I wasn't a student and had no classes to sacrifice, but it was an exciting time to be cheering the more radical ideas on campus.

Unknown to most, the Americans had been bombing and sending troops in "hot pursuit" of the Viet Cong across the Cambodian border for months, all with King Sihanouk's secret acquiescence. He'd been trying to stay neutral and play the opposing forces off against each other, but in March, General Lon Nol deposed him with CIA assistance. The war heated up with more intensive bombing of Cambodian villages which only pushed the population to support to the local Khmer Rouge rebels, who went from obscurity to complete control of the countryside. Nixon's prosecution of the war wasn't only immoral. Supporting oppressive tyrants was a losing strategy that backfired.

4

THE LONG WALK

Barb called me over to where she sat under the trees in Wilder Park. "Are you going to the Walk for Development tomorrow?"

"What's that, a protest march?"

"Not exactly. The Young World Development Committee is raising funds for worthy causes like the Havasupai Indian Project."

Jill, one of her freakier friends, said, "The tribe lives on a remote, cramped reservation at the bottom of the Grand Canyon." She nodded for emphasis. She wore beads and buckskins and considered herself part Indian.

Barb cut in, "Then, on a local level, there's Project HOPE, Homes of Private Enterprise. It's a nonprofit organization based in Wheaton, buying, and rehabilitating older homes in DuPage County for families on welfare."

Jill smacked her forehead. "Jeez, it's tomorrow, isn't it? I'm not in shape for it, but do you want to go, Ron?"

"Sure, I'll go." I'd been crashing on the campus since April 22, and it was already May 3. The gals were pretty, but our relationship was stuck on platonic. It had been a long dry spell for me, and I needed a real, touchy-feely girlfriend. Maybe I'd meet some groovy chicks on the walk.

"You need to get sponsors," Barb said. "You ask businesses, like grocery stores and such, to pledge a sum to donate for each mile you walk."

"Cozying up to business owners isn't my forte, Barb, and it's too late now. Maybe if I heard about it beforehand…"

It was to be a thirty-mile trek through several Chicago suburbs, from the start line at Willowbrook High School in Villa Park to Wheaton via Lombard and Glen Ellyn, making several loops through Elmhurst to end up back at the start line. I jogged between my parent's place in Wood Dale to Bensenville and Elmhurst College on a regular basis and considered myself in great shape for this.

Another friend of mine said, "Thirty miles? Are you fucking crazy!"

I said, "Some people would rather grab some adventure than spend every day smoking dope on the couch. Dig it?"

The student union ran a carpool shuttle to Willowbrook high where I joined the milling crowd behind the start line shortly after seven am. When I approached the table to sign in, they asked who my sponsors were.

"Uh, well, I don't have any."

She looked at me funny. "Well, you need sponsors to sign in."

"Okay," I said as I walked away from the table, an undocumented participant.

My friends Chris, Bob, and Janet also came without sponsors, but the immense crowd prevented us from finding each other. Clunky combat boots were my only footwear. I wore my Army surplus jacket against the morning chill, even though I'd have to tie it around my waist or carry it as the day and the exertion warmed me.

The crowd grew to be estimated at between 15,000 and 20,000, so many that they decided to turn us loose four minutes before the official 8 o'clock start time. We took off, walking elbow to elbow in a giant herd that soon began thinning out along the road. Most of the chicks I met in the first few miles claimed to be *with* someone. Then I got lucky, falling into easy banter with a petite brunette and her none too ugly blond girlfriend.

"We're high school students from Western Springs." The brunette said.

"I dropped out to join the Revolution," I said, hoping to wow them with tales of my heroism facing the *pigs* on the streets of Chicago. By the time we made it to the first check in station, we three seemed to be good friends. There were twelve checkpoints along the route where registered walkers checked in and grabbed free sandwiches and paper cups of fruit juice or water. Hungry, I gobbled whatever they offered, even bologna on white bread, which was my least favorite food.

Bathroom relief was on offer at specially marked houses along the route. Kindhearted family members stood outside to direct us. As other couples blew on past, I waited for my two ladies to finish and shrugged off the temptation to forge ahead on my own.

As we got better acquainted, the girls smiled more at my jokes, and I saw a flicker of interest cross the brunette's lovely brown eyes. I was plugging for her, but walking between them, I took her friend's hand too. A guy had to hedge his bets, just in case, because you never know how things will turn out. The brunette dropped my hand as we approached the third checkpoint.

"Oh, shit, that's my dad!" she said.

He waved, smiling at his precious brown-haired girl. "How are you holding up, honey?"

She forced a grin. "I'll make it, Dad." Grabbing a juice, she moved on without introducing me.

He was waiting at the next checkpoint too, and then each one thereafter. Each time she brushed away my hand to go through it alone. Little by little, this girl who'd already filled my daydreams was flagging down and becoming snippy. Maybe I'd bet on the wrong girl. Her blond friend still had energy, but since I'd directed so much attention on the brunette, she'd moved to walk on her far side and her polite smiles didn't seem meant to entice.

We climbed up and up a steep section of Hill Avenue in Glen

Ellyn and then trudged downhill as other more fleet of foot passed us. I tried pep talk to cheer the gals.

"You can't give up!" The brunette's listless eyes told me I wasn't helping, so I offered my back. "Hop on, I'll carry you."

I hoisted the pretty lass up on my back, and her friend and I picked up the pace. Even with her petite hundred pound weight, I got my second wind and felt invincible, jogging in triumph to the crowd's applause. On we flew through two checkpoints, passing many of the weary couples who'd passed us earlier, and waved at her cheering dad. Could she have been embarrassed about him seeing us like this, or was she only tired, tired of me? At the next check, she begged off.

"Just drop me here and go ahead," she said. "I'll be alright. My Dad will pick me up."

Her friend was holding up very well. I wondered if I could switch horses in midstream. I dropped the brunette and asked the friend. "How about you? Want a ride?"

She gave me a sideway glance and spoke after a long pause. "Gee, I don't know."

But I squatted and waved her aboard. "Climb on; you can finish this on me."

Her eyes pivoted between me and her girlfriend, as if weighing her options. "No, thanks, I'd better stay. Her dad is my ride home."

"Will I see you ladies again? Can I have your numbers?"

The brunette shook her head. "Maybe we'll meet again someday."

"Just maybe, after all our fun?" I couldn't let both her and her friend slip away without some hope of reunion.

The blond girl's eyes lit up. "Sometimes we hang out at the Student Union or Wilder Park in Elmhurst."

My hope sprang anew. "There's going to be a concert there on May 9th. I could meet you then or at the student union tonight whenever you like."

"Maybe we'll see you at the finish line."

With that vague promise to hearten me, I jogged onward. Unburdened and as frisky as a colt, I passed whole regiments of frazzled walkers who'd been passing us all day. Some warned me to *take it easy,* but I knew they were pooped and sour at eating my dust. I flew past one check point without stopping, then gulped down two cups of water at the next station and got the heartening encouragement of the volunteer staff. Spectators all along the last miles cheered, firing me up even more. "You're almost there, man!"

I alternated between a dog trot and a brisk walking pace; surprising even myself at the great shape I was in. As I came up on station number II, a volunteer yelled, "This is the last checkpoint before the finish line, just straight on from here!"

Galvanized, I broke into a run as I turned onto Harvard Street and crossed Jackson. The finish line was just ahead and then, with my heart bursting from my chest, I was there. Overwhelmed by a combination of dizzy exhilaration and fatigue, I joined those stalwarts who preceded me and flopped down on the grass.

I'd done it! Of the original 20,000 or so who began, only 6,000 were documented as finishing the full trek. It gave me a jolt of macho pride, or hubris, to know that I'd made it. The committee raised over $200,000 for various projects, although, being unsponsored, I wasn't in the statistics and earned them zero. But I was no middle class American. I was a rebel stranger in a strange land and was proud of defying the corporate structure.

When I got back up on rubbery legs, I searched the crowd for my erstwhile companions. My little brunette peeked around the side of her dad and gave me a curt wave so he wouldn't see. I'd have been embarrassed too. Her blond friend spotted me and waved with more vigor, so I approached, thinking I should have been trying for instead.

"Too bad you two didn't make the finish," I said.

The blond nodded. "Yeah, I needed my ride. Maybe see you again someday."

But it wasn't to be. The next day was Monday, the 4th of May, the day our sky crashed. The fast sweep of events shook America to its core. 1970 was turning into an action-packed year for all of us.

5

MONDAY MAY FOURTH

Samson offered me and a couple other guys a joyride ride in his car. He was a couple of years older than me, with the build of a quarterback out of training. His full reddish blond beard and matching shoulder-length mane made him look like a Sunday school picture of his Biblical namesake. And just like that amoral killing machine in the Bible, our Sampson could be by turns a gentle giant, or a scrapper bragging of his fighting prowess.

As usual, Sampson was on his way to some dope deal and we just tagged along for the ride and the reefer that he passed around as we drove. We'd suck it in while admiring the greening fields and red barns whizzing by. April showers brought us May flowers in the Illinois countryside.

Still resting up from my thirty-mile hike the day before, I let the joint pass me by more often than I toked on it. Moderation was my motto, but his pot packed a punch, heightening my senses. The announcement came over the car's radio like a thunderclap.

Four students are confirmed dead at Kent State University in Ohio. They were shot by National Guard troops during demonstrations against the war...

While we cruised around the countryside getting high, four

students had been martyred. Somebody in the car said, "They've killed too many of us already."

"Yeah," Sampson said. "We got to be ready to fucking die in this struggle!"

Stoned as I was, Jim Morrison's song *Five to One* reverberated in my head. *They got the guns, but we got the numbers*, as the image my own confrontation with a gun totting cop the year before flashed before my eyes. I fumbled for words to express my jumbled thoughts.

"Oh, yeah," I said. "Once you've heard a bullet whistle past your ear, revolutionary theory becomes as real as shit."

One of the guys let out a lungful of smoke. "Shit man, we've got to be ready to turn it around. Dying for the cause doesn't win the war. We've got to make the pigs die. Dig it?"

Kent State was remarkable only because the students were white. Black Panthers, like our hero, Fred Hampton, were gunned down on a regular basis with less media coverage. This time would be different. It wasn't Black or Vietnamese kids they'd slaughtered. The death of a few white, middle-class students gave a shocking wake up call to those blasé students still on the fence. We had an opportunity to radicalize them and pull them over to our side.

The My Lai massacre in Viet Nam had been too far away to register with students who now felt the crosshairs on them. The Kent State shootings did more to galvanize opposition to the establishment than the Weather underground. **Remember Kent State** became the new rallying cry against the war and all that was wrong in this country.

Some conservatives applauded the shooting of students at Kent State. Even when it came out that most had been bystanders on their way to class, one was even a member of ROTC, who believed in the rightness of the war.

Elmhurst College was on edge. Sympathetic professors turned their classes into a focused analysis of current events, but too many of our compatriots were still wracked with debilitating fear. I heard spontaneous exclamations like: *My God! They're going to kill us all.*

This front-page editorial appeared in the Elmhurst College paper, Elm Bark, issue 21, on May 7, 1970.

REMEMBER THOSE WHO DIED

The inevitable has happened. We all sat back, knew that it would happen, and waited. Four students have been MURDERED in Ohio and undoubtedly if any charges are brought against the National Guardsmen upon whose hands is permanently stained the blood of those students, the charges will read justifiable homicide, like so many charges before them. The Far Left has sufficiently aroused the "reaction" of the Far-Right as well as that good old "Silent Majority" or "Middle America."

America is reacting to something they don't understand nor care to understand. College students have been branded with that classical "Scarlet Letter" although not "A" for adultery (that's the silent majority's claim to fame) but with a "C" for Commie-Pinko or "T" for threat...

With this newest form of harassment by the military, no college student should feel safe. White college students now feel the same insecurity that many Black people feel after the undisputed murder of Illinois Black Panther leader Fred Hampton. The sad truth has been vividly brought to bear. All minority groups not adhering to the 'right' way of thinking may fear for their lives.

Then the writer veered off into apathy.

I would propose that students at Elmhurst do not strike at this time, not because they believe what happened at Kent State was right or because they believe what is happening in Southeast Asia is right, but because we will prove nothing by striking. The people who need to know the facts about Kent State or Southeast Asia will not be striking, anyway. Now is the time students need to band together and decide on a reasonable course of action to take. Staying away from classes or attacking the National Guard would not seem like reasonable actions. More dead students will do none of us any good. Signed, R.U.

Seize the time! Mobilize! Shut it down, became catchphrases as over 450 campuses went on strike. On Saturday, May 9th, I hung out at the all-day *Folk & Rock Festival* in Wilder Park and heard that President Nixon dismissed all of us anti-war organizers as bums. That did it. On Sunday, May 10th, more Elmhurst students joined the call for walkouts and even some high schools joined in strikes erupting across the nation. Students everywhere woke up to what we had to do.

6

VENCERAMOS

A pale, thin young woman dressed in combat fatigues stood next to the red and blue Viet Cong flag with a yellow star that the Doan brothers had set it up in the Student Union. Her platinum blond hair didn't quite reach her shoulders and her angelic sky-blue eyes sized me up and pulled me in. As I approached, I noticed a shiny red and white pin on the breast of her army surplus jacket. I pointed at it.

"That's pretty. Where did you get it?"

"I was in Cuba a few weeks ago. It's a Venceramos pin."

"Cuba? Isn't it illegal to go there? I've never heard of Venceramos."

She grinned. "We had to go illegally, of course. Cuba, North Viet Nam, and North Korea are the only nations that our State Department forbids us to visit. The Venceramos Brigades are made up of foreign volunteers supporting Cuba. Our government wants to create the image of Castro as a boogie man, but Canada doesn't have the same negative attitude or travel restrictions we do. The Cuban people love Castro for all he's done for the campesinos, who didn't even have electricity before the Revolution."

She smiled and extended her hand. "I'm Sandy." At her touch, a spark ran through my body.

"I'm Ron." I squeezed her hand and gave her a bow. "I'm pleased to meet a heavy movement sister like you. How many groups have gone to Cuba, and how long were you down there?"

"The First Brigade of over two hundred left in November, last year, and spent six weeks cutting sugar cane. They had a bumper harvest and its tough work, but I was lucky, and went on the second Brigade of almost seven hundred volunteers and sugarcane wasn't in season, so we did other work side by side with the Cuban people, building solidarity with them and also meeting with visiting Vietnamese veterans of the People's War. We went there in February and I just got back in April."

Her shining radiance and experience made a big an impression on me. The Doans and our RYM comrades were busy passing out leaflets and rapping with the crowd, which gave Sandy and I a chance to rap. I told her about my time with the Weathermen, which impressed her, but although friendly, she wouldn't let me walk her back to wherever she was staying.

I often saw her on campus that week, but couldn't get past the friend or brother category. With her hair cut tomboy short, and began to wonder if she preferred women, or if she was too cerebral or even asexual. Although being in her company raised my spirits, for love and sex, I'd have to seek farther afield.

7

CONCERT SEASON

Music was the glue that connected us all. As the weather warmed up, I ached to get back on the road and find a girlfriend. I'd missed the epic Rock Concert in Woodstock that claimed our baby boom generation as its own and Chris and Bob's animated description of their adventure at the Poynette concert convinced me to make the next scene when this article in the Seed underground newspaper fell into my hands.

American Bandstand

The season of the festival is about to begin, and the new wave of hip capitalism is coming to the Midwest. A whole swarm of side burned entrepreneurs is preparing to capitalize on the hip culture's twin addictions: rock music and tribal gatherings. Several rock festivals are planned for the Midwest, and two things are becoming increasingly clear: local authorities are cracking down on the possibility of any large-scale gathering of freaks, and local freaks are getting more and more uptight about the rampant shucksterism involved in most of the festivals...

Another festival, billed as only an "outdoor concert" has been planned for a site on Kickapoo Creek near Bloomington, Illinois for the Memorial Day weekend. This one is meeting the other form of local resistance – honkoid fears of hippie invasion. Local authorities have filed suit to stop the thing on the basis of a zoning ordinance that stipulates that the land in question be used for 'agricultural' rather than 'recreational' purposes. The suit is going to be hard to beat, and the event, which was to have featured a large number of local bands as well as a scattering of nationally known groups, now appears in doubt.

When three owners announced that they would hold a three-day festival near Carbondale... Immediate protests broke out, Concerned Citizens groups formed instantly, and several lawsuits and legislative measures were filed. "They'll destroy our property, rape our women, kick our dogs and generally urinate all over our way of life," cried an aroused citizenry. They'll smoke narcotics, fornicate (that's slang for fuck'), and even trespass," screamed the representatives of law and order...

The Chicago Seed, March to April 1970, page 5, signed by Eliot

Kickapoo! The name rang sweet in my ears. The story of the Kickapoo Indian tribe's determined fight against the White man's encroachment into Illinois was unknown to most people. They were pushed all the way down into Mexico by the expanding frontier, but they hit back, raiding for horses and loot across the Rio Grande until the Fifth US cavalry, *Mackenzie's Raiders* of television fame no less, subdued them at the twilight of the Indian wars. Their descendants remained in Mexico, living as traditionally as possible. We owed them more commemoration than the "Kickapoo Joy Juice" gag in the "Lil Abner" comic strips.

On Saturday, May 30, Chris, and I struck out together, hitchhiking down Route 83, for Bloomington only a hundred miles away, but without a map and only a vague notion of how to get there, we somehow ended up on Route 57 when we should've been on 55, where we got a ride with a beefy guy in his mid-twenties.

"Where're you fellas headed?"

"The Kickapoo Creek Rock Festival!" We said at the same time, and hoped that would be enough, but he only blinked at us.

"I don't know about a rock festival," he said, pulling away from the shoulder, "but I'm going to Carbondale."

Chris shrugged. "Carbondale?"

Neither of us knew much downstate geography, but the Seed article mentioned a rock festival there too, so it was probably close by. Our new friend handed us a map, which we studied as we rolled along. Carbondale was 250 miles farther south from the creek at Bloomington, but our driver was optimistic.

"Carbondale is a college town. Students will surely be heading there, so you boys will catch a ride easy." He chuckled. "I'm going to be too busy with my little coed honey to bother with a crowded concert, if ya know what I mean."

I'd heard that Southern Illinois was practically Dixieland, full of racial prejudice, but when Nixon widened the war into Cambodia, the Carbondale students rioted against it, proving they weren't all crackers. He dropped us outside the gate to the campus of Southern Illinois University and we stood, watching as a stream of northbound traffic drove by. Cars honked and people yelled out apologies. "Sorry, man, we're already full."

Finally, someone stopped and squeezed us in among the bodies in the back of their open pickup truck. We sped north along the narrow two-lane highway, through acres of lush green corn, sweet smelling hay and tidy farmhouses. Our detour tripled the 135 miles from Bensenville, but we saw more of the state, miles, and miles of it, that morning.

We finally bogged down in a snarl of bumper-to-bumper traffic approaching the Festival gate. Chris gave a cynical laugh. "We're lemmings running to the sea!"

I elbowed him. "Lemmings or not, here we come!"

We jumped off, shouted our thanks, and merged into the throng of foot traffic, but instead of approaching the gate, we circled the chain-link fence around the perimeter until we found a hole. A couple of walkie-talky totting guards stood a few feet away. Chris shouted, "Go for it!" We dove on through, ignoring their frantic commands to halt and lost them in the milling crowd of paid patrons, thus avoiding the $15 gate fee, which neither of us had.

"Music belongs to the people," I shouted in justification. The air, the land, and music were community property to be liberated in our outlaw version of People's War. But as single men, we had other needs to fill, and sought the rare unclaimed women. We approached a group of three and bantered with them until their men showed up carrying their cargo of wine and food from the parking lot. The tanned lovelies didn't ask us to stick around, so we moved on to try our luck elsewhere.

Someone yelled, "Hey! It's Chris and Ron!" We turned to see a couple of guys from the neighborhood who said, "We've been here for hours already."

Chris stayed to chat, but I wandered off to seek my fortune among strangers on those high seas of humanity. Most were white suburban kids, ranging in age from early teens through late twenties with a few graybeard hippies sprinkled in. Whenever offered, I shared a hit off a passing joint with spontaneous friends as I searched the wide environs for lady luck.

Skinny dipping couples cavorted at the creek. Bold nudity at last! They'd created a giant mud slide on which nude and semi-nude people whooped as they came skidding down the slimy surface to splash into the water. Couples embraced in amorous fondling, uncaring who watched, but the ratio of male to female was very unbalanced. Men without partners, like me, looked on in vain hopes of an invitation to an orgy. Wasn't that what free love was supposed to be about?

"Here comes Captain America!" I looked up to see a guy wearing a US flag as a cape and nothing else slide down the slick mud slide. He made a bigger than usual splash with the crowd, too. I also stripped and swam around, making a few splashes, and caught some afternoon rays, but to make my exhibitionism worthwhile, I needed an audience of appreciative chicks.

Rain showers came and went. Wrapped in soggy blankets or

huddled under beach towels, hardy souls invoked the indomitable spirit of Woodstock against the elements. We dried out in the sun between the intermittent downpours and all the while the bands played on, the music loud enough for all to hear.

Bodies packed tight against the stage. I wandered along the outer edge, enjoying the live performances as best I could from a distance. The rocking tunes were the backup for my life's drama. Seeking a mate, I came across a picturesque hippy chick. Dressed in India print fabrics adorned with multi-colored beads and feathers, she looked as if she was posing for a magazine article on flamboyant flower children. Her vibrant femininity charmed me. Here was a chick who would understand me. Our eyes met, and she seemed receptive to my hello, so I remarked upon her radiant aura.

"Thanks, dude." She flashed a disarming smile that left me tongue tied. "You look kind of cute too, but a little tense. You need to lighten up."

She flustered me, but I tried to make a good impression. "Yeah? Well, I'm a revolutionary, see, and ah, standing up to the War Machine and, ah, I just got out of jail..."

She raised a hand and cut me off with a song. "But when you talk about destruction, don't you know that you can count me out?" It was a line from the Beatles song, *Revolution*. She giggled as my face turned red. "You'd better get your own head together first, man. Love and peace are the only way to end war. Can you dig that?"

"Well, yeah, but, ah..." I stammered, trying to regain my composure. "We've tried nonviolence and look what happened. Martin Luther King, Medgar Evers, Malcolm X, and now four white students at Kent State, all killed by the pigs. We need to stand up to them."

"Pigs? Listen to your angry, hateful words! You're almost as bad as they are."

I should have shut up and agreed with her, but I got on a stupid rant. "That's easy for you to say. They're not burning your village, killing your brothers, raping you and your sisters, and spitting on you when they're done. You're white. A Vietnamese or a black woman doesn't have the option to *make love, not war* like you."

Damn my big mouth. I wanted *to touch her face, her hands and gaze into her eyes*, as the song *Cherish* by David Cassidy had it. Rapping politics instead of mouthing sweet platitudes was a sure way to lose this heavenly chick.

Then, from out of nowhere, a monkey jumped up on her shoulder, but she recovered from her surprise and her motherly instinct kicked in.

"Well, hello there, little sweetie." She started to kiss it, but it sprang into the arms of a girl coming from behind.

"Don't worry, he doesn't bite," the other girl said. The monkey's antics brought a whole retinue of joyful partiers who surrounded us, absorbing my hippie girl, who I'd lost, anyway. Someone slapped a big jug of *Bali Hai* wine into my hands.

"Come on, brother, have a swig!" It was some compensation for my loss, and I gulped its fruity sweet taste, a welcome late breakfast. Then a jug of *Mogen David* came around, and smaller bottles of *Ripple*, cheap fortified wine, and reefer, too. It kept coming, passed around with a warm communal feeling. It hit me quick on my empty stomach, mellowing me into a more relaxed version of myself. Through the haze, I remembered an often-repeated article of faith: *When you're ready for her, your lover will appear*. And she did.

"Hi, I'm Natasha." It started as just another rambling, drunken conversation with a girl.

Her long frizzy black locks shone like obsidian, cascading almost to her butt, reminding me of Rapunzel, who let down her tower length hair in the children's fable. In my stupor, I let her do most of the talking. It was the right move for once, and she had plenty to say.

"My family came from Russia. That's my major now, Russian studies. It's amazing, studying the language and culture of my own people." She rattled off some phrases, and the exotic lilting music of her words enchanted me. My mind cleared enough to shoot off my mouth again.

"What do you think about the Soviet Union?"

"It's not yet perfect, but socialism promotes equality and is a better system than our freebooting capitalism. This peace and love hippie shit is too much of a sell-out; people are dying in a neocolonial war in Vietnam and these freaks just don't get it. Castro had the right answer. We need that kind of revolution here now." Her intellect, charm and looks captivated me. We were kindred spirits. Then it started to rain again.

"Come on," she grabbed my hand. "My friends parked our pickup truck over there. Let's get under cover." The back of the truck was covered by a tarp on a wooden frame that kept out most of the rain. Snug and dry, we continued our rap-a-thon to the soothing pitter patter of rain mixed with the continuous background of Rock and Roll.

8

FROM RUSSIA WITH LOVE

Natasha warmed me with a smile. "Let me teach you some Russian, Ron. Repeat after me: *do svidaniya*." It took several tries in my inebriated state before she was happy with my pronunciation. "That's much better. It means goodbye. Now say *tovarishch*... Good job Ron! That means comrade." She had me repeating these words and a few simple phrases until my slurred pronunciation cracked her up and she fell giggling into my arms. I took a chance and kissed her.

It was a simple kiss, no tongue, just a chaste prelude, and my earnest prayer for our togetherness. I'd found love with this exotic Russian woman. Still fully clothed, we snuggled under thick blankets against the evening chill. From time to time, her friends dropped in for a few minutes' rest beside us, before going back out into the blaring music scene. I sobered up and when we were alone for a while. I slipped my hands under her clothes to caress her soft body.

"Not now, Ron." She shrugged me off. I resigned to embracing her clothed form, certain that we had plenty of time to consummate our love. She sat up and checked her watch. "I want to hear BB King. He'll be on stage at three AM."

"Me too, I feel a special connection with BB King. When I was broke and starving, hitchhiking through Ohio last year, a white guy stepped out of a car full of black musicians in his stocking feet. 'I'm in BB King's band,' he said. 'Sorry, but we're too full to offer you a ride,' and he gave me his fish sandwich. What a lifesaver." I thought for a moment. "That was seven months and a lifetime ago. I got arrested and lost touch with my girlfriend, who'd come with me from New York, and guess what?"

"Tell me what?" Her big black eyes squinted, scrutinizing my face for answers, while I weighed whether to offer my honest thoughts.

"She looked a lot like you, Natasha, a smart, tough, fearless girl."

"Oh, I'm not so fearless. I've never hitchhiked; I'm more of a bookworm."

"You're a linguist and a scholar and I'm just a high school dropout, but I'm well read on Buddhism and history. Maybe you could help me write it up in a book someday."

"Maybe," she said, and let it hang there as she laid back against me. "Get some rest. BB King is on in an hour."

Despite our intentions, we were both too tired to leave our dry nest for the stage. We let the ragged blues of BB King serenade us from afar, to doze off and on in each other's arms. When Natasha's friends returned, smashed on wine and grass to await dawn's early light, they winked and asked me how I was doing.

"Groovy" was the one word I used to describe my situation. With Natasha sleeping like a baby at my side, I felt fulfilled. Her warm presence gave me some satisfaction, even if we didn't have sex. That would come, of course. I'd take it slow, enjoy our precious time together, however she wanted it with faith in her love.

Dawn shone through a misty drizzle on Sunday morning and our wake-up call wasn't hard rock, but a new chant.

Hare Krishna! Hare Krishna! Krishna Krishna! Hare Hare!

I disentangled myself from my still sleeping Russian lady and followed my ears to its source. A meandering band in orange and saffron robes with Hindu markings on their foreheads banged conga drums and finger cymbals as they snake danced in ecstasy through the sleeping crowd. The men's heads were shaved except for a scalp lock, whereas the women, in colorful sexy saris, wore their long hair loose under flowing shawls. I had chanted with these *Krishna* devotees a few times in Chicago's Old Town and enjoyed their free vegetarian feasts.

When the Krishnas reached the empty stage, they climbed up and continued chanting. Whether they were an official performance or a spontaneous act, I didn't know. A few spectators joined in, however far more heckled them. I spotted people munching on bananas, which reminded me that I was starving, and I scored a few for myself and my Russian lady before they were all gone.

Natasha and her friends were up by the time I returned. We gobbled the bananas, and she shared some granola with me, assuaging my hunger for food, at least. I repressed my other hunger, confident of its full satisfaction at my lady's pleasure.

"We have to leave soon," the guy getting into the driver's seat said. My Russian lady shot me a demure, almost bashful look. "Are you coming along with us?"

"Where are you going?"

"Freeport, ever been there?"

I took it as an invitation. "No, but I'd love to check it out if that's alright."

"Sure." She gave me a brusque hug, as if embarrassed. We were still getting acquainted. From my all too brief relationships, I'd learned that a guy could never be too sure where he stood with a chick. I had to keep fighting for her interest and build a nest in her heart.

The driver backed the truck up through the tire sucking mud, swaying over bumps, and sloshing through potholes, meandering slow and careful around the collection of pup tents and somnolent bodies lying in the open until we reached the gate and joined the growing bumper to bumper caravan of early departures.

With the blankets over our heads, Natasha and I kissed, but she kept pulling my hands out from under her flannel shirt. The others were asleep, paying us no mind, and I wanted to know where I stood.

"Look, Natasha, you know I'm not some male chauvinist pig, or a selfish jerk who only wants to have his way with you. Don't you think we can give each other some love and pleasure? I mean..."

"Shush, Ron, I'm tired. Let's not talk about this now."

I'd found a woman as interested in world events as I was, someone who understood what I was talking about when I rambled on about the Revolution, and I assumed our far-ranging conversation meant as much to her as me. But what was I to make of her lack of interest in sex? Was she uptight about it or was I stuck in her *friend* category? I'd have to be patient and win her over.

We sped north to Rockford, then due west to Freeport, as I dozed off. The Kickapoo festival ran from Friday, May 29 to Sunday, May 31.

Illinois State Police said that only about 25,000 of the crowd, estimated at various times to range anywhere from 40,000 to a high of 80,000--- remained at the L. Davis farm, site of the festival.

The Chicago Tribune, Monday June 1, 1970, section 2, col. 1

9

FREEPORT

As we approached Freeport, Natasha banged on the cab's back window and shouted, "Pull over at the next house." Then she turned to me and said, "I've got to drop you off with some college students and take care of some business."

We pulled into a driveway where three long-haired guys were loading a car. "This is Ron," she said. "I need a place for him to crash a couple of days. Can he stay here with you?"

"Well," the blond guy said, stroking his Christ like beard. "We're leaving town for a couple of days, too. He'll have to stay out of our nosey landlord's sight."

"Why's that?" I asked.

"If he knows you're staying, he'll jack up our rent, because we pay per person to live here. So, unless you can pay, you'd better stay out of sight. Okay?"

This lease agreement seemed slanted for the property owner. I'd assumed people rented at a flat rate and the more bodies came to chip in, the more affordable it should be.

"But you're still paying the same rent while you are gone. Right? I'd be the only one here. It doesn't sound fair."

"Who said capitalism is fair, man?"

I promised to come and go by the back door and keep a low profile for a couple of days until they got back. Natasha gave my heart another hard wrench when she kissed me on the cheek, more like a sister than a lover.

"Bye Ron!" Her voice sounded chipper, but I saw a tear on her cheek and wondered if it was a token of sorrow at leaving me there. "I'll see you soon, just a couple days."

Without further explanation, she climbed back into the truck. Stiff and mute as a statue, I watched the truck back out and roar away; wondering if this was a loyalty test, or her way of dumping me. I thought we'd forged a deep connection on our long day and night together and didn't want to lose this elusive Russian girl, despite the fact that she'd abandoned me in that mid-sized town in the Corn Belt. She was gone on a wing and my prayer for her speedy return. What else could I do but wait?

The three students finished packing, handed me a key, and drove off. The sudden silence enveloped me. Once again, I stood alone, a stranger in a strange land, wondering why everyone had to leave town. Maybe it was a school holiday. I swallowed hard and put on a brave face, masking my confusion, masking all my raging turmoil below the surface, as if I'd expected all along for Natasha to dump me like an abandoned dog. I went inside and sat alone in the empty house, haunted by my bad luck, which once again had stolen my love. I already had an extensive list of disappointments.

Back in September, my girlfriend, Bonnie, had been forbidden by her comrades to admit me into her radical collective in New York, after we'd hitchhiked in from Chicago. Then I'd met Karen, and she joined me on a grueling journey back to Chicago, which ended in disaster with my arrest. Still aged seventeen, I lost my freedom and had no way of finding her when I got out. A series of new loves in the mental hospital had been frustrated by the administration, but I was free at last and sick of being alone. Therefore, I hung onto my hopes for this Russian girl. I could wait a couple of days, and when she returned, she would have time for me.

Meanwhile, I'd use my time to focus on meditation, maybe even achieve the sidhi, the psychic power, of precognition or astral projection. If Natasha failed to come back to me, I could hitchhike back to the Chicago area. It was only 80 miles to the West End neighborhood, a straight shot due east along US 20, which became Lake Street, the umbilical cord linking me to the closest thing I had to a *home*, so near and yet so far.

The guys had told me the larder was empty, but I knew that when spoiled middle-class kids said there was no food, they omitted things that only a desperate rat would munch. But this time, the cupboard held absolutely nothing except a half empty bottle of Karo corn syrup and a few slices of extremely hard stale bread. I was a revolutionary yogi, wasn't I? I would FAST and seek divine nourishment.

Although my conception of these yogic techniques only came from my books, I received flashes of inspiration, spiritual insight, and waves of blissful reward rained down at times, but hours later my mind became hazy as my rumbling, empty stomach cried for mundane nourishment and my brain craved sleep.

The next morning, I took a swig of karo and half a slice of bread. Remembering my disciplined military heroes surviving on hard tack or iron rations during the war, I ignored my hungry sensations. Every day I applied myself, sitting cross-legged in full lotus position, until my legs became numb, then I went to half lotus, but I found it hard to stay awake and gave in to sleep more than usual. I took walking meditations around the house, and slipped out the back door after dark, so I'd remain invisible to the nosey landlord, and walked around the silent neighborhood, meeting no one.

On the third day, the bottle of Karo stood like a lonely sentry on an empty pantry shelf, staring me down until I finished it. When the students said *a couple of days*, I thought two, but when they hadn't returned, I splurged, spending my last two dollars on what meager food I could afford in a market some distance away. That scratched my hunger for a few hours, but it returned, although I was drinking lots of water to compensate.

The students finally came back on the afternoon of June fourth. I'd reached the limit of my endurance, but they had brought food and, after some hesitation, allowed me to join them in a nourishing meal.

"How long are you staying here?" they asked.

"Gee, I don't know. When's Natasha coming back?"

No one knew. She was just a friend's friend to them. They called a house meeting, warning me that the landlord was going to show up and when he did, he said he knew that I'd been staying there and laughed when I insisted that I was just a visitor.

"We need to list you on the lease to start paying rent if you're going to stay."

My benefactors didn't want to make waves with him, so I agreed to leave. Everything seemed *unreal*, illusory, like I was on a heavy acid trip as I walked out the front door. Then, just like in the old movies, the cavalry arrived. My Russian lady drove up. She'd come to save me from my lonely exile. Or so I hoped.

"Do you have time to stick around, Ron?" she asked, as if I had pressing business elsewhere.

"Sure." I kept as cool as I could. "I've nothing cooking at the moment."

"Good, I'd like you to meet some of our people with the anti-draft resistance."

"Okay, let's go." I was bleary-eyed from days of isolation and hunger, but my life was starting up again.

10

SALVATION

Natasha drove me to an office staffed by both freaky long hairs and straight collegiate students. Dazed from my long, hungry isolation, I only half listened as she rushed through introductions and discussed demonstrations, draft card burnings, and other rallies she was organizing. Her attitude was impersonal, all business, until she stopped, took a deep breath, pulled me closer and spoke in a low tone.

"Ron, I am *sooo* sorry. This must have been *very* difficult for you." I nodded my head in agreement and she went on. "Look, I'm going to turn you over to this other girl, Audrey." She smacked her lips and let out a weary sigh. "I've told her all about you, and she's happy to show you around."

Someone walked into the room for a file of papers and Natasha waited until he passed through the room and back out to the hall before she continued.

"This girl, she's a friend and, well, pretty loose sexually, kind of a slut, if you know what I mean." She giggled and put her hand over her mouth. "And well, she can, ah, take care of your *needs* much better than I ever could."

I couldn't believe my ears in my semi-lucid state. Maybe I was delirious, hallucinating, but if it was real, I didn't want to overreact and blow it, so cool as ice, I nodded my calm acceptance of her generous offer, as if it was an ordinary thing for a girl to hand me off to another woman with the promise of sexual satisfaction. Throughout my adolescence, I'd dreamed of wild scenarios like that, but never expected to experience it.

A cheerful blond girl bounced in. Natasha took her arm and led her to me. "Ron, this is Audrey." She gave me a sly wink. "You two should get along fabulously."

Audrey gave my hand a squeeze and smiled as she looked me over from head to toe.

"Excuse me now," Natasha said. "I have things to do, so run along." And she disappeared down the hall.

My new dream girl giggled and, with a gleam in her eye, said, "It looks like you're all mine now. Would you like to take a walk around Freeport?"

"Sure, let's go."

Her warm hand still held mine, and the touch convinced me that Audrey was *real* and I noticed she was much prettier and curvier than Natasha. It intrigued me that Natasha described her as a slut. Some women loved to denigrate other women, calling them whores and sluts, which they consider shameful, accepting the double standard that divided women into categories: *bad* girls who *did*, and *nice* girls who *didn't* have sex, at least not until they had a marriage ring on their finger. It made *nice* girls who became haughty women insecure about their sexuality, even ambivalent or frigid.

And men? They were given license to fuck all the *bad* girl sluts they could handle, at least until they *finally* settled down with a nice, boring *good* girl. However, in my experience, having talked to men all over the country, those married men, as often as not, complained that their nice wives were cold and no fun in bed and continued seeking sluts. That situation seemed counterproductive and anti-social to me, but I prided myself on my nonconformity to inhuman morals and, as an adolescent, I swore that I would only fall in love with a slut.

Natasha had proven to be too *nice,* but frigid or not, I owed her tremendous gratitude for giving me Audrey as a consolation prize after all she'd put me through. Audrey was fresh air, an absolute angel, and I would take a so-called slut any day over an ice queen.

As she led me downstairs, Audrey half turned to give me a leer that filled me with renewed hope that my situation was improving. Her warm hand clasped mine tight, as she went through the motions of showing me downtown Freeport. Then we came to a park bench where we sat, smiling at each other.

"She told me so much about you, Ron. How you've been in jail and all around the country. She said I should get to know you better and, ah, sure, I'm looking forward to that."

"Well, I'm happy to meet you, too." I said, and kissed her hand like a continental swain, then I continued smooching along her bare arm all the way to her neck, like Gomez on the Adams Family TV show, and we both laughed.

"Oh, that was nice," she shivered, running her tongue over her lips. "Keep going, man." That was all the encouragement I needed to keep kissing, and I put my hands where Natasha forbade them. Kissing Audrey was better, sexier, no holds barred, compared to Natasha. She opened wide, inviting my deep tongue and replied in kind, giving my hands unimpeded access to her luscious bosoms, her nipples stiffening to my touch, arousing me even more. God! They felt even better than I had hoped. She pulled away with a crooked smile, her melting eyes drinking me in as her hand groped the engorged bulge in my pants.

"Please make love to me, Ron." Her straightforward request bowled me over, multiplying the hot turned-on rush I felt.

"You bet. I'll make love to you." I was dizzy, my words slurred, as the gates of heaven opened to me, and yet, after all I'd been through, I felt disassociated from the intensity of my feelings like an observer as much as a participant in these heady events.

Audrey saw someone she knew and bummed us a ride to her grandma's place. It was in an upscale mobile home park on US 20 east of town, a double wide manufactured home, much roomier than a regular trailer home, with a bedroom up a short flight of steps from the cozy living room.

Her voice sounded husky in my ear. "My Gram is going to be out for a couple of days, so we'll have the place to ourselves." We stripped and got down to the business of enjoying each other. Her body intoxicated me, just looking at and running my hands over her warm flesh, spurred me to give her as much excitement as she gave me. I felt more alive than I had in ages, loving her like no one before, and our initial intense coupling produced a jagged orgasm, after which we took it down a notch to last longer and try alternate positions: front, back and sideways. Then we showered, rested, and went at it again, building back up to a roaring finish.

This wildcat of a woman seemed perfect for me, my uninhibited, gorgeous slut, which was not a slur but a compliment. Forget Natasha with her prim intellectual isolation. Audrey was the woman I had been seeking to love forever. In the afterglow of our climax, we relaxed in each other's arms, chatting.

In a jocular mood, I asked her how it felt to be "fucked like a slut." She laughed, and I followed up with "You are my beautiful little whore," all in playful fun, of course, or so I thought. She giggled at my words, but I may have gone too far and would pay for it.

After our night together and breakfast in the morning, we went out to meet her girlfriend, Lynn, who had the car that Audrey borrowed from her grandma. They asked me to drive them around. I'd had a driver's license since high school, a full two years before, but I had lost my glasses and hadn't driven since then, which made me a little nervous backing up and pulling out into traffic. Audrey chided me.

"What's the matter with you, man? Can't ya even drive?"

"Of course I can! I'm just a little out of practice."

"Well, be careful with my grandma's car!"

"Leave him alone," Lynn said. "Just let him drive, alright?"

I was grateful for Lynn's sympathetic words that crosscut Audrey's sarcasm. After all I'd been through, I needed all the encouragement I could get. Lynn understood how stressed and insecure I felt below my fake calm. I had to cover up my insecurity or lose points with Audrey. If my manhood slipped even a notch in her eyes, I could lose her, having learned that love has no conscience. The law of the jungle ruled romance and lay behind the fickle hearts of women and men. I couldn't risk losing my new girl, as I had so many others. After all, I had no car, no money, no job, and no prospects of getting any of that soon and I had no illusions about what my poverty could do to our relationship.

Back at her place, we three plopped on the couch and watched TV, and then Lynn waited on the couch while Audrey and I went upstairs for another, more subdued round of lovemaking. Audrey was more than I could have hoped for, and I'd been unwanted and sleeping alone so long. Our sex was great, and my jokes made her giggle. Afterwards, I went down to watch TV. Audrey said she'd rest and pop down later, so I sat beside Lynn against the couch on the floor. She looked at me with a serious face.

"Audrey has a pretty big mouth sometimes, Ron, but don't worry, she doesn't really mean it."

"Thanks, Lynn. I appreciated your encouragement. You could be a good referee for us to keep around." She smiled at that.

When Audrey came down, we threw some dinner together and drank a bottle of wine. All went well. I felt like part of the family. Saturday morning, we just hung around the house, making brunch. The girls chatted with excitement about upcoming concerts.

Audrey nudged Lynn. "The first free concert of the year is in Lincoln Park tomorrow at noon." Her voice lowered, but I could still hear. "Gee, I wonder if *you know who* will be there."

Lynn gave me a furtive glance that I pretended not to notice and whispered close to Audrey's ear. "Sure, all the black dudes will be there." She turned to me, sitting across the table. "Do you wanna come with us to the concert in Chicago, Ron?"

"Sure, Chicago is my turf. I'll show you gals around."

"Oh, don't bother," Audrey said. "We've already got plenty of friends in Chicago." She giggled. "A couple of our, ah, black friends are heavy into the music scene."

Lynn cut in. "We'll introduce you. They're pretty cool dudes."

I read between the lines. They had to be boyfriends, current or former lovers. The casual mention of a boyfriend would have gotten an angry reaction from some guys I knew, but I was tactful, and didn't question it. Of course, she'd had other guys. I believed in being inclusive, not possessive. Maybe I was too smug, but as far as I knew Audrey and I *dug* each other with mutual intensity, we made a great couple, and I didn't want to spoil a good thing.

Even if Audrey hooked up with someone for a while, that meant Lynn and I could get together, too. Fair is fair, and I could dig some open sharing in the love department, as long as it didn't blow me out of the picture. We would be an inclusive, loving hippie tribe, maybe even have kids.

11

FREE CONCERT IN LINCOLN PARK

Grandma returned late Saturday night. Audrey said she was *cool* with everything and not to worry, but as a precaution, she had me sleep on the couch while she and Lynn shared the upstairs bed. The past few days with Audrey had been amazing, the best continuous love fest I had experienced, and it had to be only the beginning of our togetherness.

Early Sunday morning, we got up and Grandma cooked a quick family breakfast. Then we walked one hundred feet to the highway that ran by the trailer court and stuck out our thumbs. Grandma needed her car, so we couldn't drive, but with two beautiful girls, the rides came fast. In less than three hours, much less time than it took a male hitchhiker alone, we pulled to the curb beside Lincoln Park on Lakeshore Drive.

The park was already teeming with an eclectic mix of white, black, and Puerto Rican Freaks, young and old. A few were pounding their conga drums and playing trumpets, the organic music of the masses, which created a cozy feeling of being together in a spontaneous community. The tangy aroma of Reefer pervaded the assembly as grinning benefactors passed around joints and wine to enhance the electric atmosphere. But despite all this, a sense of unease crept into my heart.

Audrey scanned the crowd, searching for someone, and refused to hold my hand. She whispered to Lynn, her co-conspirator, and my flirtatious efforts to regain her attention fell flat. Her pretty face twisted into a snarl at me, as if she had bitten a sour lemon. I needed to give her some space. Then I spotted Chris and his brothers with John W.

"Hey," I said, beckoning at the girls. "Come meet my good friends." I walked over, but the girls shot me a glance and didn't follow.

Chris grabbed my shoulder. "Where've you been? Nobody's seen you since Kickapoo! We thought you got lost, killed, or maybe even got lucky."

"Well, it was sort of a mix of all that." I forced a laugh and tried to sound upbeat. "I did get lucky, big time, and came here with a couple of cool chicks."

"Oh yeah? Where are they at?" He evidenced more than casual interest.

"See over there." I pointed to where they had been standing twenty feet away, toward the stage.

"Which ones?" he said.

The girls were moving away, as if trying to lose me in the crowd. My heart sank, but I put on a brave face. "Too late, man, they're, ah, looking for some friends. I'll go and try to bring them over."

Chris pulled me aside. "Look at John over there." He sounded concerned. John sat crouched against a tree, tears streaming down his cheeks, the music drowning out his sobs. I was sure it was drugs.

"Is he high or something?"

"Naw! He's just a fucking mess, is all. Been like that all day without any reason. I can't get through to him. He just sits there and cries like a baby."

Some deep, internal problem sabotaged John. Maybe Eva's death, two months ago, had something to do with it. Eva told me she was in love with John the night before she died, and he was the closest thing to a boyfriend the thirteen-year-old girl ever had. Whether or not he felt the same for her, or even knew about her crush on him, I didn't know, but she started acting suicidal, running into traffic. The next day, she got hit on a busy highway. John must have felt partly responsible, although he never said so.

I was a loser, too. We all had problems, even if we didn't acknowledge them. The world we lived in was a madhouse, but it was home and we were in it together. Buddhism explained our common situation best; we are all experiencing the same traumas through birth and death on the wheel of Karma, spinning through this messy, interdependent life together. Only altruistic love can ennoble and save our wretched existence.

I kneeled beside John. "Hey man, what's wrong?" There was no response, so I shook him. "Talk to me, man! It can't be that bad." He looked up at me like a wounded animal, his eyes streaming tears, useless, self-pitying tears. I failed to snap him out of it and went looking for my Freeport ladies.

They were jabbering away with a trio of older, graying Black dudes dressed to kill in pink and velvet shirts and leather beanies atop their Afros. Audrey didn't look at me and ignored my hello. Lynn gave me a stiff *Yeah okay, hi*, without enthusiasm, loyal to her girlfriend above me. Neither of them attempted to introduce me to their snazzy companions. I didn't crowd them. Whether the men were old friends or brand-new acquaintances, they enthralled our ladies.

Although missing the warmth they had bestowed on me just the day before, I hung in there, a fool for love. No matter how many lovers Audrey took, my love remained steadfast. I couldn't regret a moment of our passionate interlude, if that's all it was, and wracked my brain for why she was cutting me off so cold. Was it my driving, which improved after my first fumbling moments, or my poverty? I wracked my brain until I remembered something I had said in jest.

I'd called her my *little whore*. It was all in fun pillow talk while we clowned around after the best sex I'd ever had, and her moaning climax had led me to believe I'd satisfied her as well. Stupid words that I meant as adoration came back to haunt me. Somehow, I had to salvage the situation and win her back.

Chris found me. "Hey man, we're gonna take off." He looked around at the people nearby. "I thought you said you were here with some chicks?" He sounded doubtful.

I led him to Audrey and put my hand on her shoulder. She shrugged it off as if I were an impertinent stranger, which I hoped Chris didn't notice.

"Audrey, this is my pal, Chris. I think I told you about him."

She snapped a wan smile at us. "Yeah, hi Chris." She turned her focus back to the black guys. Chris shot me a quizzical look and brought his mouth to my ear. "She's a stone fox, man, but you've got trouble in paradise, huh?"

"Chicks, Man. You know how they are."

Chris shook his head. "I know too well. Good luck!"

It was embarrassing. If he hadn't known me better, Chris might have thought I'd made it up. I wasn't the kind of guy to pretend a chick went for him when she didn't.

The band began a mellow, bluesy tune, and the girls began dancing with their trio of studs. I thought about inserting myself into the mix, but they weren't acknowledging me, and that would make me look as desperate as I felt and fuel Audrey's contempt for me.

Chris' brother came over and blurted, "Let's go, we're ditching John." He glanced at me. "Unless you wanna stay and keep an eye on him?"

"Sure, I can't just leave him to his fate on the mean streets of Chicago." Then I snickered at a wicked thought. "Or could I?" We laughed at that. "Nah," I said. "Tempted though I am, I'm too nice a guy. But maybe that's what John needs, to make it on his own like a big boy."

With Audrey shunning me, I didn't have anything better to do than take care of John in the state he was in. He could say the stupidest things to the wrong people at the worst times. You never knew what could pop out of his mouth. Chicago was gangster city. Someone could take offence for any reason, so I had to watch out for him, but I'd drop him off where he wouldn't be robbed or killed.

John still sat against the tree. He seemed better, changing into his usual manic self, slapping his thighs in time to the music.

"Come on John, let's go," I said.

"Where're the other guys?" He sounded like a naïve child.

"They're long gone, man."

"Gone? But things are just picking up! Man, listen to those drums!"

Small groups of people playing bongos, horns, and guitars were still at it. It was organic, unpretentious people's music, but I wasn't in the mood anymore.

"You wanna stay, John? Go ahead, but I'm splitting this scene." I started walking, and he jumped up and tagged along, rambling on about how much he dug the music.

"Feeling better, John?"

"What do ya mean? I'm cool." He acted as if he hadn't cried all morning.

I took him over to meet Audrey, but in those few minutes, they were already gone. Without a goodbye, she'd cut me loose. It felt like a knife sliced through my heart and a lump grew in my throat. I had to gulp a lungful of air and hold it tight to keep from losing control and weep like John had been doing. I couldn't show that side of myself. Not me, I was a fucking revolutionary and a goddamn Tantric yogi, not some whinny brat.

John and I walked to the exit of the parking lot onto Lakeshore Drive and tried hitchhiking together. Cars honked and cheerful people leaving the concert waved at us, but no one stopped. Finally, a car pulled over, and we ran up. Looking inside, I couldn't believe my eyes.

Audrey sat in the front seat, her face blank, between a couple of the suave black guys. I wondered whose idea it was to stop for us, and what, if anything, the girls told them about me and did it matter anymore.

Lynn sat in the back behind the driver, with the other guy on her right. He motioned us in to sit beside him. I climbed in with John at the door. Unsure what to expect or how I should greet them, I stammered, "Ah, hi Audrey."

"Oh wow," John blurted out. "You know this chick? She's a real doll, man!" He tapped the shoulder of the guy in front. "You're a couple of lucky studs with a hot looking chick between you. Do you know my pal, Ron? How'd you guys meet? That's synchronicity, man, to be picked up by friends, coincidences like that don't just happen, it is destiny. You dig?"

The guy by the right front door turned and looked over his dark shades at John with a bemused smile on his face and the driver moved his rear-view mirror to glance at him. Even Audrey turned her head and for a second our eyes met. I attempted to relay a telepathic message of my love before she faced front again. John kept rapping away.

"You black guys are way cool with me, man. I'm not prejudiced. No way, man! I think white freaks and black cats should chill out and jam together. Black chicks are beautiful too. Why can't we all just be friends? We aren't all that different from each other. Are we? Just our skin and you guys have kinky hair is all." His motor mouth ran on and on without let-up, embarrassing the hell out of me. I needed to distance myself from him before he ruined whatever chance I had.

I shook the hand of the guy on my left, mouthed a quiet hello to him and rolled my eyes, so he knew I thought John was a character. Lynn flashed me an anemic smile, the warmest sign of affection, or commiseration I got.

Whether they were amused or overwhelmed by John, the guys didn't appear hostile. Although no one mentioned a destination, they seemed to be heading to Freeport. I hoped the girls would say something in my favor so they would take me back with them. I hadn't figured out if I should mention going back to Freeport with the driver as we whooshed across Chicago on the Eisenhower expressway. When we got off and headed west on Lake Street, Audrey finally spoke.

"Where should we drop you guys?"

"Just a little farther," John said. "I'll tell you when."

As we approached the familiar landmark of Fischer's farm, I was still wrestling with what to say to salvage my relationship with Audrey, but John beat me to it.

"You can let us off here," John said as we crossed Route 83.

Getting out of the car, I turned back. "Bye Audrey." I tried to sound cheerful, but not gushy. "Maybe I'll see you again sometime. Huh?"

"Yeah, maybe, bye." She sounded perturbed.

I hadn't gotten her phone number, assuming there would be plenty of time for that before she had frozen me out of the equation. I wondered if I could ask for it without giving myself away as a desperate loser, when John slammed the door, and they tore off. The experience felt more psychedelic than real. This moment couldn't be the end of our encounter.

John and I ran up the embankment to the Sunnyside Church of God to find the basement coffeehouse closed. There was nothing there to fix my broken heart, anyway. It was just me and John. Wracking my brain, I came up with a new mission.

"Let's walk down to Elmhurst, John. My friend Sandy should be there."

"Sure, man, I'm up for any kind of adventure." He had recovered his balance and would be company of some kind.

I'd been interested in Sandy since I met her, but she'd kept me at arm's length, locked in the friend category. She was hanging around the student union, passing out leaflets with some other RYM guys, when John and I showed up. I introduced her to John, trying to explain to Sandy in an aside that he was a little off.

She sounded doubtful. "Crazy, you say? He seems okay to me." She called him *Brother John* and treated him with marked consideration, which reminded me that we were all brothers and sisters in the Movement.

Sandy pulled us toward a bench and sat down. "So, what have you been up to, Ron?"

"I went to the Kickapoo concert and made some new friends and hung out with them in Freeport." I left out my romantic adventures and framed it as seeing what their draft resistance community was up to. That piqued her interest.

Sandy smiled and said, "I think I need a road trip."

"Well, okay then." I tried to hide my surprised excitement. "Let's go to Freeport."

"Let's go," John said. And so, that same Sunday, we three mixed up adventurers began our strange road adventure.

12

BOOMERANG

Maybe I still had a chance to win Audrey back. Showing up with the slim, politically savvy Sandy could help. Audrey might assume that Sandy was my *old lady* and at least I wouldn't come off as a total loser and it might make her want me again. Jealousy works as an aphrodisiac with some women.

It could work the other way, too. If Audrey became interested, Sandy might see my value as more than a friend. They each had something the other lacked. Maybe I'd even get both. We'd build an open, loving, sexy partnership, a revolutionary family together. It was easier said than done, as I'd seen in the New Mexico commune I joined a year ago, but I'd learned from that disaster and was confident we could pull it off.

Filled with song and high hopes, we three stuck out our thumbs headed west on Lake Street as the late afternoon sun began its descent. With pretty Sandy facing traffic, guys stopped for us, but at that hour on Sunday, our rides took us only a few miles farther into the green countryside before the glorious sunset ended our day and darkness embraced us.

Sandy scanned our surroundings. "We'd better find a place to camp for the night."

I nodded in agreement. "Yeah, we're only a little more than halfway there and the traffic has wound down."

We hunkered in a culvert under the highway that blocked most of the wind. None of us had sleeping bags, or anything more than light jackets. This was the least prepared road trip I'd blundered into, but at least we had each other.

"Ah, the pleasures of the hobo life," I said, trying to lift our flagging spirits. We were boon companions, rebels *with* a cause. Sandy pulled out her harmonica, and we took turns making noise on it in our vain attempt at playing the Blues.

"We stink," John said.

Sandy shot him a look. "Hey! We don't need any negative criticism, man!"

"It's organic People's music," I said, flashing on old cowboy flicks of playing harmonicas around the campfire, but without a campfire to warm us, we snuggled together, and fell asleep in each other's arms.

In the sun's pale warmth, we emerged like trolls from under our bridge on Monday the 8th of June. It hit me how crazy I was to be chasing after Audrey so soon after she dumped me, but life was nothing but a wild, crazy ride to the far side, and all three of us had nothing better to do then to chase illusive rainbows.

We caught a ride and got dropped off in Freeport just as a main street bakery turned its closed sign to open. Sandy bought us some day-old bread, pasties and coffee for our breakfast. I was flat broke. John had a few bucks and said he would catch our next meal. We wandered around like lost tourists until I recognized Natasha's old brick office building. She wasn't there, and I didn't see any familiar faces. Sandy laid her *Revolution Now* rap on a few guys we met, but they weren't interested.

"Freeport is a drag," she said.

I shrugged. "Well, there's a cool chick we should meet."

"Is she into the movement?"

"Well, yeah, sort of." I lied, not at all sure where Audrey's head was at. I'd have to brazen it out. "Come on." I directed us back to the highway.

A guy stopped. "Where to?"

"Could you let us off at the trailer court?"

"Which one? There are two trailer courts."

Lucky for me, the first try was the right one. We marched up to the familiar trailer and I knocked on the door. Grandma eyed me with suspicion, as if she didn't recognize me.

"Is Audrey here?"

"No, she's not back yet."

"Do you know when she'll be back?"

"No." As she looked me over, her face lit up in recognition. "Didn't she leave with you on Sunday?"

"Well, yeah, but she got a ride back with some other guys."

Grandma didn't invite us in. Without her granddaughter to vouch for me, I was just a stranger standing there with two other complete strangers.

"That's all I know. Bye!" she said as she shut the door on me. Hearing the door's bolt lock chilled me with a sense of finality. I turned around and hesitated, wondering if I should wait around for Audrey to get back.

"I guess she isn't back yet," I said, expressing the obvious.

An idea formed in my head. Maybe Audrey had told Grandma to lie, but was hiding inside. But more likely she was shacked up with her friends somewhere and even if she wasn't, she wouldn't welcome me back.

"Jeez," John said. "What do we do now?"

Sandy crossed her arms, sighed, and shot me a baleful look. "So, this is your big scene, huh? It looks like we came all this way for nothing."

True, I'd led them on a wild goose chase and felt lost, with no place left to go.

"We might as well head back to Elmhurst," John said, making perfect sense.

We trudged back to the highway and stuck out our thumbs. From where we stood, I kept an eye on Grandma's trailer, in case a blond head popped out, but of course my hopes were in vain.

Sandy seemed stiff and distant, but there was nothing lost, because I'd never had a chance with her, anyway. Free spirit John borrowed her harmonica and blew out some caterwauling blues.

Sometimes I feel like a motherless child. It fit my mood.

Getting a ride to Chicago with Audrey and her girlfriend had been a snap, but three people hitchhiking together is not recommended when two are dudes. We languished at the side of the highway, becoming far too familiar with individual trees and cracks in the pavement as we awaited our benefactor. After a long hour's wait, we got a ride and left Freeport and an enormous chunk of my heart behind.

Although I tried to make light of it, the camaraderie of the night before was missing. At our next stopover, I took a turn on the mouth organ, blowing the blues as best I could, which was far from great. John and I cavorted like monkeys or jesters in the Queen's court to keep our long-faced lady amused, but all our attempts to impress her fell short.

Nightfall found us back in Elmhurst. Sandy didn't want to bring us to her place. I assumed because we weren't cleared by her comrades in whatever collective she belonged to. She took us first to Wilder Park for the night, but then remembered that the pigs rousted everyone trying to sleep there.

"There's another park," she said. "I heard they don't hassle people there."

Sandy led us far from the familiar campus to an unknown edge of town. There was no one else but us there and we huddled, freezing cold, without blankets under the lone tree we hoped would block the chilling wind. I'd assumed comrade Sandy would bivouac there with us. Maybe she had every intention of doing so, but the cold ground was even more uncomfortable than our companionable night under the bridge. After a brief hug, she left for her warmer digs among better situated friends.

My thwarted feelings for Sandy melted away in the chilly damp, and I wondered what I saw in her. Yet I still longed for my lost Audrey, the girl I should have beside me forever.

John and I did our best to zone out into unconsciousness, but the tree offered too little protection from the wind. We shivered, and our teeth chattered from the cold.

"Forget it!" John stood up and jumped to get his circulation moving. "Let's get the hell out of here, man."

We picked ourselves up and stumbled back to the West End. For once, the cops didn't hassle us on our trek across Elmhurst. On the way we found new companions.

Jeff J and another dude I didn't know walked up with a pale and frail, pimple faced girl. I hadn't met her before. Her blond hair was hacked short, and she wore a brand-new oversized jean jacket. Jeff snarled in apparent irritation.

He yelled at her. "Go home. We don't want you tagging along with us!"

"Jeff," I said. "What's the poor girl done to you?"

"This stupid bitch has been chasing after us like a lost puppy all day. Her name is Sue, says she's running away from home, but we don't want her around."

Sue was like a little sister who wanted to play with the big boys.

"Doesn't be an asshole, Jeff," I said. "You're no prize either, you know."

Stories circulated about his drunken plead for affection from a girl who wanted nothing to do with him. The other amorous couples in the car with them that night laughed as they told me how he begged.

"Oh pleeease! Pleeeease let me touch you, just once!"

His whining made a sickening display that only worsened the girl's revulsion with him. It was a night of weakness that he had to live down. How sad for Sue to be undesired, even by such a desperate fellow as Jeff.

"You want her?" Jeff said. "Okay, Ron, you can have her."

The girl was no bombshell, but the poor desperate thing wouldn't resign herself to such sneering treatment if she had anywhere else to go.

I told her, "You can stick around with us if you want." That seemed to upset John. "Shit, Ron, we've got enough to deal with." But I prevailed. John could go his own way for all I cared, but he, too, didn't want to return to his parents' house. We had nowhere to turn but my usual refuge from life's storm, the warm darkness of the Tree house in Fischer's Woods.

It slept four or more comfortably, two to each side of the tree on each of the two platforms, plenty of room, but as far as I knew, no female had yet succeeded in climbing up. I handed her the rope and supported her from behind, but her strength failed in the crucial exercise of hoisting herself over the parapet, and despite several tries, she slid back down.

"That's okay, I'll stay down here." And so, she sat exhausted against the tree on the log among the mosquitoes. They swarmed thicker on the ground, although John and I had our share of them in our higher elevation. The mysterious forest noises may have held some terror for her in the night, but she proved her grit by sticking it out, surviving for yet another day.

13

BACK TO CHICAGO

On a perch eighty feet above the sleeping platform, I watched, thrilled, as the blood red dawn light silhouetted the shadow of the Hancock building in downtown Chicago. It was Tuesday, the ninth of June, and I allowed the dawn's splendor to inspire me for a new day's bold adventure before I descended to rouse John. Together we climbed down to find Sue, still sitting on the log where we'd left her.

Her face, puffy from mosquito bites and crying, betrayed the agony of her night, but seeing us, her eyes lit with fresh hope. "Let me come with you guys! Please, I won't be no trouble."

"Forget it," John said. "I know a place we can crash, but she might get in the way."

"That's okay, John. We'll bring her along." I had to find her some refuge in this cruel world.

"Okay, Ron, she's your problem."

My paltry possessions consisted of several shirts, a couple of frayed pairs of jeans and an olive-green Army surplus jacket, which I gathered from Chris's house, and stuffed it into a borrowed knapsack with a worn-out sleeping bag that was a spontaneous gift. Sue already had her basics, and John met us dressed in fresh bell bottoms, a top hat he had picked up somewhere, and a peace medallion around his neck. His jean jacket was stuck like a pincushion with buttons carrying revolutionary symbols and slogans: Peace Now! Right On! Power to the People! Black Power! Make love, not war. One was a raised middle finger, and another was a black flag on a red background that stood for anarchy.

"You look like you escaped from the set of *Laugh-In*," I said.

"Why?" He blinked, clueless, but he couldn't help being himself.

We headed into the rising sun on Lake Street. Our first ride took us all the way to the downtown Loop. Wandering up Clark, we spotted another vagabond like us, panhandling for spare change, who had a story to tell.

"Just call me Weed," he said. That was a slang term for marijuana, with connotations of being free, natural, and uncultivated. "I just got out of the Navy after being wounded in Nam. My patrol boat got a direct hit that killed everyone else on board and blew me out into the Mekong River. See here." He raised his trouser leg to reveal jagged scars. "The MASH surgeons put my leg back together with a steel rod to replace a chunk of my thigh bone, leaving this leg a couple of inches shorter than the other one, but shit, I'm alive and I got the fuck out of the war zone."

Weed still wore green military fatigues, and his tussled mop of yellow hair was just starting to grow out, which lent credence to his story. He seemed haunted, like someone who had seen death up close and personal and learned to appreciate the simple joy of just being alive. I came to know him as a generous, unassuming guy who didn't ask much of others.

"I've already made a few bucks and I'm hungry. Come on, guys. I'm paying."

He led us to a nearby greasy spoon joint where we breakfasted and shared more of our biographies. Weed too needed a place to live, and we invited him to join our merry band. With our bellies full, we walked north to Old Town.

"I'm trying to remember how to get to a house where we can

crash," John said. "The Doan brothers took me there a couple of weeks ago."

He took us in circles and, knowing John, I became doubtful that he would find it.

Weed walked slowly, limping on his shortened leg. By his contorted face, I knew he was in pain, but after taking a short breather, he pushed on without complaint and we continued north on Broadway.

John suddenly pointed ahead. "I remember that blood bank. We're close! Come on, guys."

We turned east on Waveland Avenue, then north on Pinegrove Place, passing a couple of houses. "Here we are," he said, as Weed and our exhausted Sue sighed with relief.

A Freak sporting extra-long black locks answered the door and smiled at John. "I remember you. You're a friend of the Doan boys. Your friends aren't narcs, are they?"

"Of course not, man," John said, and motioned to me and Sue. "These are my West End pals. And this is our new buddy, Weed, who made it through the hell of Vietnam!"

"I'm Thomas, come on in." He introduced us to his *old lady,* whose long dark hair was parted down the middle, like his.

"It'll be cool for you to stay here," she said. "If you contribute what you can to our kitty for rent and food. The two bedrooms are taken, but you can make yourselves at home on the carpeted floor. It's a nice area, just a short stroll to Lake Michigan with a growing hip community. Tonight, we're having a rent party. Everyone who comes gives a donation; give us what you have and stay for the party."

"Groovy," John said, and we all nodded our agreement. Weed contributed the rest of his morning's take to cover all of us. I found our new digs more than adequate for our needs compared to the dives I had become accustomed to. We were street folks, the wandering, un-possessing nomads of the open road, who, by mutual design and opportunity, rolled out our sleeping bags to find repose wherever and whenever we could.

We were home at last, or at least we had a base to jump off from.

This couple had set up the rental agreement with the landlord and they were the official tenants. They claimed the nicest bedroom in back as their private reserve and a single guy we'd meet later when he got home from work claimed the room next to theirs.

"You look totally spent, Sue," Thomas said. "He won't mind if you flop in his room until he gets back." Exhausted, our blond Orphan Annie fell across the neatly made bed, snoring in no time.

They called their place the Waveland house, although the old single family brick house stood northeast of Waveland on Pine Grove. It didn't look run-down like a typical crash pad. Varnished sliding room dividers could separate one large community room into a living room in front and a dining room behind. It had a separate kitchen in back and two small bedrooms with a back porch overlooking the backyard and a couple of trees.

John and I decided to sell our blood at the blood bank we'd passed on Broadway. They paid ten dollars a pint for positive blood and twenty for negative. It was a royal sum for a few minutes of inconvenience. We sat in the office and filled out the required questionnaire about our present and past health, and then I had the pleasure of being interviewed by a pretty nurse. Everything went fine until she asked me, "Have you ever feinted?"

"Sure, I have," I said too soon. "Hasn't everyone?"

Although I didn't remember feinting dead away, I'd swooned, seen stars and entered a spacey twilight zone when I got clubbed on the head in the riot the year before. I assumed that was a normal occurrence in most people's lives, as everyone gets a bump on the head now and again. Looking at me with what I hoped was aroused sexual interest, she asked, "How often have you feinted?"

"Oh, not too often," I said with a straight face. "Maybe once or twice a month."

She looked disappointed. "You'll have to see the doctor."

He said, "Son, we can't take blood from anyone who's feinted even once."

"Well, that was a misleading question. Man!" I revised my story, said I'd misunderstood the meaning of faint, but it was too late. Later

I tried the other blood bank on Clark, close by, but the first place had called and blacklisted me. Although most of their donors were outright winos, they would not even accept my clean blood for free.

John and I were hungry. Mayor Daley had set up a Free Lunch program at a few locations in poor neighborhoods. One was a block west of Wells Street in Old Town, and we headed over there, taking an ill-advised shortcut through the Westside ghetto. Three black dudes came slinking up, dressed in floppy hats, and wearing shades to hide their emotions. They tightened a menacing circle around us.

"Hey Man! What you Honkies doing here?"

John, ever glib, spoke up with naïve innocence. "Wow man! You dudes look so cool in those shades! Where d'ya get 'em?" He jabbered on with enthusiasm, like he was their long-lost cousin.

The biggest one eyed him with suspicion. "You got any weed on you, man?"

"I sure do!" He produced a joint he'd been saving, lit it, and handed it to him. All the tension subsided as it made the rounds. Thanks to John, we'd managed to hit it off with them. He even offered them a few of his buttons.

"Are you guys hungry?" I said. "We're going over to get some of Daley's free food. You wanna come?"

"Daley stole that idea from the Black Panther's free meal program," One of the guys said. "He just wants to win votes and make himself look like he's supporting the people."

"True," I said. "All people everywhere need to unite in the Panther's Rainbow Coalition to fight in the common struggle. But food is food, and eating it don't make us supporters, we're just taking back some of what's ours.

"Yeah," John said. "I bet that fried chicken tastes good, too. Let's go!"

With our new companions, we got in the line to be handed an aluminum tray with fried chicken, mashed potatoes and peas or carrots, as good as if we had paid hard cash for it. It became a regular meal stop for me during my time in Chicago.

Racial tension simmered just below the boiling point in most cities, and it wouldn't change overnight, but a cooperative relationship between white, black, red, and yellow was possible.

14

THE PECULIAR ATTRACTION OF AN UGLY GIRL

Back at the Waveland house, Sue met us all smiles in the embrace of the other male resident of the house. He was a late twenties guy as skinny as she was. With his Fu Manchu mustache and blond hair combed down along the side of his bald cranium, he reminded me of Bozo the clown. His denim jacket had *Power to the People* emblazoned on the back and a Black Power button on his front. He was the master of the bedroom where Sue napped, and we had stowed our gear. Like magnets, they'd connected to each other and were enjoying the bliss of their newfound romance.

Sue kissed my cheek and squeezed my arm, grinning ear to ear. "I wanna thank you so much, Ron, for bringing me to Chicago with you." She stuck her tongue out at John, who shrugged and walked away. "If I didn't get away from home, I don't know what I would have done, but everything in my life is falling into place now."

A surge of pride filled me that I had helped her get away. And that brought these two lovebirds together. Unloved in her hometown, Sue was in his loving hands.

"See you at the party," Sue said. "We're going to walk along the lake."

Almost as soon as they left, another girl flounced in the back door. After a quick glance around, she giggled and batted her eyelashes at me. With a lusty grin spreading across her face, she gave me a careful look over before plopping beside me on the bench at the kitchen table. She was a short squat, thick bodied thing with acne scars and a bulbous nose set over coarse meaty lips, but she had plump breasts that stood out at least six inches from her chest. Squirming in her seat, she contrived to make it seem like an accident when she brushed her nipples against my arm, and she opened her eyes in fake alarm.

"Oh, sorry. Did I bump you?"

"No bother, it feels real nice."

She brushed against me some more and a flood of heat pumped into my brain. *Gawd*, I felt her nipples harden as her chest heaved against me with her hot breath on my neck. She was flirting like a brazen hussy straight out of my dreams, taking my breath away in a delirious rush.

She was no classic beauty. By the standards of the time, I considered her ugly, but the expert way she flaunted her body enhanced her allure, and my needs were more overtly sexual and less romantic than the cuddly affection of Sue and her new guy. I wasn't looking for a lifelong partner, not with her, just an uninhibited fuck, and it appeared, to my happy surprise, that our desire was mutual.

Ignoring the shocked look on the faces of those around us, we took matters into our own hands. I slipped my hand under her blouse and pawed her proffered tits. The feel of her warm flesh inflamed my desire to fever pitch. I wanted to take her with rough abandon, without bourgeois social niceties.

"Wanna fuck?" My words came out huskier than I expected.

She giggled. "You bet dude." Her hand brushed over the growing bulge of my crotch. "I'm ready for what you've got in there for me, handsome."

Her flattery added to my turn-on. Without further ceremony, I stood up and lifted this giggling wench off her feet. She wrapped her legs around me as I carried her like a sack of potatoes to the bedroom claimed by Sue and her new guy. He owed his lady love to me and shouldn't mind us baptizing his bed with our rash lust. In a spirit of bravado that felt new and refreshing to me, I tossed her onto the nice clean bed in his well-ordered room. We wasted no time on formal introductions, modesty, or a dishonest pretense of shame.

I manhandled her, which excited her and she let me do whatever I wanted. Pulling her clothes off, I paused to savor the sight and feel of her body, which more than made up for her zit ridden face. Then I rammed into her, eliciting a gasp, followed by a cry of pleasure as her pussy rippled, gripping my dick with each thrust.

Her eyes rolled back in her head while her body responded, and bucking like a mare in heat, she cried out, "Oh, yes!" which assuaged my tardy conscience at using this unnamed girl for my selfish pleasure.

Ugly enjoyed a great fuck as much as I did. Too bad she wasn't as attractive as any of my former lovers; I would have tried to keep her if she was. She became my surrogate for Audrey, my beloved whore. This ugly girl, panting below me, became beautiful, a worthy receptacle for my pent-up passion as I punished Audrey for leaving me through her. Rage helped transform my thwarted love into lusty fulfillment. Fast and furious, I slammed into her until I shot my load, and even then, I kept pumping until my rod grew flaccid and I dropped like a dead man beside her.

She giggled and grabbed my wet cock. "Wow, that was something!"

Smiling with satisfaction, I rose on my elbow above her. "Do you want more?"

"Sure, dude, give me all you got."

"Play with it and tell me how much you want it, baby."

She soon had me hard enough for another go. Our human brain is the biggest sex organ we have, and great sex needs psychodrama. Ugly had a carnal beauty sufficient to help me forget my broken heart, if only for a moment. I worried I had let my standards down, that I'd end up as a permanent couple with her. Too bad, but I wanted a trimmer, less thick-set girl for a keeper. I wouldn't own her, so I had to remain aloof and discourage emotional attachment, which bothered my conscience anyway.

We got up and dressed in time to meet some people arriving for the party. One of the guys she seemed to know invited her outside to smoke dope and away she went. Despite myself, I felt a twinge of jealousy, which I tossed aside. Maybe she'd screw somebody else right away so that it would be clear that she wasn't my *property*.

Sue and her bald guy floated back from their stroll, holding hands and smiling. She looked more composed, and prettier, than when I first saw her, a forlorn waif derided by unchivalrous classmates.

"You look exhausted, Ron," she said. "Why don't you lie down in our room a while?" She'd already taken charge of her new lover's room. Baldy winked and nodded. "Go ahead, man. What's mine is yours."

15

THE RENT PARTY

I t had been a long day, a longer week, and a long night lay before me, but I'd become accustomed to little sleep and jumped up refreshed after an hour's nap. I found the room divider open. The house was crowded with people who spilled into the kitchen and out onto the back porch. The Doan brothers arrived from Elmhurst, and with them came Marvin, the guy I suspected of being an undercover agent. I pulled Tom aside and whispered.

"Why'd you bring Marvin? He's a pig."

"Oh, him?" Tom said. "He's our ride. He brought us some killer weed, too."

That made Marvin popular and all I could do was whisper warnings.

"Don't be paranoid, man," our housemate Thomas said, shaking his head when I told him. "Here, try some of this terrific shit he brought." I inhaled, sat back, and tried to mellow out.

"Oh, wow, that is some heavy shit," I said, exhaling a long trail of smoke. It pulled me into the zone where words and images seemed mere echoes of reality, and it was difficult to keep track of time. Whether something had just happened or happened hours ago, I couldn't always be sure. People began sentences that trailed off in the middle, unfinished. There was cosmological speculation aplenty offered by those all around me. It may have been full of insight, but in a heartbeat it vanished, forgotten but for a vague memory that something profound had been uttered and then lost in the cosmic ocean. It was a *head trip* and nothing more substantial.

Although the counterculture touted marijuana as our sacrament of enlightenment, it gave me uncomfortable body sensations and made me too withdrawn and introspective, ineffective in the social sphere. My mind gravitated to spiritual concerns, to the transformation from carnal to cosmic realities. Events around me unfolded as in a surreal dream.

Hard rock music blared from the stereo. People danced like whirling dervishes in the crowded room. Among them, I spotted a cute chick the color of cinnamon. She glanced my way, and I smiled, so she homed in on me through the crowd to shout over the music. "It's a cool party, isn't it?"

"Yeah." I took her hand. "Wanna dance?" We started moving with the music, then she clasped her hands around my back, and said, "I like slow dancing better."

"So do I." With my hands around her waist, I pulled her close, my cheek against her head, inhaling the sweet narcotic smell of her hair.

She had to shout over the throbbing music. "I'm Maria."

"I'm Ron. You're very pretty. Are you Puerto Rican?"

"You guessed it. Let's go outside to hear each other better." We stepped into the fresh air on the back porch, leaning beside other couples against the railing. She ran her fingers over the back of my hand, deep in thought. "I've got to leave the party early tonight. Would you like to walk me home soon?"

"Sure." I kissed her forehead. She nestled in my embrace, her head on my shoulder. Our being together seemed so natural and inevitable, and I knew she was a keeper. I was falling in love with Maria, as I had so many times before. She was a slim exotic beauty, so unlike Ugly, the girl who had surrendered herself to my harsh, raw lust with such wild abandonment.

Sweet romance, and wild lust, were diametrically opposed to

emotions that social convention isolated from each other, but they swirled within me and I needed both.

Down in the yard I spotted Ugly smoking dope with another guy against the fence. She looked at me and quickly turned away. Contradictory feelings tumbled around inside of me. Maria and I had found the magic of love at first sight, and I hoped Ugly wouldn't intrude and spoil it. I couldn't afford an embarrassing scene that could cost me Maria and yet I felt a warm concern, a deep indebtedness to Ugly for the satisfaction she had given me when I needed it.

As I watched, Ugly grabbed the guy she was with, and in my full view, she leered at me over his shoulder, rolling her eyes like she had when I fucked her such a short lifetime ago. She cupped her breast and ran her tongue over her lips, then stuck it out at me, like a naughty girl, before she pulled his face to hers and kissed him.

Her lewd display was meant for me, and it turned me on. Feeling guilty, I attempted to suppress my errant lust for Ugly by looking deep into Maria's warm brown eyes, a comfortable pool that I could drown myself in, but even there, like watching a split screen, the image of Ugly followed me. The memory of her pulsing pussy muscles massaging my cock sent me back into delirious joy, a joy that assailed me with guilt, cradled as I was in the arms of a new love.

Reality and fantasy danced together in my pot stewed brain. Scenes from my past and blurry visions of an idyllic, if impossible, future vied for my heart and mind. The present eternal moment hadn't seemed possible a week ago when I'd been starving in Freeport, waiting for my idealized Russian princess to return. And when she did, she surprised me with the gift of another woman as she dumped me and my love for her, which blossomed instead for Audrey.

That love, too, a glorious moment of fulfillment, crashed when dearest Audrey dumped me in Chicago, without as much as a kiss on the cheek or a *see you later*. Life rushes on, but I needed to treat Ugly better than I had. She deserved at least my heartfelt thanks.

Maria squeezed my hand. "Hey, space man; come back to earth with me!" I realized that she'd said it several times already.

"Wow, I guess I lost it a minute. Huh? I'm stoned out of my gourd."

"You sure did, man, but don't worry, I'll take care of you. Walk me home now."

She led me west on Waveland to Broadway, where we turned south a block to continue west on Addison Street. Our footsteps rang hollow on the pavement, like we were the only living beings in a silent city. A sudden moment of panic hit me. Maria was too perfect for me. Maybe she was only an apparition who would vanish and leave me stoned and bewildered, like a lost child in the big, bad city.

Pot always made me paranoid. I had to reaffirm my spiritual refuge in the Buddha and remind myself that I had made vows to become an altruistic bodhisattva. Whether Maria was a phantom angel, or a being of flesh and blood, she was part of my karmic journey. I tried to explain some of this to her, but I was too stoned to talk. My words came out mangled and disorganized. So, I let her do the talking, and followed her lead like a dumb beast.

Maria tugged at my sleeve. "Have you ever been to Wrigley Field?"

"No, I've never been to this neighborhood before."

"My brother's really into baseball, so it's great that we live so close, and he can come to games. See it there?"

Up ahead on the right loomed the silent concrete monster, Wrigley Field. I'd never cared about baseball and wondered if I should mention that. She was rattling on about her brother. I was the silent man at her side, afraid that any wrong word from me could blow my scene with her. I didn't want to be lost in Nowhere Land again.

We walked beyond the stadium two or three blocks to confront a series of decrepit old apartment buildings several stories tall. They stood grim and dark on the northwest corner and for their run-down dinginess; they seemed to belong more in New York than the north side of Chicago.

"We're here!" She pushed open a heavy wooden door that stood ajar and we entered the dark, musty foyer. "Shit! The goddamn Super was supposed to fix that overhead bulb last week!"

I had heard that the term Super instead of Manager was used only in New York, never in Chicago. Up the rickety stairs we climbed, past two or three landings. She fumbled with her keys and opened a door I couldn't even see in the darkness. We entered, and she flipped on a light. I found myself in a small, well-furnished living room. She led me over to the couch beside a stereo.

"Have a seat. My parents are away and my brother, ah, I think he should be home, probably sleeping by now." She nodded toward a room across from the couch and pointed me to a stack of LP albums. "Look through them for something you like while I check on him."

Leaving the door ajar, she tiptoed in and kneeled beside the bed, whispering in Spanish to someone I couldn't see. Her accented voice beguiled me, but I only understood the word amigo, in reference to me. She turned and closed the door.

"I told him I brought home a friend. It's okay, we can play some music."

"Wouldn't that keep him awake?"

"No, he can sleep through anything. Maybe he'll come join us. Did you find something you like?"

"Oh, still looking." I resumed shuffling through her albums with unfocused eyes. I'd expected to find some Latin music, but all of them were rock and roll, which made me wonder if she felt as free of her roots as I was of mine.

"I'm going to the kitchen. Want anything?"

"Water or a coke would be nice."

She returned to sit against the couch beside me like she belonged there and pulled a record out of my hand.

"Look, I just got this one!" She put it on the turnstile and handed me another reefer to light up. Stoned as I was, it was the last thing I needed.

"Let me check on my brother once more. He works late."

Then I realized that her brother wasn't a child as I first imagined. With a job, he had to be around our age. If only I hadn't gotten so stoned. Paranoid thoughts assailed me. Over the years I had heard so many garish tales of Spanish jealousy and revenge, rip-offs, and switchblade murders. Maybe she was setting me up. Her brother might be waiting until she had put me in a compromising position and come out with a switchblade, screaming that I was violating his sister and he'd kill me to defend her honor. But no, I pushed that crazy thought away as another barged in.

What about my honor? My head was fuzzy and distracted, and in my unease, contrary parts of my personality argued with each other. While I didn't believe in absolute monogamy, I felt honesty, and fairness were critical in relationships, sexual or otherwise, and it hit me again that I'd treated Ugly unfairly, disrespecting her as much as Audrey treated me. I owed her a proper farewell before I took up with Maria. Maybe I'd been reading too many old Victorian books that espoused a chivalry made obsolete by the new age of liberated women taking charge of their own destinies.

The marijuana haze inhibited my thinking, making me withdraw into jumbled feelings that my voice didn't work well enough to express. I'd let Maria take the reins. If she gave me an opening, I would use it as an excuse to slip away to bid a proper goodbye to Ugly. Then I'd come right back with a clear conscience, free to merge my future with Maria's.

She yawned and took my hand. "Come on, let's go to bed."

Her room was kitty corner to her brother's. I stood at the foot of her bed and watched as she stripped off her dress and lay across the open bed, arching her back, supple as a cat. The dark nipples of her pear-shaped breasts were visible through the sheer fabric of her black bra. She still wore her see-through black bikini panties and her skin looked warm and inviting. But I hesitated, wanting her, yet needing to clear my troubled conscience before I could give Maria my full, loving attention as she deserved.

It's a myth that marijuana loosened your inhibitions and made you a sex maniac. It numbed my physical sensations and shorted out my lust to make me to be almost an indifferent observer to Maria's erotic display.

"You can join me here, you know," she said, pouting at my delay. She stretched her arms above her head, as if inviting me to remove her bra and panties. Still, I hesitated.

She sighed. "Well, I had better warn you. I *might* have crabs, although I did the treatment, and we do not have to make love if you don't want to chance it."

She'd just given me an option to refuse her with grace. Although she didn't seem concerned about them, I wasn't sure what crabs were. Sure, I'd heard the term bandied about, but never understood if it was a venereal disease like gonorrhea or syphilis. Asking for clarification would open me to ridicule, or so I thought. Later, I learned that crabs were only spidery lice, and a simple application of A-200 killed them.

"Ah, I'd better get back to the party," I said. "I want to be with you, but I just need to take care of something first. I will be right back, I promise."

Regardless of the crabs, I intended to rejoin her. Her doe eyes registered confusion as I slipped out, an image that hounded me as I ran down the stairs and out into the street.

16

PARTY ANIMALS

A couple blocks passed the Stadium, the fresh air revived me enough to realize what an idiot I was to leave Maria. Maybe in the morning my mind would be clear enough to find her apartment.

Marvin's high-powered joints were making the rounds to a thinner crowd by the time I got back. He smiled as he finished rolling another joint. "Have another on me, man."

I waved it away. "No thanks, I've had more than enough."

The more I realized how I'd blown it with Maria and probably lost her forever, the angrier I got at myself for cheating me and her out of what should prove to be lasting love, all for an ugly girl whose name I didn't even know. My exasperated rage functioned as an aphrodisiac, engorging my cock. I decided to take it all out on Ugly, as if she'd cost me Maria and I'd make her my consolation prize.

Several couples sat along the wall, making out, while others danced. Ugly squatted in the middle of the floor, flirting with the same long haired guy who seemed more bored than interested in her. The crazy juxtaposition of watching her watch me as she French kissed him while I cozied up with sweet Maria exploded in my mind, like a tableau of society's sexual double standard, a concept that I had internalized despite my idealistic denial.

She smiled up at me. "You back already, Dude? Bet she didn't put out, huh? Wanna dance?"

I pulled her up and began grinding my pelvis against her. She giggled, enjoying the attention, which encouraged me to run my hands under her clothes and whisper my impertinent demands more forthright than I ever had. "I want to fuck you right here on the floor."

"Here?" Her eyes grew wide, and then a crooked leer crept across her face. "Okay wild man. Anything you say."

Indifferent to the roomful of people, I pulled her down to the carpet, and she didn't resist or complain. The line from the Beatle's White album popped into mind, which I whispered in her ear. "Why don't we do it in the road?"

The dancers stopped to stare as I unbuttoned her blouse and grabbed her melon sized tits, her most appealing feature, and pulled them out to munch her nipples. Her giggles turned to moans as I yanked down her jeans and found her pussy dripping wet. Once again, I mauled her; rough, not gentle, as even *good* girls wanted. She was a *bad* girl, and I punished her with delight, satisfying that secret, primal desire that was long denied by modern social norms. More than a few women as well as men feel a wicked pleasure in violent conquest. We inherited it from our ancestors and would pass it to our descendants, along with the rest of our wild instincts.

Right there in front of everyone, we fucked with as much intensity as before. Ugly dug her fingernails into my shoulders and became beautiful in her throes of passion. She was the honest expression of our common *Ur-Mutter* passed down from beginningless time, from before humanity even evolved from apes.

Our shocked audience recovered to shout, *Fucken A, Man. Go for it dude,* the evocation of victorious tribal comrades. Hearing this, Marvin ran in from the kitchen, open-mouthed shock on his face. "What the hell!"

I paused my thrusting, looked up at him and grunted, "Hope we didn't freak you out."

"Just get yer nut, man!"

"Huh?" That's the first time I'd heard that expression.

"You know, get your rocks off, man. Knock yourself out!"

And I did. Ugly arched her back, shuddering into a perfect orgasm as I let loose. Bliss rained through my body and the crowd roared approval. My mind cleared into a sublime, satisfied composure as I rolled to her side. The sweet scent of sandalwood incense mixed with the reek of community sweat and our bodily love juices filled my nose.

The guy she'd been flirting with took a sudden renewed interest in Ugly. He helped her dress, and they gravitated into serious talk before taking off together. I never saw either of them again, but I suspected that I'd helped match them up, like I had with Sue, but I'd blown my own chance at a lasting romance with Maria.

Crabs be damned, dark, and beautiful Maria was more my type, and of all the girls I'd met, she belonged at my side. The music had been so loud and with all the grass I smoked, remembering names was never easy for me. I began to wonder if Maria really was my dream girl's name, or if I'd mixed her up with the girl in Westside Story.

In the early morning I went back out, retracing our route, but all the apartment buildings looked the same and I couldn't find an unlocked entry door. Over the next several days, I tried again with zero results. I could only hope she'd turn up again, but like so many others, she vanished from my life.

17

PANHANDLING

After the crowd left, we closed the varnished partition to give us private space, and I bivouacked on the floor near the kitchen with Weed and John. My sleeping bag cushioned me on the hardwood floor with my rolled-up pants for a pillow. I was used to privation and slept as well as ever. In the morning, Tom Doan came up with the idea of painting freaky revolutionary art on the varnished woodwork of our pad.

"Cool idea," Sue said. "Do you think it'll be okay with the landlord?"

"Sure," her bald lover said, to impress his new lady with his *right on* attitude. "We're paying the rent." She wanted to express her artistic side, and he became enthusiastic.

Together with the Doan brothers, they painted revolutionary slogans: "Power to the People---Off the Pigs!" And the ubiquitous "War is not healthy for children and other living things," which Tom called too peacenik. Sue and her man outvoted him, so he crafted a large red and blue Viet Cong flag with the yellow star in the middle and below that the blood red flag of North Viet Nam, to make his hard line politics clear. The place took on the look and feel of our new counter-cultural identity.

Then the landlord walked in to collect the rent. He was a dark haired, well-built thirty something man. He stumbled around with a bewildered look on his face as Sue and Tom took pride in showing him their project, as if unsure what to make of his tenants redecorating.

"You will, of course, wash everything off before you people move out. I want it left the way you found it."

"Of course," the couple who'd signed the lease assured him as he handed the full rent collected at the party to our liege lord. "Don't worry about a thing. Me and my old lady are working, and we will be here a long time."

The landlord shuffled his feet and cleared his throat. "Just how many people are living here now? Most landlords wouldn't tolerate so many tenants dwelling in this two-bedroom apartment, you know."

The lease holder pointed out that the place was being kept clean and undamaged, except for the artwork, which he insisted added charm to the house. "And with these extra housemates" –he waved his hand at the rest of us– "we'll be sure to pay on time from now on."

That seemed to mollify the landlord, who seemed like someone who'd stepped into the Twilight Zone. Outnumbered, he may have been concerned for his safety. The Doans, never willing to swallow their politics, even in the presence of a landlord, their *pig enemy*, were putting out hostile vibes. I put my hand to my throat, trying to motion them to chill out. We needed his goodwill, and he seemed an agreeable guy, or he wouldn't have rented to hippies in the first place.

To committed revolutionaries like the Doans, there was no gray area. You were either part of the solution or part of the problem. I saw that as a simplistic, self-defeating attitude. After the landlord left, we held a house meeting and discussed this practical reality of pleasing our landlord enough so that he'd be willing to rent to people of color and other alternative communes.

"If little compromises are sell-outs, how are we going to organize the community and grow in strength to confront the bigger issues?" I said. Such discussions became commonplace among us. Then we started on our domestic issues.

Sue, our little blond waif, having coupled with Baldy, became of equal status to her senior sisters. These feminine halves of our lease signers were in their element, more concerned with running the household than us men. They took on the traditional division of labor as House Mothers and required us single male newcomers to chip in most of the income for food and other expenses. John, Weed, and I took the hint and went out to panhandle.

"Spare change?" I implored well-dressed passersby. "Anything you can spare will really help."

They answered, "Get a job," as often as, "Get lost," or "Leave me alone."

It irked me that I had to panhandle. That's what Weed, John, and I did for hours on that second day at Waveland. We took opposite sides of the street to cover more territory, hitting up everyone who looked promising all the way downtown. Weed was in his element, playing up his bad leg, but I never raked in as much as him or John. How could we build a new society if we were dependent on the largess of the old?

In the bus station, I gritted my teeth and approached a well-dressed guy only a few years older than me and went into my routine, raising my voice to a desperate whine. "Any spare change, buddy? I really need it."

He was the personification of my capitalist enemy, and yet I depended on him for support. He looked into my eyes with more contempt than pity and for a hellish moment I saw myself as the lowest of the low, a groveling beggar. Reaching deep into his pants, he pulled out a handful of change and handed it to me. It was more than a dollar, the most money I had gotten from a single request, but the nausea of self-loathing overwhelmed me. I was determined to find a better way than begging to make money.

"My leg is killing me," Weed said. "I haven't been out of the Veteran's hospital long and am still recuperating. Let's get home, Ron."

When we got home, I gave my few dollars into the common fund and found a pretty, freckle faced girl with frizzy brown hair had moved in. She had a lot on her mind, processing the recent breakup with a boyfriend and joined us single men camped on the living room floor. John, Weed and I couldn't help but be interested in her.

Mulling over my *nowhere man* situation, I told the others that I needed a job to feel like I wasn't a deadbeat and contributing something, and Thomas said, "You should join the IWW, the Industrial Workers of the World like I did. They began right here in Chicago back in 1905 and are making a comeback."

"Yeah, the Wobblies! I dig their One Big Union concept. We need to unite all workers under one banner to fight for our rights. I've been to a couple Rockfests at their union hall on Lincoln Avenue, but I didn't have enough for an initiation fee, much less for regular dues."

Thomas nodded his head. "Well, there's always work at the day labor place. It gets crowded and you've got to sign up super early or you'll sit there the entire day for nothing."

"That sounds better than begging, even if the work is dehumanizing. I'll go there tomorrow."

"Me too," the new girl said. "Let's go there together."

Someone had given Weed a big hit of acid. He sat cross-legged, meditating on the floor in Sue's bedroom, facing a glowing candle.

Later that evening, someone called me, looking worried.

"Hey man. You better go check on your friend."

The candle had burned to a stub, but Weed was as I had left him, sitting aloof in silent meditation. Below his yellow mop of hair, held in place by a red bandana, his wide-open eyes were dilated. His whole body quivered as if from a fever and his cheeks glistened in the candlelight, bathed in sweat and tears that streamed down and dripped from his chin. I wondered if he was crying from intense emotion, an attack of malaria, or the effect of staring unblinking at a flame for so long. I hoped staring at the flame wasn't damaging his sight, but I had done that too, and mine was still okay.

"He's been sitting like that all fucking night, man," John said. "What if he explodes like a time bomb?"

I shook him. "Weed, did you drop that whole tab of acid?"

Weed turned his head to me without a speaking a word and

nodded without blinking before turning back to his candle. Whether or not his Mekong River patrol story was true, the dude had been through some real shit and something heavy was going on in his psyche. I admired his noble determination to break into the spiritual plane where his shipmates had gone before him.

I changed his candle for a fresh one and joined him in meditating on it. He finally changed position to lie on his belly, resting his chin on the backs of his hands while staring at the candle and continued quaking. Weed made it through the night and got up early to sally forth with us the next day.

18

ADVANCE TEMPORARY LABOR SERVICE

I n the predawn light on Thursday the 11th of June, John, Weed, the new girl, and I arose from our bivouac on the floor, sloshed down some coffee, Carnation Instant Breakfast, and toast, before setting off to find income. We shuffled over to the great manpower hiring hall below the sign that advertised daily work for daily pay on 4510 North Broadway and joined the hushed throng of haggard, unkempt men and a few frumpy, disheveled women slumped along the sidewalk, waiting for the locked glass doors to open at six o'clock.

A job couldn't be guaranteed. It depended on the fluctuating demand for labor. Few of us possessed skills in high demand. Companies paid $2.00 an hour gross for unskilled jobs that otherwise paid $3 to $4 an hour. After income tax and other expenses were subtracted, the agency pocketed the remainder. That left about $1.60 an hour in net earnings for the worker. Unless we were hired early and worked a full eight hours, we made little enough for our trouble of waiting all day. Then again, we could get hired into a permanent job and make the going rate if we wanted steady work.

As newbies, we had to fill out registration forms first, while those already registered signed the daily roster and snapped up the first jobs in an initial flurry of activity. Then, as the rest of us huddled masses sprawled in the ranks of folding chairs, things quieted down through long hours of waiting. By eleven am, I was hungry, but lunch would have to wait. We spent the long morning slumped on folding chairs in the great hall of the unemployed, listening to the mixture of bragging and whiney complaints from our companions.

Some of them were down and out winos. Others sober, tattooed, and macho refugees from Appalachia or the Great Plains, who attempted to impress the few women present, bragging that they were *permanent* temporary laborers. Like me, they were willing to put up with much for a little bread of life. As the hours crept by, many bored or wiser souls left for home.

Weed stood up and harrumphed. "I don't need this shit, man. I can make more scratch panhandling!"

John shook his head in agreement and joined him. Our pretty girl wilted beside me but hung on for half an hour more before she too gave up and slipped out without a farewell, leaving me alone to contemplate the futility of sitting so long for naught and I almost gave up too when a voice startled me out of my reverie.

"Ron Schulz! Get up here."

Almost disbelieving my ears, I swallowed hard and came to the counter where the dispatcher, a bespeckled woman in her late forties, appraised me over her glasses with hard angry eyes.

"Some asshole didn't make it to the job I sent him to, and I need a replacement fast. Think you can hack it? I've put up with too much shit from you people, so you'd better not fuck this up."

I forced a smile. "Well, I didn't sit here all morning for my health."

Without cracking her hard lips, she pointed to a shy young man of about twenty-five on my side of the counter. "He'll drive you to your assignment. Now get!"

The younger man ferried me to a noisy factory warehouse where an impatient, balding boss took over, throwing a long-handled broom at me as he listed my duties. It was similar to work I'd done at Beeline Fashion the year before, crushing boxes, tidying up and running an incinerator for scraps. I'd come full circle to remain lost in the scramble for bottom scale jobs.

The boss hounded me from nook to cranny in the dark and unfamiliar hellscape. "Get over there. Grab that. No, the other thing, goddamn it! Move it, man, I don't have all day."

From sweeping and burning trash to loading trucks with heavy boxes, the boss wanted me to catch up with tasks the no-show employee hadn't done, doing anything to get his money's worth from me before the day ended. But with as much time as he spent chasing me around the premises, he could have done it all himself and saved my wages.

With my belly growling, I wasn't sorry for the five o'clock whistle to end the day. The shy guy who drove me there was the son of the boss, and he dropped me back where he'd fetched me. The still angry dispatcher handed me a check for eleven bucks, just as much as Weed made on a slow day of panhandling, but I'd earned it through honest labor. On the way home, the pretty girl stepped out of an alley that I passed off Broadway, as if she'd been waiting for me, or maybe we were predestined to meet.

"How'd it go, Ron?"

"Well, they finally called me, and I made a few bucks."

"Oh, yeah? I feel bad for having left so early. Maybe I'll try again tomorrow."

"So will I," I said with rash haste. The torture would be worthwhile with her beside me.

She came with me to cash my check at one of those places that take a healthy cut out of your earnings, leaving me about nine bucks, but without a bank account or enough cash to open one, I had no choice. I owed my share of the rent and food and should have turned it over to my housemates right away, but I thought to hold on to it for another day. I'd work better with a lunch for some glucose in my system and earn more if I got called early.

All four of us single people were beat and turned in early, scattered around the floor, our bedrolls spaced wide enough to allow easy passage so no one would get stepped on in the dark.

I took off the loud, plaid dress pants I'd worn that day and keeping my wallet with the cash deep within the front pocket, I rolled the legs around it into a ball for a pillow and, after giving a reassuring squeeze to it, I nestled down into my sleeping bag and drifted into contented sleep. My money should be safe, the doors were locked to outsiders, and I was a light sleeper among friends.

"Coffee's on," the pretty woman shouted. Groggier than usual, I felt around for my pants pillow. It was missing.

"Has anyone seen my pants?"

The pretty woman chuckled. "Who would take those gaudy plaid pants? We are all friends here."

"It's not the pants so much as the dough in the pocket, my share for our kitty."

"No one saw anyone come in. The doors and windows are all locked tight, and nothing else is missing."

I questioned everyone, Weed, the two lovey-dovey couples, John, but no one admitted it and I had no proof. I suspected John, but he was a sound sleeper, and I didn't think he was slick enough to pull it off. Everyone mobilized into the search while I put on my other pants.

Eureka! Thomas *found* my pants up on the roof, of all places, but the wallet was gone. Then Thomas's old lady *found* the empty wallet on a garbage can in the alley. No money, but at least I had my draft card and driver's license.

Weed pulled me aside and whispered, "That is too damn suspicious. I bet they were planted to make it look like an outsider took it."

I agreed. Whoever ripped off my bread was one of us, a comrade, and that hurt. I'd slaved for that dough and with its loss, I had no heart to go back to the meat market that morning. The pretty girl gave me a sympathetic glance as she went out alone. I went with John and Weed to panhandle, but when I passed the hiring hall, I saw the pretty girl standing outside, looking sheepish.

"I've got stomach cramps," she said, as good an excuse as any to evade the cattle pen. She and I panhandled together until some kind freaks gave us enough to duck into a luncheonette and commiserate over food and coffee. She thought Thomas and his old lady took my money.

"Yeah, it couldn't be Weed or Sue and her dude, and if Thomas took it, I owe him my share, anyway."

We walked around the neighborhood together. I wondered if I should put the make on this pretty girl. She wasn't Maria or Audrey, both of whom weighed heavy on my mind, and like me, she was recovering from her own broken heart. Hoping to impress her, I bragged about my hitchhiking adventures on the open road.

That evening the weather wasn't too cold, so I brought my bedroll out in the yard. The new girl came out and laid down three feet away, just being coy, I assumed. After a few minutes, I log rolled in my bag close to her. She feigned sleep, but I knew she was awake and just lay beside her a while before I nestled in, cuddling her. Stiff and unresponsive, she turned her face away, ignoring me.

"Come on, baby," I whispered in her ear, then I reached inside to let my hands do the talking, caressing her cold, still form. She just needed encouragement to relax and get into the groove. I thought I was making some headway when she finally spoke through clenched teeth.

"I'm tired, man. Leave me the fuck alone!" I felt as if she slapped me, then she shrugged my hands away, curled up and turned her back like a great barrier reef against me. We were strangers again, strangers lying beside each other below a romantic Milky Way sky. An hour later she picked up her gear and moved to the far end of the yard, an eloquent rebuff.

19

THE LAIR OF THE WHITE PANTHERS

W alking down Wells in Old Town the next day, a one-page flyer blew along the street and caught my eye. It featured a famous Old West photograph of a group of Plains Indians in full feathered regalia set below a proclamation addressed to Woodstock Nation. That was the recent designation of our hippie-freak Rock and Roll generation. It said we were a people made up of many tribes bound together in a common desire for positive cultural and political change. The 10-point program of the White Panther Party followed. It was founded in Michigan by John Sinclair, which I had first learned about the year before. Reading on, I discovered that a chapter was forming in the Chicago area. My heart jumped. Joining this radical organization was just what I needed.

It was Saturday, June 13th, my lucky number. I ducked into a phone booth, pulled out the last of my hoarded dimes and dialed the number.

"Hello," a cheery voiced woman said. "This is the People's Information Office Switchboard."

"I found this number on a flyer to reach the White Panthers."

"Well…" Her voice lowered, and I heard her rifling through some papers. "Why do you want to contact them?"

"I'm not a cop, if that's what you mean."

She laughed. "Yeah, I wonder why they don't just give out the number, because the cops already have it. So, who are they fooling?"

I had to bum another dime and dialed the number she gave me. A young man's voice at the other end began a brief rundown of what the Party stood for, nothing that wasn't already on the flyer.

"Yeah," I said. "I already know about John Sinclair and want to join up."

"You can come over and we'll *rap* about it."

"When can I come?"

"I'll have to screen you. We don't just let anyone in off the street."

"Hey, I'm cool man. Meet anywhere you want."

"Well, okay, you can come over here to our headquarters. It's on the west side of LaSalle Street, a couple of doors south of Division, just north of a gothic church. I'll be waiting."

It was only a few blocks from where I stood and I soon found myself before the heavy, windowless unmarked door of the unremarkable building that housed the Illinois Chapter of the White Panther Party. I knocked and rang the buzzer. A muffled voice asked, "Who is it?"

"I'm Ron, the guy who called a few minutes ago."

A minute elapsed, during which I overheard a muffled conversation between two men.

"You didn't tell me someone's coming over."

"Okay, just a minute."

But then I heard another voice, "How do you know he's not a *Pig*?"

"We'll have to check him out."

It took a minute while I heard the sound of heavy bars sliding out and deadbolts being unlatched before the door swung open, and I was face to face with a medium-sized youth with short, wavy red hair. He pulled me inside, slammed the door behind me and latched it with two deadbolts and slid two heavy timbers into the welded steel brackets on the door frame.

"For security, man," he said. "Ever since the pigs murdered Fred Hampton and Mark Clark in their beds, we've adopted the Black

Panther principal of Armed Self Defense." He chuckled as if it was a joke. "Let the *fuckers* use battering rams if they really want to come get us! That'll slow them down and we'll be ready."

Behind him stood a dark-haired youth of seventeen whose face was covered in beet red acne and blackheads, who clasped my hand in a brother's handshake, thumbs interlaced as in Indian wrestling.

"I'm Steve Smith; the guy you talked to on the phone, but everyone calls me Schmitty." The other guy finished locking up and said, "I'm Jeff, Schmitty and I are from Albany Park. What makes you interested in joining the White Panthers?"

I gave them a brief rundown of my time with the Weathermen and in jail, which impressed them. Jeff said he was on guard duty, but Schmitty would take over and show me around. We climbed a few steps to a landing, then up a short staircase on our left that led to a space above the door, just big enough to hold the double mattress placed before a full-length window.

"This is our crow's nest to overlook whoever is at the door," Schmitty said. I suspected it was also a cozy place to take a nap. Looking out the window across LaSalle Street to the east, Schmitty pointed out the sign proclaiming "Sammy's Red-Hot Vienna hot dogs."

"Sammy's is the most popular junk food of the soul around here, Ron," he said. "Their greasy fries are legendary, and we'll pick up a bag to munch later." It stood in the alley back of the Mark Twain Hotel, which aroused fond memories from the year before, when I'd spent a night there with Bonnie. Our brief life together had been so perfect, and here I was again, back full circle, starting over.

I followed Steve down into the small living room to the left of a staircase going up. "This house has history," he said, flourishing his hand over the tawdry furniture. "It used to be a busy whorehouse. Then it was a crash pad for junkies before the rent got cheap enough for hippies to move in. The staff of the seed took it over for a while and we moved in when they left to move beside Alice's Restaurant. The building's been condemned for renovation."

I'd noticed that the decaying two-block neighborhood to the west of LaSalle on Division was composed of abandoned storefronts, a ghost town awaiting demolition.

"Dig it, Ron, we don't even pay rent!"

The kitchen was beyond the living room and another bolted and timber braced door guarded entry from the back porch and an L shaped alley wide enough to park a couple of cars. Following Schmitty upstairs, I found two sets of metal bunk beds in a barracks like area at the top of the first landing and an assortment of dilapidated beds or mattresses laying in each of the enclosed bedrooms on the third floor. We climbed out one of the second story bedroom windows onto a flat roof above the kitchen and gazed over the back alley. It dead-ended beside a telephone pole at the building's rear. Up on the third floor was a large bedroom with a grand bed enclosed with India print curtains.

Steve flashed a conspiratorial wink at me. "This is the residence of Chairman Bob himself."

"Who is that?"

"Bob Rudnick is a radio DJ on WEAW and the Chairman of our Chicago Chapter of the White Panthers. They call him Righteous Bob." He winked. "He's the one who decides if you join us, but that shouldn't be a problem."

Bob Rudnick had a busy life, and I wouldn't meet him until the next day. The spacious rooms needed more thorough sweeping, a re-plastering of the gaping holes in some of the walls and a fresh coat of paint, but I loved the dilapidated, narrow three-story brick building. It had lofty ceilings, popular in houses built a century before, and it breathed a roughhewn, picturesque charm, befitting Steve's whorehouse story. I could envision smiling lovelies half dressed in Roaring Twenties, or even turn of the century finery escorting their paramours upstairs. Too bad that the house was due for demolition. It gave the vibe of Chicago's wild history that I felt connected to, but meanwhile it was a launching pad for revolution, and social experimentation by our merry band of Panthers.

Schmitty said he worked with the Euphoria Blimpworks, who set up local rock concerts. Although not on a par with the fabled Black Panthers in terms of community programs and services, the White Panthers offered a Rock and Roll cultural dimension to channel the growing anger and frustration of those who identified as hippies, or freaks, at the perceived *pig* harassment.

He escorted me back to the kitchen and offered me a bottle of beer at the large wooden table, where we were joined by others as they trailed in from wherever the day had taken them. Jeff took part in the conversation when he could, but each time someone came home, he had to go to the door to let him in, because a key was of no use without the bars being removed.

Bill Johnson had long, straight black hair tied in a ponytail far down his back. It surprised me to learn that he was from the White Pine neighborhood in Bensenville, just north of where I'd been staying with Chris by Fischer's Woods. Bill was quiet and reserved, less likely to pounce on someone with self-righteous rhetoric than the others, me included. He was slightly older than the rest of us, except for our elder statesman, Chairman Bob.

Fuzzy came from the Ann Arbor collective, but his accent was from Kentucky or Tennessee. He permed his strawberry blond hair into a giant Jimmy Hendricks style Afro that stood out around his head like a lion's mane. His skin was as pale as porcelain, one of those guys who didn't tan and avoided the sun, and he was rail thin and sparked with electric energy. I later learned that Fuzzy was a switch-hitting bisexual, a fancy dresser hyperconscious of this adornment, which attracted women and some of the men he meant to influence.

Pretty auburn-haired Tracy was the only woman in residence at the time, but Schmitty told me she wouldn't be staying long.

"She doesn't count as a serious *cadre* of the Party," he said. "But she'll have to do until we get some more committed, politically *heavy* chicks."

His dismissive attitude toward her struck me as odd, and I wondered if she had rejected his advances. If the White Panthers didn't aim to be an all-male club, they needed some feminine representation. With plenty of spots available for guests and visitors, the sleeping arrangements were fluid, leading me to understand that we had the potential for an active sex life. This Chicago group was new and just starting out. Including me and the absent Chairman Bob, I counted six men and one woman. We would have to fill up the ranks.

20

WHITE PANTHER BACKGROUND

The White Panther Party had formed in Ann Arbor, Michigan under the leadership of the charismatic champion of Rock and Roll "Youth Culture" John Sinclair, who'd been sentenced to *ten* long years in prison for the possession of a minuscule amount of marijuana, nature's sacred herb. I'd first read about John and Pun Plamondon, his "Minister of Defense," back in 1968 in a book I found in my high school library. The Hippies, published by Time-Life, showed how the relationship of those once pacifist hippies to the police had changed in the years since 1967, before the founding of the White Panther Party.

The recognized guru of Detroit hippies is John Sinclair, a 25-year-old former beatnik. Sinclair is usually up at noon, scurrying around Detroit gathering accouterments for a new hippie entertainment spot he is to front, called the See. For a hippie, Sinclair is pretty autocratic, particularly when supervising some minor repair work to his new place, or in handing out painting or sweeping jobs to buck-private hippies.

One reason Sinclair may seem so forceful is his size. He stands 6 feet 4 inches in his bare feet, weighs 230 pounds, and it is obviously fortunate that he is nonviolent. His hair grows wild in long tufts, bristling around his head, and naturally, he has a beard. He wears rimless glasses.

There are thousands of hippies in Detroit and the suburbs," Sinclair said, added "—a lot in the suburbs. We're not organized in any way." ... (He) feels hippie relationships with the police are "pretty good except for the narcotics bureau." ...

...Sinclair can't remember how many times he has been busted. "I pled guilty to possession the first time and got two years' probation. The second time I got six months in the House of Corrections and three more years of probation."

Sinclair's probation runs out Dec. 30, 1969, but meanwhile he faces another charge of selling and possession of marijuana. The narcos made this arrest by planting an undercover agent among the hippies, and they charge Sinclair supplied the pseudo-hippie with pot. Sinclair feels aggrieved about it. "It's the same case other hippies are fighting," he said...

Pun Plamondon, 22, a hippie sandal maker, speaks up to mention that he also has been run in by cops about 10 times, though not for anything serious. "Cops haven't bothered us too much," he said. "After all, we don't believe in fighting or getting drunk. We have more trouble with the average guy, the drunks, than with the police."

Pun was not exaggerating. He had just come from a restaurant where a guy had knocked him down a couple of times. Although Pun is hefty, 185 lbs. And 5 feet 11 inches, he did not fight back. He does not believe in it. Because of the way they look, hippies get a lot of lumps from hostile straights in Detroit. For safety, they usually travel in pairs, like cops...

Though Sinclair is their leader, Detroit hippies recognize no single spokesman; no one speaks for all of them: "We don't feel people should go to tribal living again, for instance," Pun said. "We want the luxurious living, radios and records."

Sinclair feels the hippie way is an enduring way, that hippies will live and die---from youth to maturity---as hippies. He also believes that hippies will eventually become a major voting bloc, and the first thing they will do is legalize marijuana. Eventually, they will change the world...

The Hippies, 1967, Time-Life Books, pages 132-136.

By 1970 the peace and love idealism had worn off as hippies across the nation confronted police repression. John was in prison and Pun, the peaceful sandal maker of 1967, was on the *lam* and made the FBI's list of ten most wanted fugitives. The WPP aspired to be a national and even international organization and made common cause with Black Power movements, especially the Black Panthers. In early 1970 the Chicago SEED ran this piece about them in a music article titled "TASTY TREATS":

...After renouncing the revolutionary politics of their mentor and former manager John Sinclair, Michigan's MC5 seem to be jinxed. Their teenage pap single "Tonight" bombed, their album is only doing so-so, and nobody has anything good to say about them. Last month they played to less than 300 people at Detroit's Grande Ballroom, where they had been the house band for over a year, while this month less than 100 fans came out to one of Motor City's sultry movie houses for a spectacular that billed them with Frigid Pink, Rumor, and a W.C. Fields flick.

Meanwhile, White Panther Chairman Sinclair is being transferred from Marquette State Prison in the wilderness of Michigan's Upper Peninsula to Jackson Prison, about 25 miles from his Ann Arbor stronghold. Transfer is related to his upcoming conspiracy trial for bombing a CIA Recruiting Office. Also indicted were Detroit White Panther Captain Jack Forest and Minister of Defense Pun Plamondun, who is to be congratulated for making the FBI's Ten Most Wanted List after going underground.

The White Panthers join the Hog Farm as a security, bad trip, and survival force at the Miami Pop Festival, March 27-29.

Seed Volume 5, number 1, page 21, signed by "Stanley."

WHITE PANTHER PARTY 10-POINT PROGRAM

We want freedom. We want the power for all people to determine our own destinies.

We justice. We want an immediate and total end to all cultural and political repression of the people by the vicious pig power structure and their mad dog lackies the police, courts and military. We want the end of all police and military violence against the people all over the world right now!

We want a free world economy based on the free exchange of energy and materials and the end of money.

We want free access to all information media and to all technology for all the people.

We want a free education system, utilizing the best procedures and machinery our modern technology can produce, that will teach each man, woman and child on earth exactly what each needs to know to survive and grow into his or her full human potential.

We want to free all structures from corporate rule and turn the buildings over to the people at once!

We want free time and space for all humans – dissolve all unnatural boundaries!

We want the freedom of all persons held in federal, state, county or city jails and prisons since the so-called legal system in Amerika makes it impossible for any man to obtain a fair and impartial trail by a jury of his peers.

We want the freedom of all people who are held against their will in the conscripted armies of the oppressors throughout the world.

We want free land, free food, free shelter, free clothing, free music, free medical care, free education, free media, EVERYTHING FREE FOR EVERYBODY!

We believe that the only solution to the problems of the earth now is through the establishment of a free economy throughout the world in which the only consideration is the needs of all the people all the time, and that any social system which does not provide for the needs of all the people must be abolished and replaced by a free social order.

John Sinclair, Minister of Information

BOB RUDNICK HAD OPENED the Illinois Chapter of the Party about a month before I met them. Chicago was where the action was during the 1968 Democratic convention, and the repressive police riot had radicalized Bob, as this taste of his doggerel, posted in the East Village Other can testify:

I hit my first cop with a rugged red brick
broke a store window and rioted
running wildly free down Chicago streets...

In Chicago, the radical paper Rising Up Angry ran a couple of articles about the new Chicago branch of the Party in their spring issues.

PIG HARASSMENT ON WHITE PANTHERS

On the night of May 19th, in the alley behind the White Panther Party's commune, a brother and sister were stopped and asked about the owner of the car they were driving. While the Panthers were explaining that the car was loaned to them---another brother came out to inquire about what's happening and asked the badge numbers and names of the pigs. The pigs said "This one knows the procedures too well, we'll take him in." The bullshit charge was disorderly conduct and the ransom was $25.

The next morning, May 20th, the same brother was busted while driving a friend's car. The 3 charges were: driving on a boulevard, illegal license plates and no registration. More bullshit! The ransom this time was $100.

Later that afternoon, the WPP commune was raided by 18th district pigs. They entered by saying they were from the Telephone Company and were at the front and back doors with loaded shotguns and revolvers in hand. They put everyone up against the wall, frisked them and then tore the house apart. The search warrant was for the same brother that was busted earlier. The whole scene lasted 2 ½ hours and no one was busted. They were questioned by the GIU and Red Squad pigs about their brother John Sinclair (in prison) and Pun (wanted) so it's clear the heavy harassment is coming from national pigs as well as local pigs, including the building inspector who came in during the raid and told us we had 30 days to leave because the building was condemned.

Repression has been heavy on the Black Panthers and its getting heavier on all of us. We have to tighten the fist.

POWER TO THE PEOPLE!!!

Rising Up Angry Vol. 1, number 9

THE GIU WAS the Gang Intelligence Unit of the Chicago Police, otherwise known as the Red Squad, Chicago's political police. They were charged with tracking dangerous radicals who threatened the status quo with ideas like equality and cooperation between the races.

WHITE PANTHER PARTY

On June 11, 2 pigs from the Task Force stopped our van because our door handle was missing. They asked for ID's and hassled one of us for wearing an NLF *(Viet Cong)* flag on his jacket. They made us all line up and searched us. I was pulled over to the back of their car by pig Zingarelli and he said the White Panthers 'suck niggers dick'. I called him a raciest pig! He and his partner grabbed me, hit me, tore my shirt, and threw me in the car. They charged me with assault and battery, resisting arrest and driving an unsafe vehicle.

These are the racist pigs that patrol our streets under the slogan; 'we serve and protect.'

All Power to the People!!!

White Panther Party, Illinois Chapter

Rising Up Angry, Volume 1, number 10 on page 7

I would soon become acquainted with the Rising Up Angry, RUA organization, whose motto, besides *Power to the People*, was *To Love We must Fight*.

21

ACID TEST

Schmitty sat at the kitchen table inhaling cigarette after cigarette as he regaled me with how they'd stood up to the police during the raid. Although he used an empty beer can for his butts, he had a peculiar habit of flicking his ash onto his jeans and rubbing it into the fabric. Later I saw others doing the same and wondered if it had some purpose, like giving their jeans a rugged, faded look. Unlike most freaks, or society in general, I didn't smoke tobacco due to the health risks and cut down smoking reefer as much as I could without raising suspicion that I was a narc.

"So, what do ya think, Ron?" Schmitty dropped another butt into his can. "Wanna join our White Panther collective?"

"Sure, I need to get back in the Revolution."

"You seem okay to me, but the decision is up Chairman Bob and the others."

That gave me an idea to speed things up. "When I was with the Weathermen, they talked about using acid as a truth serum. An undercover pig would be afraid of blowing his cover while under the effects."

"That sounds like spacey, punk-hippie jive to me, man. I'm leery of freaking out on acid too. I've never tripped and not sure if I could handle it."

Jeff popped back into the kitchen. "Hey, did I hear someone mention LSD? A guy I know laid a few hits of LSD on me. Maybe Ron and I should go tripping in the morning."

"That's a great idea," I said, launching into a monologue. "Freaks like us are reincarnated Indians come to take back our country, acid trips can help us commune and give us insight into our mission." I continued rambling on about the theme of a sacred visionary quest aided by Indian Peyote rituals, LSD, and mescaline.

Schmitty looked nervous as he lit another cigarette. "Well, you can count me out." He leaned back and blew smoke at the ceiling. "Anyway, tomorrow's Sunday. I've got a meeting with the Blimpworks."

"That's okay," I said, hoping to allay Schmitty's fears. "You need to be ready for an acid trip. A bad trip comes from a bad conscience, something we need to resolve on our journey to the deeper parts of ourselves. We may enter a dark night of the soul before we can reach the bright dawn of transcendence over negative forces. Can you dig that?"

"Fucking A man!" Jeff said. "But why wait until morning?"

The others drifted off to random beds in the huge house as that first day became a warm June night. I followed Jeff upstairs to the roof, where we each dropped a hit of acid and rapped about thoughts and the sensations that came over us as we *got off* under the influence of that powerful hallucinogen.

I presented my ideas of cultivating psychic abilities to give us outgunned cultural warriors of the left some edge over pig repression. The prophecies of Edgar Cayce, who died in 1945 but was well regarded by elements of the hippie movement, jibbed with my vision of the natural calamities in store for us, due to our civilization's destruction of the natural order. Perhaps they could aid us in tearing down this Pig Empire so we could rebuild on the ashes.

Schmitty, who'd replaced Jeff on guard duty, kept checking on us during his roving patrols. His worry creased face, as if he expected to find us *freaking out,* became exaggerated into a bizarre caricature to us under the influence of LSD. Absorbed with our inner visions, Jeff and I passed beyond the words with which to explain it to him. Repeating "WOW" was the best we could do.

Jeff and I were still tripping as the dawn beckoned us to roam Michigan Avenue and along the Lakefront where I saw the tall buildings hemming us in on all sides shimmer and begin to melt before our *righteous* spiritual magic. Alas, 'twas only a vision, a prayer, a hallucination of my hope for transformation. The ramparts of Chicago would remain standing no matter how much acid I took.

That afternoon, De Paul University held what they called a "Peace Rock" event. It was an opportunity for us Panthers to mingle among our Woodstock tribe, passing out leaflets and rapping the Revolution. Still coming down from our acid trip, Jeff and I floated through the gathering more like disembodied spirits observing life on Planet Earth than revolutionaries on the make. Here, for the first time, I met members of Rising Up Angry. They were Greasers, with slicked back hair and leather jackets. Greasers from my hometown tended to be apolitical tough guys spoiling for a fight, but these fellows had been radicalized by Michael James, a former SDS cadre, who directed their anger at the *real enemy*, Corporate America. Abe Peck of the Chicago Seed wrote this about this legendary leader in his book, *Uncovering the Sixties:*

> The day after the Democratic convention's conclusion, a leather-jacketed guy named Michael James came into the *Seed* office. Mike had grown up in a Connecticut suburb, and his neo-hillbilly accent belied an education at upscale Lake Forrest College. He'd played football there, had worked in SDS's JOIN (Jobs in our Neighborhood) project in Uptown, Chicago's poor-white Appalachia, and had been very active in the convention streets.
>
> I'd published an article of Mike's called "Take a Step into America" that asked freaks not to ignore working-class people. The Seed staff was trying to step as far out of America as possible, but James's piece had been energetic and humane, worth running. Now I

told him that I was bitter about the convention carnage. Michael was confident; reaching across my rickety wooden desk, he took my right hand and bent two fingers outward to form a peace sign. "That's over," he said. He bent the fingers back, then turned my hand, so it formed a raised fist. "That's what's happening now."

Abe Peck, Uncovering the Sixties, Page 126.

Stoned as I was, I bonded with my new comrades in Rising Up Angry and the White Panthers. Michael's Greasers were our revolutionary brothers and sisters, who blurred the line between *hip* and *straight*. Most of them smoked weed and a few even *tripped* on acid. Their Rising Up Angry newspaper bore the masthead "To love we must fight!" Our bi-weekly White Panther paper, the Ann Arbor Sun, supplemented by pamphlets, was aimed at raising the political consciousness of the hippie-freak "Woodstock Generation" with an appreciation of psychedelia and Rock and Roll. Side by side we hawked papers propagating our message of solidarity with all liberation struggles, to build a class consciousness opposed to the corporate war machine.

22

RIGHTEOUS BOB

Back at the house, I met Stanley G. Rudnick, our Chairman Bob. Kinky, coal-black locks radiated about his head like a brunette version of Fuzzy's blond Afro, except that Bob didn't put as much time into combing his, so it hung limp around his head. From the buildup they gave him, I expected a bigger man than the short, roly-poly, beer-bellied elf of a man who grinned, shook my hand, and said in a booming voice, "Welcome to the White Panther Tribe!" His rich, baritone erupted from deep in his belly, perfect for his radio disc jockey alter ego, Righteous Bob, whose radical reading of the news over the airwaves had created a stir across the Midwest.

He'd gotten fired for his views on a Michigan radio station, where he'd joined the White Panthers, so he moved to Chicago to set up a new chapter and took a job at WGLD FM radio in Oak Park, Illinois. It had switched to a full-time progressive rock format in January 1970. David and Darlene America's column entitled *in the streets* in the Ann Arbor Argus had this to say about him in the Feb. 24th, 1970, issue.

> While staggering on down to the corner diner, Righteous Bob Rudnick (1/2 of the famous Kokaine Karma Kids) and his friend Joel were kidnapped by the Chicago pigs and busted for 7 joints. Luckily,

they emerged from the ordeal unshorn. Says Rudnick, "Those punks will answer to the people for this!"

Ann Arbor Argus, Vol. 2 number 2, page 15, column 3

The Chicago Seed ran an ad for his program below a picture of a bored lady on an opera balcony, written in commix style:

"Fuck dis shit!" Sez Myrtle. I'd rather listen to **Kokaine** Karma with Bob Rudnick, 5 to 9, Monday thru Saturday on WGLD, 102.7 FM. 'N' don't ferget KOKAINE KNOOZ KODAY, Saturday evenings at 7!

Seed, Vol. 5 Number 1 on page 21

The next issue of the Seed related how it came crashing down in a lengthy article.

Instant Karmel (?)

About two months ago, the Seed ran a story on the advent of "Progressive Rock" on WGLD-FM, in the form of Bob "Righteous" Rudnick's Kokain Karma show and a new 24-hour format. Hopes ran high that WGLD would become the community Station that Chicago needs so badly --- that it would be Radio Free Chicago.

... With the issuance of the memos pictured here, freedom of speech was thrown for a big loss... after word of a CBS -TV News presentation on WGLD's "radical" format and personnel reached Augment Sanderling, the owner of the station. In addition to banning all news and comment, the corporate management has also banned all guests, interviews and satire from the airwaves; not to mention banning the name of Rudnick's show. When Righteous was shown the directive, he lived up to his name by reading over the air, playing "Street Fighting Man", and walking out of the studio --- for good...

STATION COMMUNICATION

Date: 3/31/70
From: Charles E. Manson

To: Steve Stafford

Effective immediately no longer will there be a show on this station
known as Kokain Karmel *(sic)*. You may call it the Bob Rudnick show,
as you do with the other shows, but there will no longer be a Kokain
Karmel show. Please see to it that Rudnick is informed and all the
jocks, so that the name Kokain Karmel is not aired again
As stated in the memorandum addressed to the staff, WGLD does not
advocate anything. All statements made by WGLD will be made by
me, as general manager. The staff will not comment on any current
day issues. Failure to abide by this law will mean immediate
dismissal. (Chicago Seed Vol. 5 number 2 on page 6)
Rising up Angry ran a short piece about this in their "Winter 1970"
issue on page 5, below a picture of Bob, clowning, elf-like in his
cowboy hat.

RUDNICK-PEOPLES D.J.

Bob Rudnick, popular disc jockey on WGLD-FM, is no longer on
the air. He refused to compromise with station owners who came
down on him for giving political interviews, rapping about RUA and
other political groups, for playing 'banned records,' playing Malcolm
X tapes, supporting the Panthers, for his political satire and his news
show (which is nothing like the Huntley & Brinkley reports.) They
also told him he had to drop the name of his show - Kokain Karma.

Rudnick, however, is now negotiating with other stations and he
feels he'll be back on the air soon--with the same kind of out-of-sight
format his old show had. Watch for him--dig him (if you haven't
already). He's our kind of people.

To the strains of Gene Autry's *I'm back in the Saddle again!* Bob got
back on the air with Radio Free Chicago, airing midnight to 5 a.m. on
WEAW, 105 on the FM dial. We'd stay up late to listen to his
broadcasts.

Bill Johnson told me that Bob had been a heroin addict, but
beating his addiction added another feather in his cap. Bob Rudnick

was two distinct individuals. In person, he was a fleshy man with obvious weaknesses, but over the radio, his disembodied voice called on us, like a prophet of the new age, to step forward into the dawning consciousness of Woodstock Nation.

With Bob Rudnick's baritone welcome, it seemed I'd found my true home at last. We were a small band, but I felt confident that we'd grow into something meaningful that could benefit the beautiful Aquarian-Woodstock New World order. Bob was committed to the ideals we shared, but we saw little of him. He had a busy schedule of meetings, hanging out with a variety of *straight* and underground or Avant guard media luminaries when he wasn't on the air and he slept late. I only had the briefest of chats with him, and found that our chapter muddled through with little direction from him or the National Party.

23

WAKEUP CALL

"Hey, Ron," Bruce called me over. "Since you're on guard tonight, can you wake me up in the morning?" (I'm shielding Bruce's true name in this short piece to protect a still living comrade's feelings.)

"Sure thing," I said. It was my first turn on overnight guard duty.

"Great, I've got an important meeting and can't be late." He sighed. "I'm not a morning person, but keep trying to get me up, even if I tell you to go fuck yourself."

Schmitty overheard this and waved me into a bedroom with a finger to his lips. "I'd better warn you. Bruce goes crazy when he's woken up. He even punched me! That's why he never gets to his meetings on time."

Bill came over laughing and told me the same thing. "Watch his fists! Both Schmitty and I have gotten clocked by him. Be careful or he'll take a swing at you too!"

"Okay." I chuckled at the thought. "I'll watch out for his fists, but I'll get him up even if I've got to throw water on him."

Morning arrived. I banged on his open door. "Time to rise and shine, Bruce!" There was no response. He was lying on a mattress under the half open window, sprawled out under a sheet, and snoring as loud as a freight train. I shook him. "Come on man, get up!" Still no response. I pulled off his sheet and shook him like a rag doll with increasing violence.

Bruce yelled. "Get the fuck away and leave me alone!" With his eyes shut, he fumbled around and pulled his sheet over his head. But he asked me to get him up for his urgent appointment and by god I would, even though nothing anyone did before worked. It was my duty.

I grabbed his foot and dragged him off the mattress to the bedroom door. He thrashed and swung at me, sputtering like a naughty child.

"You wanted me to wake you up," I said. "And that's what I'm going to do. Get dressed!" I left him there to get dressed, but a minute later, when I came back, I found him back in bed with the covers over his head.

"Come on, man, get the fuck out of bed now!"

He swung and kicked, but I stayed clear. I'd never met anyone so impossible to wake up and had to up the ante. I ran to the bathroom for a pitcher of ice-cold water and splashed some into his face. He cursed me but still wouldn't get up, so I tossed the full pitcher in his face, soaking him, but sputtering curses, he still refused to get up. I'd never seen such thing and was sure he was faking it.

Schmitty ran upstairs. "Whoa, Ron, aren't you taking this too far?"

"Too far? We're supposed to be hard core revolutionaries, not wimpy, undisciplined hippies. Do you have any better ideas?"

He shook his head. "No."

"This is ridiculous," I said. I've been up all night. "Grab a foot, Schmitty, and help me drag him out."

Schmitty backed away, so I made a last appeal. "Look Bruce. This is your last chance. Get up now, or I'm dragging you down the stairs." I pulled him by his feet as he punched wildly in the air. His head went *thump, thump, thump-a-bump* on the steps and I expected him to snap out of it, but he didn't. I stopped on the first landing. "I didn't want to hurt you. Snap out of it."

At last, Schmitty came to my assistance, lifting Bruce's head for the last few steps to the living room. Only after we hauled him into the kitchen did he stand up, soaked and disheveled and mad as hell.

"What the fuck are you doing, Ron," he raved at me, and Schmitty took his side, and said I'd overreacted. I was the new guy, being put on the spot for doing what they'd begged me to do the day before. I looked around at their accusing faces and launched into a lecture.

"What are we running, a damn kindergarten, or are we a party dedicated to revolution and offing the pig? What about revolutionary discipline? How are we gonna make a revolution if we can't even get out of bed?"

Wordlessly, Bruce got dressed and walked out, slamming the door behind him, but at least he was on time. He never again asked me for a wake-up call. I didn't think that I was a hard case, but we needed some basic discipline to put our brave words into action.

24

THE HOUSE MEETING

Talk of discipline became a weighty issue at the next house meeting, my first since moving in. It was a warm morning, so the meeting was held on the roof above the kitchen. We squatted in a circle in the sunshine on the tarpaper roof with a view over the L shaped alley.

Chairman Bob called us to order, and the first thing on the agenda was Tracy. His booming voice accused her of outlandish charges, like "counter-revolutionary behavior," of not being totally committed to the cause. The vague charges were couched in such high-flown rhetoric that I couldn't grasp the specifics of what she may or may not have done to deserve such a dressing down.

She was no pig or enemy agent. I'd already experienced some harsh criticism sessions during my stint in jail with the Weathermen. We radicals were supposed to be open to criticism and self-criticism, which lent the aura of an almost religious confession of sins to the proceeding, meant to spiritually cleanse us and make us stronger in our purity of faith in the "People's struggle."

The Weathermen recommended their cadre form tight affinity groups to prevent infiltration by undercover agents and claimed monogamy was divisive. Everyone within the group should share sexual love to create an unselfish one for all, all for one bond. I hadn't heard that spelled out in our White Panther collective yet and wondered if that was the goal. If so, poor Tracy was the only woman in a men's club, and that didn't seem fair.

I waited for someone to defend her, but Bill and Jeff were silent. Perhaps they, like me, couldn't formulate the required jargon to couch her defense. My instinct was to jump in, but I was the new guy, unsure of the situation, and kept my mouth shut.

The White Panther Party advocated Women's Liberation as well as Gay Lib. We needed women in our chapter and auburn-haired Tracy had plenty of the girl next door sex appeal, if the girl next door happened to be into hard jamming Rock and Roll. I doubted she'd stick around after Bob's tongue lashing and feared our collective would remain a boy's club.

The next item on the meeting's agenda was our defense strategy. If Bob hadn't already clapped me on the back and assured everyone that he trusted me, I probably wouldn't have been there for this top-secret discussion. The police had already raided the house before I came, and they could be counted on to come again. Their raids on the Black Panthers had been deadly, Chairman of the Illinois Chapter Fred Hampton, founder of the Rainbow Coalition, along with Mark Clark had been murdered in bed and, and Bob assured us that we could expect the same, despite our *white skin privilege*.

How should we react to a pig assault? That boiled down to reiterating the necessity of keeping doors locked and bolted and not letting potential pig agents inside. The problem was how to recognize an agent who could be undercover and posing as a friend or ally.

We discussed Armed Self-Defense, the merits of refusing entry to all police demands to open up, stalling and making them resort to battering the door down, rather than admitting them without a struggle. I wondered what kind of firepower we had to hit back with. Even if we were armed with double-aught shotguns, like the Black Panthers swaggered around with, how realistic was it for us to hold off well trained police marksmen. They'd be better armed with far superior weapons than whatever arsenal we may have stashed around. It sounded like a do or die, almost suicidal Alamo situation.

Bob agreed that the best we could do was delay an assault long enough for at least some of us to escape out a door or window on the opposite side of the house, if and it was a big if, the cops had left it unguarded. Better yet, we could cross over the roofs to melt into the community like a fish in the ocean, to paraphrase Mao.

Schmitty dragged out a plank he had stashed to demonstrate how we could bridge the sidewalk-wide gap to the closest building.

"The last one to climb over should pull the plank after him, or drop it below to cut off pursuit," he said. That was our only plan, and I wondered if we could pull it off.

Bob lectured us. "The *Man* has real bullets in his guns. If we're going to *get our act together* and stand up to the Pig, not just brag about it, we need preparation, martial arts and firearm training to prepare ourselves for the inevitable next phase of *armed struggle*, and yes, we need a hell of a lot more discipline *for when the shit hits the fan.* Dig it!"

We shouted *Fucking A! Right on, man!* To punctuate Bob's rousing pep talk.

Then he made an announcement. "I'm leaving tomorrow for an Alternative Media Conference at Goddard College in Vermont. Maybe I can spread the message and find some new recruits there."

Bob Rudnick had to pack, and the rising sun began melting the roof tar to hot and sticky, so we wrapped up the memorable meeting and went back inside. Afterward, I hung out with Tracy to hear her side of the story. She didn't want to talk about Bob's accusations at first, but finally spilled a jumbled story of refusing Chairman Bob's sexual advances.

"I'm not a prude, you know Ron, but I'll only sleep with a guy who turns me on."

It shocked me a little, not that my faith in human nature was shattered. I'd long accepted how fallible we all are, but "Righteous" Bob Rudnick had been touting the party line on combating male chauvinism and sexism, and this seemed too transparently hypocritical. Whatever their faults, I decided to stick it out with this collective and hope that they outgrew this apparent male chauvinism.

We fancied ourselves guerillas and looked to the Viet Cong for inspiration. The NLF used whatever antiquated weapons they had and were still holding out against the most sophisticated weaponry on planet Earth, but American forces claimed a huge body count, which, even if inflated, was lopsided in favor of the Americans winning the battle of attrition. We were behind the lines, trying to sabotage the monster from within, and although they couldn't drop napalm on us, the same logic of attrition applied. As the Doors *Five to One* song went:

> *No one here gets out alive...*
> *They got the guns*
> *But we got the numbers*
> *Gonna win, yeah*
> *We're taking over*
> *Come on!*

25

THE ARAGON BALLROOM

The Aragon Ballroom at 1106 W. Lawrence Avenue was the place to go for music even back in the Big Band days. Although getting a bit run down, it remained popular with the psychedelic rockers of our generation. The Aragon was a place where the Chicago tribes of Woodstock Nation could gather to hear heavy rock. The White Panthers shared a concession table with our Rising Up Angry partners, and on Friday June 19th, I joined them there for the first time. I'd never had the *scratch* to afford a ticket before, and this was my chance to get in free.

We sold anti-war buttons and radical books by a host of luminaries from Abbie Hoffman to Eldridge Cleaver and Mao Tze Tung, as well as underground newspapers geared to educate *our* people, that is hip white youth, on the social realities of oppression, racism, and sexism. We did this by rapping, rapping, and more rapping, jiving for the Revolution with stone hippies, and even straight kids whenever we could.

Tracy turned up and sat at the table with us for a while. Her disarming smile and pretty looks produced more successful book sales than either Schmitty or I achieved. If someone perused our literature and asked enough *Right on* questions, we'd sometimes give it away, although sales and donations were our collective's main income. We were revolutionaries first, businessmen last, and only by necessity.

Schmitty and Jeff came there often and once the incoming rush died down, they offered to let me wander into the auditorium with Tracy, where we were immersed in primal darkness pierced by flashing strobe lights playing over colorful slide images. It was a psychedelic light show that turned everything around us into a hallucinogenic collage of altered perception, bathed as we were in an ocean of loud, pulsing rock music.

We danced with wild abandon, working up a sweat jerking and bouncing into other couples who were jammed together on the crowded dance floor. We were among our own people and I was starting to really dig being with Tracy, even if Rudnick accused her of being less ardent about the Revolution.

We took a break, slipped our arms around each other, and took a few drags off a joint that made the rounds and then we kissed, sharing a sweet, refreshing interlude of bliss, uncaring whether we were acting as dedicated revolutionaries, or *jive-ass* punk hippies, in the parlance of the times. We just hung out until Schmitty called and I went back out to help load our tables and literature in the van. Then a fat, balding, middle-aged man in civilian clothes approached me.

"Well, hello there Ronald Schulz."

The silky seductive male voice had a sarcastic lilt to it, and I swung around to confront this stranger, wondering how he knew my name. With his overhanging beer belly and ill-concealed revolver and radio, he was an obvious cop.

"It *is* Ronald, right? Or do you prefer Ron?"

He spoke like an old friend who was happy to see me, but from all my run-ins with the law, I couldn't place him. When I didn't answer, he continued in the same mock familiar tone.

"Oh, let me congratulate you for getting off on that Weatherman rap back in October. Who was the judge? Saul Epton, wasn't it?" He grinned like a cat with a mouse. "Maybe next time you won't be so lucky. Huh? You're a smart kid. Maybe you'd work out a deal with us."

He'd emphasized how much he knew about me to intimidate and show me I was under scrutiny, my every move known to them, but of course he exaggerated, or so I hoped. I walked away and pointed him out to Schmitty.

"Who is that fat guy?"

"Oh, that's Mori Daley, the Red Squad pig."

That's how I got to know him on the first of many encounters to follow. I suppose his real name was Morris. I wondered if he was related to *hiz honor* the Mayor, Richard Daley, but I was assured that the name and looks were only a coincidence.

The Red Squad turned up at every social or political event, shadowing us, dogging our steps, snapping photos to update their files on everyone involved in the movement, badgering us with sarcastic comments, as if to sweet talk us into trusting them, to seduce some of us back into the fold of the red, white and blue-blooded American mainstream. The Seed later ran a piece with Mori's face on the cover.

The Red Squad

...The Red Squad is here. Plain clothes pigs so uptight proud of what they are doing that they're wearing P.I.G. buttons, even though they are supposed to be undercover. G stands for guts. A tall skinny undercover pig, his tape recorder poorly concealed, follows us around for a while. "Hey pig, you're pretty skinny. You don't look very strong. How'd you ever get to be a pig? Oink, oink." When the tape is replayed there will be a lot of false *yuks*. The wound will last longer and go deeper than any rock or bottle cut. We're proud.

Chicago SEED, volume 5, number 6, top of page 3

By the time I looked for Tracy, she was gone. She moved out of the LaSalle house right after that and worked sometimes at the Seed. Much as I was tempted, I didn't follow up with her, being too stuck in my head for my own good.

26

PICK UP THE GUN!

Schmitty sat across from me at the kitchen table with a frown on his face and stubbed out his cigarette. "I guess you're one of us now, Ron. We needed to be sure we could trust you, but you're ready, so I'll initiate you into the last secret of the Chicago collective."

I nodded in solemn agreement. Our revolutionary brotherhood had to be built on trust and mutual support. We were at war with the Mother country fighting against racism and class barriers and might even have to die for each other when the time came. We had something worth fighting for, not for some *rag* of a flag, or a way of life that was based upon keeping others down, in the mad materialistic competition enshrined in this "Land of the Free."

"Follow me," Schmitty said, as he led me upstairs to Rudnick's vacant bedroom on the third floor. With a finger to his lips *shushing* me, he whispered, "This is top secret, tell no one about this unless we've discussed it." He removed a wooden panel that was part of the doorframe and reached into a space in the wall. When he pulled his arm back, it was clutching a rifle. He beamed at me as he ran down its particulars, sounding like he'd memorized them straight from the manual.

"It's a Springfield model, 1903 bolt action rifle." He pulled back the bolt to show me the firing chamber and how to work it. "The sight's a little off, and the stock has a crack. iIt needs oiling, but we've taken it out to the country for shooting practice."

Like a new father showing off his baby, he handed the aged rifle to me. To my untrained eye, the barrel looked a little warped and would be outclassed by whatever shiny weaponry the pigs brought.

"It fires okay," Schmitty said to assure me. "I managed to hit some bottle targets, and you'll get a chance to shoot next time." After I joined, we had our hands full with other issues and had no chance to get to a firing range.

Taking a page from the Black Panther Party's program of *Armed Self Defense,* the White Panthers had to be ready to fight when *the shit came down,* not go like sheep to the slaughter as the Jews in the holocaust had done. As far as I saw, this Springfield rifle was our sole defense, our only gun to practice on. We'd load; cock the bolt and sight along the barrel without firing it inside the house. Even if we had another rusty flintlock or two stashed away somewhere, we'd be outgunned by the police.

Schmitty agreed with me. "The lowliest patrolman in Chicago is able to spend more hours on the shooting range than we can."

If the pigs ever came crashing in with murder on their minds, the best we could hope is that a marksman of our own would race upstairs and fire a few shots to make the pigs take cover long enough for us to escape over the roof. Ours was not a war of equals. A guerilla insurrection, like the Viet Cong, had to choose their battles carefully. We had to bide our time and avoid every conflict that we couldn't win. Our Indian brothers in the "Old West" had been outgunned facing the US Cavalry, and yet they offed Custer and most of his regiment. Despite that, they lost the war and had to surrender.

One gun seller who catered to the defense needs of *our* community was advertised in Rising Up Angry and later in the Seed.

HARPERS FERRY ORDINANCE
  shotguns, rifles, shooting accessories

open every Saturday,
180 N. Wacker Drive, Chicago, Ill.

27

ENTER THE GODDESS

I was on guard duty when there was a loud knock on the front door. I opened the window at the bed sized perch above the door and looked out. A couple of girls dressed in black, with berets cocked at a rakish angle, looked up at me. They were encumbered with several white carry-out bags and large sodas. The aroma of delicious fried food wafted up to me. They looked harmless, but I had to make a show of screening them, and called down, "What do you want?"

The one with a red star on her cap called up to me. "We brought you guys cokes and some hot, greasy chow from Sammy's, but if you don't want it, *screw you*, we'll eat it ourselves!"

"Just a second." I went down, unlocked, and unbarred the door. As I swung it open, the girls called out. "One-two-three!" Splash! They tossed two full sized cokes, ice and all, in my face, and burst out laughing. "Got you man!"

That refreshing hello confused me a moment, but dripping wet as I was; I kept a dignified bearing, because we Panthers represented the teeth of the revolution.

"Is anyone expecting you?" I said with a grave voice, unruffled by being drenched with coke, as if I was the butler, which I suppose I was, and that cracked them up even more.

When her laughter subsided, the one with the red star on her beret said, "Sorry about that dude, but you must admit it was funny as hell!"

Charmed and disarmed by that pretty, poised young woman, I was once again smitten with love at first sight. I racked my brain, unsure what my duty or my heart required me to say.

The other girl, smiling like a mischievous elf, spoke up. "Sorry, we thought Fuzzy was gonna open the door. Is he here?" I nodded in the affirmative and she smiled. "I'm Barbara, by the way."

Maintaining my composure, I reached out to the other girl. "Who's this rabble-rouser?"

"I'm Kay. We're from Hyde Park."

Pulling a paper napkin out of one of the sacks, she wiped my face and patted my shirt dry while I stood dumb, enjoying her fragrance and touch. She finished and looked up at me. Her cool, green eyes pulled me into her cool oasis, where I lingered for a second that lasted an eternity.

With a curt bow, I said, "I'm Ron, won't you please come in?"

My butler act put them in stitches again. These chicks were a breath of fresh air. We needed some female input to balance our intense male energy.

Kay was about my age but had the worldly demeanor of a worldly woman, exuding the confidence of knowing what she wanted and how to have fun getting it. She dressed like a beatnik, in black tights and sweatshirt, her long straight black hair streamed down from her beret like Che Guevara on the iconic posters. Her voice, as husky and sultry as Lauren Bacall's, enraptured me.

I ushered them into the kitchen, where the others joined us at the table to gobble the greasy hot chow they brought. After my two-cup shower, however, there weren't enough soft drinks to go around, so we popped open a couple bottles of beer we had in the refrigerator and toasted each other like good comrades. After eating, I slipped out of the room and made my rounds of the doors and windows like I was supposed to, until Kay found me.

"Where do you think you're going, Ron?" She purred the words using a sultry voice.

"I'm still on guard, but, ah, it's ending in a few minutes."

"Fuzzy and I are going for a walk. It should be a beautiful sunset. Wanna come?"

"Gee, I ah, guess I can, sure," I stammered like a tongue-tied schoolboy, transfixed by her dreamy eyes.

The sun was low on the horizon when the three of us trooped out the back door and down the wooden porch steps to the L shaped alley. I was in the lead, and when I turned around, my heart skipped a beat as I saw Kay linking arms with Fuzzy. Noticing my discomfiture, she took my hand and gave it a squeeze as she reeled me in beside her.

"I just love alleys, don't you guys?" she said as we took a right past several abandoned buildings on Division Street, where we took another right toward the Lake.

"Sure," I said. "Alleys are the trippy backside of the urban landscape."

Fuzzy laughed. "That's a cool perspective."

With Kay between us, we strolled, arm in arm, chatting about nothing, until we stood in silent awe, watching the sun slip below the tall buildings to the west and the cityscape turned dark. We circled back to our alley, where a dim gray form appeared out of the darkness on the porch. Approaching closer, I saw it was a long-tailed rat, big as a cat. It reared up on its hind legs before waddling down the steps toward us, showing no fear, before scurrying off into the jumble of weeds and broken concrete to our right.

"Did you see that?" Kay quivered with a mix of horror and illicit delight as she squeezed against me.

With a silent thanks to the rat, I said, "It's the biggest rat I've ever seen."

"Me too," Fuzzy said. "Although they get damn big in Detroit."

"It's a bit of urban wildlife," I said, taking the rat's side, although the size of it was unsettling and I better understood how scary those rascals could be, posing a threat to a child in a crib, or even a grown man, if the stories were true.

"We humans are just bigger animals," Fuzzy said. "We're all trying to survive in this man-made wilderness."

28

THREE WAY LOVE

After our walk, we hung out in the kitchen. Kay and Fuzzy were on familiar terms, laughing and joking, but Fuzzy was intruding between me and the woman who'd stolen my heart, and I couldn't seem to slip into the conversation. A surge of jealousy rose in me, which I suppressed, for it was a selfish, counter-revolutionary emotion, opposed to my attempt to cultivate selfless love.

I withdrew to the living room where I sat in a daze, trying to chill out, give Kay and Fuzzy their space, and pull myself together. My mouth always got me in trouble with chicks, and I needed to keep it shut and play it smooth. I picked up a random book and tried to focus on my eyes to read, but I just stared, unseeing, at the page. Kay popped in and her sea breeze of a smile quickened my pulse.

"Oh, there you are Ron. I've been looking all over for you." She flounced beside me on the couch and took the book from my hands. "What's this?" She giggled and looked at me. "You're reading it upside down, dude!"

I managed a chuckle. "Wow! I guess I'm stoned or something."

In her even, matter-of-fact voice, Kay came right to the point. "Fuzzy and I were wondering if you'd like to join us in bed tonight." I sucked in air, wondering if I was hallucinating or my dreams were coming true. She went on before I'd formed an answer. "If you don't want to, that's okay, because, like, I can understand, you know."

"Oh, no!" I blurted. "I mean yeah, sure, I'd love that, really!" I took another breath, to get some equilibrium.

"Good." She squeezed my hand. "Fuzzy, will be glad to hear it."

She went back to the kitchen while I wondered if this three-way meant sex with Fuzzy too, or if we'd both focus our attentions on Kay as the glue in male bonding. He was said to be bisexual. I felt I could share her, but sex with a man wasn't for me. I'd let Kay take the lead and see where it led.

Feminists said men had to let women call the shots. I could dig that better than fighting for sole proprietorship as men throughout history have done. Sex didn't always have to be exiled behind closed doors. We could celebrate it out in the open without shame, like the Weathermen said; and improve the one for all vibe in our tight little collective.

While our housemates trooped upstairs to bed, we three sat around the living room, discussing which of our many options made the best arena for us to bunk for the night.

Kay said, "I like that cute little observation post above the front door with a view of LaSalle Street."

"That's where I first saw you and Barb," I said. "You're a couple of dangerous *feme fatales*."

Kay giggled and winked. "You don't know the half of it yet."

Fuzzy cleared his throat. "Ahem. I guess it depends on who's on duty tonight."

"I am, Fuzz," Jeff said, bouncing downstairs. "I suppose if you guys keep an eye out for trouble. You could hang out up there."

"We wouldn't be doing much sleeping," Kay said, getting a nervous laugh from us.

I'd read Lawrence of Arabia's book, *Seven Pillars of Wisdom*. He contrasted the noisy marching sentry duty of the British Army to the relaxed, but observant Bedouin style of snoozing around a smoldering campfire with ears primed to every noise. There should be no reason our night of pleasure had to interfere with our vigilance.

We climbed the short flight of steps to the nest above the door. It was just wide enough to fit us cheek to jowl on the single size mattress, illuminated by the streetlamp glowing through the window without curtains. Anyone glancing up from the empty street below could be in for an X-rated treat. As we pulled off our clothes, I chuckled at the idea that popped into my head and out of my mouth.

"I wonder if the pigs are watching. They're developing some sophisticated surveillance equipment."

Kay glanced out into the dark street and chuckled, "So, what? Let's blow their little minds!" I loved her unflappable, forthright attitude. We joked about recruiting the pigs to our side using sex. Maybe it would work.

Free of her shapeless sweatshirt, Kay's full, ripe bosom, her taut, smooth abdomen, and rounded hips entranced Fuzzy and me. We began stroking each other's bodies, murmuring exclamations of wonder. Naked and eager, Fuzzy and I lay down on either side of her, and our four hands stroked Kay, who was the epicenter of our interest. She kissed each of us in turn, her tongue probing deep, even giving my lip a playful bite, but then Kay sat up and pushed me aside.

"Wait," she said to me, and turned to Fuzzy. "Just lie back." Then she set to work on him with vigor. I could only watch, spellbound, as she ran her tongue over his chest, around his nipples, and down along his stomach, then his legs and finally back up to his cock. It was a real *trip around the world* like I'd heard described and yearned for as a fifteen-year-old run-a-way in New Orleans.

With slow, languid, and loving expertise, she sucked his cock, rolling her tongue over the tip and then, glancing up at me with a wink and a smile, as if to say she hadn't forgotten me, she took him deep into her throat.

Aah, Fuzzy moaned with satisfaction, arching his pelvis up as she went down and came back up with a slurping sound. As they rocked ever faster, a strand of her hair fell over her face, obscuring my view. I didn't want to miss a thing, so I gathered her luxuriant mane and held it as she pumped a steady beat, focused on her task.

Watching the woman I craved suck another man's cock aroused conflicting emotions in me. I couldn't deny that it turned me on, and yet I felt left out, a spectator rather than a participant.

Fuzzy arched back and his torso convulsed. "Oh God, I'm coming," he shouted, as if all his vital energy poured out in a volcanic eruption. "Yeah, oh fuck yeah, baby."

Kay rose up from a job well done, droplets of sweat dripping from her forehead, and turned to me, proud of her performance and confident that it aroused me.

"Taste this, Ron," she said, her voice muffled by a mouth full of cum. She brought her lips to mine. I was a little *weirded out*, not being gay and never having tasted sperm before, but since it came via Kay as her gift to me, I couldn't refuse it and opened my mouth wide to receive Fuzzy's salty protein shake as we French kissed.

She pulled back. "How does it taste?"

"It's okay." I said, fighting my gag reflex as I gulped down my share of it.

Kay turned back to Fuzzy and kissed him. "How's that?" she said. "Did you ever taste your own jism before?" He laughed, leaving me to wonder if he'd tasted another man's sperm.

These two seemed to be into their own thing, and I wondered if I was just along as an audience to their act and maybe they were finished with me already when she whispered something in Fuzzy's ear.

"Okay," he said, gathering his clothes. "I'd better go up to bed now."

For a moment, I worried that Kay would go with him, but she remained curled up beside me. Fuzzy's pale body looked ghostly in the streetlight's feint glare as he clopped down from our love nest in his untied shoes and then on upstairs. Schmitty told me the house had been a bordello, and I imagined their lascivious haunting spirits blessing our erotic communion as they watched over us with nostalgia.

Kay crawled over and cooed in my ear, "I told him that I'd finish him off fast because I want to spend more time making love to you, Ron, alone. If that's okay with you?"

She'd answered my secret hope, and I breathed out my worry to inhale some buoyant anticipation, which delayed my answer. So she asked again.

"That *is* okay with you, right Ron?"

She sounded afraid that I'd say no, which gave my ego a boost, so I answered, "Damn straight it is." I gave her a kiss.

She took my cock and while gazing at me with those cool green, sexy eyes, she squeezed it back to life and guided me deep inside her. I moved slow and easy, even though she was wet and ready. I wanted to relish the moment and delay my orgasm as long as I could, while hurrying hers. It paid off. She gripped my shoulders and writhed in ecstasy. Her ever more ragged, throaty voice came out like a plea. "Fuck me harder, faster, now Ron!" Like the gentleman I was, I began banging her with more urgency. She swung her legs around my torso, lifting herself up to my thrusts, our bellies slapping together in a beat of joyful abandonment. I paced myself, restraining my release until she was shuddering in ecstasy, then I shot my load deep within her.

Spent, I lay beside her, catching my breath while Kay snuggled on my chest, purring like a kitten. "You're so quiet when you come, Ron. Most guys groan or shout something."

"Yeah, I guess the meditation I do trains me to distance myself. It's like I'm watching my emotions happen without getting too carried away."

"That's weird." She licked my neck and giggled, "Your sweat tastes salty." I ran my tongue over her breasts, making her quiver, and said, "Yours too." Kissing, we mingled our juices, and the words I longed to say popped out of my mouth.

"I love you, babe." A long moment of silence followed. I wondered if I'd screwed up. A beautiful girl like her probably heard those words a lot.

Finally, Kay sat up and tickled my ear with her long, black hair. "Would you like to eat me now?" she said in a purr.

I knew what I should say, but hesitated. Pussy is an acquired taste and the faint odor of tuna fish put me off. Sharing Fuzzy's cum with her had been a big enough deal for me, enough for one day, and I was embarrassed to admit what a sexual novice I was to this girl of wide-ranging experience. Tired and contented fool that I was, I stalled.

"I'm tired, Kay. Do you really want me to?"

"Only if you *really* want to," she answered in that *you better goddamn well know what I want* tone that women have.

I took her words at face value, and said, "Maybe later, okay?"

Kay was the uninhibited woman I'd longed for since I was fourteen and I and never imagined that I could be lying sprawled in a minefield with delayed action fuses. Words had the power to make or break us.

Hours or maybe moments later, she woke me to make love again. Taking charge of her, I grabbed her long black hair, twisting it around my wrist like a dog's leash or a horse's reins, and turned her around to try doggie style. The soft, cool feel of her buttocks against my belly was pure pleasure, variety spices sex, so it never gets stale, but I wanted to behold her divine face, so I flipped her around as she arched her back and shivered, clenching me to her sweaty bosom as her eyes rolled up in rapture. I let myself go, my body joining hers in trembling ecstasy.

She whispered, "Stay inside as long as you can." Her pussy muscles gripped me tight, and I stayed medium hard for a long time inside her sacred chamber.

Throughout the night, I only had to raise my head a few inches from Kay's warm body to peer out the window and fulfill my duty by assessing the situation outside, and be assured that our love nest in the Panther fortress was secure from external threat for the moment. Then I laid my head back down on Kay's breast, my sweet life raft. The sound of her heartbeat lulled me back to sleep until dawn's early light broke over the roof of the Mark Twain Hotel.

29

LOVE AND SACRIFICE

"I'm going to bed," Kay said that evening to no one in particular, and trotted off alone without beckoning me to join her.

Her cool, placid features were difficult for me to read. My heart fluttered as I wondered if I'd fallen from grace. Not knowing where I stood with her drove me crazy. The day had been filled with political discussions and denouncements of bourgeois culture. We had to struggle against the *pig* within ourselves. Although there were plenty of empty beds, maybe even an empty room to choose from, I hadn't yet claimed a permanent sleeping place for myself, for such a thing could be seen as materialistic, although Bob for one, had his own room with a king-sized bed on the top floor to retreat to when and if he made it home.

I waited for a discrete time to pass before I followed Kay, worried that expressing my desire, my need for her, could expose my lack of collective spirit. Kay watched me come up the stairs as she lay on the lower bunk of one of the metal bunk beds in the open "barracks" on the second floor.

"Is this where you usually sleep, Ron?"

I swallowed. "Yeah. Want to, ah, crash here with me? We could find another bunk."

She didn't answer, just put her finger to my lips as if to shush me and pulled me down beside her on the bed. Her mind seemed far away, yet her body was here with me – for now.

Silence was golden, and discretion is often the better part of valor. We lay holding each other in silence, as *kick out the jams, motherfucker* music blared downstairs, and our comrades came and went around us. We were an island of peace in our stormy, rocking house.

She remained passive in my arms for a while, but then she sat up, her eyebrows arched as she peered into my eyes.

"Do you want a blow job?" Her directness caught me off guard, and I felt myself blush.

"Ah, yeah, sure. That would be nice." My words sounded weak and stupid to me, and I wondered how better I could have phrased it. Yes, I wanted the same glorious treatment I'd watched her give Fuzzy.

She came up and kissed me afterwards; sharing my ejaculate like the precious nectar it was, before fixing me with her quizzical gaze. "Gee, Ron, you *get off* so quietly."

I forced a laugh. "Maybe I'm the silent, Gary Cooper type."

"That makes you a deeply inhibited guy. You need to loosen up."

Kay wasn't a frilly kind of girl. She could be sexy and accepting and then stony and withdrawn, but she exuded a mature, matter-of-fact sex appeal infused with a subtle sense of humor, but I hesitated to tell her too much about me, the wild swings of fate my love life had taken and the insecurity I hid within. She might be disappointed if I spilled my guts, and expressing my honest feelings could have seemed bourgeois and I would lose her.

As if reading my mind, Kay perched her chin over her folded hands atop my chest and stared at me like an artifact in a museum. "You're a puzzle, Ron. I dig that you don't jabber as much as some guys, but you need to let it all out when you fuck."

It was easier said than done. To build our new utopian future, I, like all men, had to sacrifice some of my personal feelings, dubbed macho or chauvinistic, or god forbid, whiny and childish. We had to figure out what it meant to be the *new* man and what equality of the sexes entailed. That was my duty to the cause and to her as a liberated, independent woman, for I must never attempt to "own" a woman. I heard over and over again, "If you love someone, her let her go, and if she's really yours, she will come back to you."

There were no guarantees. Life is a balancing act between expressing a slice of our deepest feelings and the necessity of trimming it, making it palatable for our audience, those for whose love we need to impress, lest we find ourselves abandoned. That's Mother Nature's tried and true way and to survive, we must respect it.

I awoke as I felt her get up beside me. To the bathroom, I assumed and tried to slip back asleep, but when she didn't come right back, I couldn't relax. I listened hard and heard her voice and lilting laughter from somewhere nearby. I arose and pretended *not* to look for her while I did just that, finding her in an adjacent bedroom laughing with Barb and Fuzzy. There was no denying my hidden jealousy, not to myself. I could share but feared losing her and it can be hard to know the difference. I hid my anxiety under a lighthearted mask and joined them, laughing at a joke I didn't get.

These were my people, and I both loved and feared them. The tie that binds us all is an invisible connection, an obsessive, primal longing buried deep within that can rip open our heart to bleed out a rich blood offering like from an Aztec sacrificial victim. It was ever thus and ever shall be in our world without end.

30

THE CHICAGO HIP COMMUNITY

The hippie counterculture was still growing all around the country and the world. Everywhere guys were growing their hair long and longer as an identifying flag of cultural rebellion. Our people were forming communes and non-monogamous families, traveling on the road, forging open-ended ties across the country and the wider world, cross-pollinating ideas and personnel with our brothers and sisters everywhere we roamed, but we had enemies too.

We were part of a growing group of young Americans who expected *the shit to come down* at any moment, like it came down hard on Martin Luther King, on Fred Hampton and Mark Clark, on the village of My Lai in Vietnam and on untold others, targeted, wiped out with impunity by the pigs. We had to stand together. Solidarity forever!

Chicago was the Heartland of America. It wasn't as freaky as San Francisco. The Chicago Freak community tended to be less *in your face* than on either coast, largely due to the repression on alternative lifestyles in the Midwest. We were always losing people who fled elsewhere, but those who stayed or came back were fierce. We White

Panthers only had a handful members, but saw ourselves as the leavening in the bread who made shit happen.

As for other organizations, the granddaddy of them all, SDS had split into three parts in 1969, first into the Revolutionary Youth Movement and Progressive Labor, and then RYM itself split in two. The Weatherman, as the former RYM I became known, went underground to conduct guerilla warfare. Their RYM II former comrades in SDS were more pragmatic and said we were less ready than the Weather *dudes* to "pick up the gun" and initiate the "Armed Struggle" phase of the revolution.

We worked together with the other organizations in the community, especially Rising Up Angry, RUA, who gave us as much help and guidance as our national headquarters in faraway Ann Arbor. The Angry guys were more organized and disciplined. They knew more about guns and attracted people to the cause better than the White Panthers seemed able to in Chicago. Maybe working-class greasers liked guns and cars more than typical hippies and were less pacifistic and identified with the need to defend their turf. Community self-defense was a huge part of the Black Panther creed, which the White Panthers hoped to emulate.

Then there were the Young Lords in the Latino community, whose headquarters we often visited as well as their rallies for a free Puerto Rico. The Black Panthers were the real movers and shakers in the Black community who cleansed whole neighborhoods of pushers and pimps, ridding the black community of the hard, addictive drugs that undermined their community.

Marijuana and psychedelics like LSD, psilocybin and mescaline weren't considered a threat, but inspirational and were deeply entrenched in the counterculture. Many hippies, however, were too spaced out on psychedelics, or *on their own trips* to be effective in the grand design of our revolution.

The Chicago Seed underground newspaper ran a regular page entitled FREE CITY DIRECTORY in which they listed social and political organizations that were part of the *hip*, alternative community. A glance at it gives some perspective on the many facets of the Progressive Movement in Chicago at the time. The White Panther Party didn't get listed until July. On Volume 5, number 6, column one on page 8, which has the image of a scowling Geronimo crouched, rifle in hand, superimposed over the page, I found the following informative entries.

FREE CITY EXCHANGE is the Chicago community switchboard. Anything you need to fuck the system, stay alive, make the revolution, or be just a little bit happier may be available from someone they know. Call 281-7197 or stop in at 2261 N. Lincoln. They need money for phone bills and rent and volunteers so the service can be expanded to 24 hours/day.

FREE CITY NEWS is a weekly sheet...

FREE CITY MUSIC is currently being run by the White Panther Party, with the help of Euphoria Blimp Works to provide free music for the community. If you need a band or want to play a free gig, call Steve at 787-7197.

FREE CITY OFFICE SUPPLIES has a glut of paper clips...

FREE CITY CLOTHING is at the Seed...

FREE CITY RADIO from 12 to 5 am 7 days a week. Tuesday from 12 to 2 presented by the Suzy Creamcheese Women's Lib. Collective. WEAW 105.1 FM. Community news, rock music & right on raps. Call Bob Rudnick at 929-0133.

THE ILLINOIS CHAPTER of the BLACK PANTHER PARTY publishes a community bulletin, operates 6 community centers, 3 breakfast programs, a medical center, and the National Committee to Combat Fascism. They need money, breakfast foods, office equipment and supplies, mimeos, typewriters, cars. The office is at 2351 W. Madison, call 243-8276 for more info.

THE CHICAGO COMMITTEE TO DEFEND THE BLACK PANTHERS has been organized to help provide legal and political defense...

WHITE PANTHER PARTY is an organization paralleling the

Black Panther Party in the white community. Chicago chapter can be reached through Free City Exchange.

YOUNG LORDS ORGANIZATION fights for the right of Puerto Ricans to exist in decent conditions, as well as for a free Puerto Rico. 834 Armitage, 549-8505

PEOPLE'S PARK at Armitage & Halsted (sic) needs loving care along with playground equipment. Feel free to just go and work on it or see the Young Lords for specifics.

I skipped over to the 3rd column, 2nd entry.

RED STAR PRESS prints for the community. Low rates. Can do color up to 17 X 22. Stickers, posters, leaflets, papers. Joel will teach. 180 N. Wacker.

OMEGA POSTERS prints for the community...

WOMEN'S REVOLUTIONARY ART CO-OP is forming to "help women break the chains of the colonizing brainwashing that we have been subjected to all of our lives" and to "open up another front against the Amerikan fatherland. We say ART BELONGS TO THE PEOPLE." Call 642-9456 for further information.

AGITPOOP—revolutionary graphic arts for free or what you can give. Leave message for Lester at 929-0133.

Joel ran Red Star Press on which lay like a mysterious dragon's cave underground, below Wacker, and he'd been busted with Rudnick in February. We see listed here many artists and printers donating their efforts to "the community." The last entry, Agitpoop, was a name derived with a healthy sense of humor, from "agitprop," short for Agitational propaganda. Lester, offering his work for free or a donation, exemplified the idealism of artists and printers in the counterculture. Agitpoop was the brainchild of Lester's friends and partner, Skeets Millard, and his girlfriend, Kay Hughes.

Skeets hailed from a wealthy family, and he'd tied up with Kay, a hard driving hip businesswoman. Kay had the distinction of having opened the very first "Head Shop" back home in Joplin, Missouri – a town that she claimed had even banned the ubiquitous Life magazine as being too racy and controversial from its town library.

When Skeets inherited a hefty sum of money, he and Kay decided to buy a farm up in Wisconsin where, together with Lester and a few others, they intended to start a commune in the countryside and put their cooperative ideas of an alternative lifestyle to the test.

31

POLITICAL EDUCATION

Agitational propaganda was the means to inspire and expand the movement. We were for *all* the people, every class, but our generation, rich or poor, was the key, for it is always the idealistic youth who build revolutions. We needed to inspire the apathetic, apolitical, confused or drugged out *stoners* of our Woodstock generation. Articles published in RUA and elsewhere described effective ways of putting up inflammatory posters.

Going out alone at night, I'd find and smear a can of evaporated milk over both sides of an inflammatory poster and plaster it on a wall that was in prominent view. When it dried, it would be difficult to tear down and could inspire our people to bold action.

One late night I almost got nabbed. I stood outside the wire fence of a factory loading dock, smoothing out the wrinkles on my wallpaper, when a loud shout startled me.

"Hey! What the fuck are you doing over there!"

Over my shoulder, I caught sight of a uniformed man, whether a security guard or a cop. I didn't stick around to find out and ran off at top speed. Later that night, after putting up my other posters, I circled back to discover that the poster had been peeled off before it was dry.

As I contemplated putting up a new one, flashlight beams zeroed in on me from two directions and gruff voices rang out.

"There he is! Get the son of a bitch!" It was a close race, but my youth and speed outran my would-be jailers, all older big-bellied men.

The week of June twenty-second through the twenty-eighth was Gay Pride week. Officially, us White Panther Freaks, like the Greasers in Rising Up Angry, were supportive of Gay Liberation, but we'd grown up in the old society and "struggled with our internal contradictions," such as homophobia or gay bashing. These blinders to tolerance prevented us from acknowledging our sexually oppressed gay brothers and sisters, living untraditional sex lives, in our common struggle of liberation. We were creating the tolerant version of the "New Socialist man and woman" in the post-revolutionary society.

Our political education included preparations for the coming storm. We were in alliance with the Gay Liberation movement in Chicago, so it was not surprising when Schmitty announced that a Gay Liberation martial arts collective would hold classes in our house.

Two guys sporting great drooping walrus mustaches arrived, wearing rakish Aussie bush hats with the wide brim turned up at one side, and matching khaki cutoff pants and tee-shirts. It looked as if the legendary Chindit commandos of World War Two had passed through a time warp and wandered from the Burmese jungle to the hot streets of Chicago. They looked martial enough. Anyone who thought homosexuals were sissies was in for a rude surprise. They bagged about *trashing* homophobic toughs in street fights and said they looked forward to opportunities to "kick pig butt," and offered to share their expertise in martial arts.

"We need to be ready for whatever the pig throws at us," the one with the longest mustache said. "We'll start with blocking moves, but remember, we will be blocking not just fists, but nightsticks and rifle butts as well, knocking them out of the way before closing in and counterattacking." They lined us up, facing partners. "There are two ways to block, using the outer or inner side of the forearm, and we will train you in both."

We rotated our forearms up and out to knock the punch or police baton away using our outer arm. "That's the safest way, but using the inner arm below the thumb is more effective. The problem is the bone has less flesh covering. Not only can it break with severe punishment, but there is a big vein running across it."

To toughen this area, they had us perform a bruising regimen, repeatedly banging a suspended lead pipe with the bone below the wrist, to desensitize the body to pain and build protective calluses to protect the bone. They insisted that such intensive workouts would not only strengthen the bone but cause the vein that crosses over it to move out of the way.

I never discovered the truth of that claim. None of us followed through with such intensive practice, we had plenty to keep us busy. Each of us had a radical reading list to wade through and we attended discussion classes on these books, with topics ranging from Imperialism, Colonialism, Racism, and Sexism, to give a good intellectual and historical grounding in the Revolution we were trying to build. I'd already read some of them a couple of years before while a student at Fenton high school.

They included Franz Fanon's *Wretched of the Earth*, *The Autobiography of Malcolm X,* and *Soul on Ice*, by Eldridge Cleaver. I'd also read Mao Tse Tung's book on guerilla warfare, which I'd been surprised to find in my ultra conservative school library, but I hadn't read his little Red Book, *Quotations from Chairman Mao Tse-Tung,* which became a bible of the Left. I thought it's stilted, overly complex language was quoted too often to give a voice of authority to whatever vague point a comrade was trying to make. "Keep it simple, stupid," made better sense to me than whatever obscure point Mao made. We rapped a lot about Theory versus Practice, arguing whether the Ends justified the Means, trying to develop a sound theoretical understanding of Marxist thought, as well as grounding in practical aspects of revolution. The rationale expressed in Marxist terms was that a successful revolution involved taking over the economic

"Means of Production," which required seizing state power first to carry this out, not a walk in the park. As if that weren't enough, we had to fight the inner revolution of consciousness for personal and sexual rights that ran parallel to the external fight going on within our ranks.

32

THE RADICAL CHIC CHICK

Bob was at Goddard College in Vermont for the four-day Alternative Media Conference that ran from Wednesday June seventeenth to Saturday the twentieth. According to the New York Times, over 300 AM and FM radio stations sent DJ's or other representatives to the conference.

The Rolling Stone article, *Media Freaks Meet The Movement*, by the ominously named *Black Shadow*, gave interesting details of the confrontation between the "uptight" and very cerebral politicos and the more exhibitionist hippie cultural warriors, including the Hog Farmers. Some of the latter attempted to "turn on" the straighter politicos with a live porn show and encouraged the rest to join in a "Fuck-in" orgy. Despite their best efforts, the prudish politicos freaked out, and the escapade backfired. The Hog Farm "leadership" responded by purging the orgy makers from this increasingly more organized tribe. Heretofore, they had the policy of operating *without* designated leaders.

The mind-blowing Free Love and uninhibited sexual expression days of our Cultural Revolution seemed to have drawn to an abrupt close, and the tightly wound left brain people had taken over. I stood with those who refused to abandon our sex positive attitude.

"If those blue nosed pundits could screw up a wet dream," I said. "What would they do to the revolution?"

At the end of this media conference, Righteous Bob, and White Panther Libby from Ann Arbor, picked up a young female hitchhiker as they drove back to Chicago. Leslie Brody, a recent high school dropout, was seventeen, and had also been at the conference, where she was invited to speak at a radical high school organizing conference in Chicago, but rather than accept the less adventurous ride with her friends, she decided to strike out on her own, hitchhiking.

Bob and Libby took her under their wings and educated her on the wonders of the White Panther Party and invited her to check it out. Leslie published her account of these events in her book *Red Star Sister*. I'll quote the passages from her book where she describes her first impressions of us White Panther men under the chapter, titled *Sneaks and Spies*.

1970, summer

At first I felt like I'd arrived at an outpost of the Foreign Legion. My brothers, as I was encouraged to call them, had turned the house into a fortress, a shrine to "armed self-defense," where the military symbolism I'd flirted with had suddenly sprung to life. We lived on the thrilling edge between paranoia and possibility. It was an accepted fact that the revolution might come tomorrow. (It might already have been declared and the news just not have reached us yet.) We used the Phone box in the grocery store because ours was undoubtedly tapped. Police cars were frequently parked on the corner of our block, and at any moment, we expected a SWAT team to burst in shooting. In preparation, we hid guns in holes in the walls. At night, when everyone else slept, one of us would stay awake and patrol the shuttered windows for an ambush.

What I wouldn't realize until much later was that I'd been recruited like a missionary, imported, with my buttons and feminist dogma, into a swamp of male chauvinism where I was expected to instruct and convert the natives. I was, after all, assistant minister of education. It was a social experiment devised by a mad scientist. And although I wish I could say that I tucked into my job with the crisp authority of Wendy among the lost boys, I felt more like Annie Sullivan with five Helen Kellers (except I didn't have a stiff spine or a teacher's dedication). I hadn't set out on this road to be a schoolmarm or a nurse. I wanted to be a soldier too.

...While I thought that, if the need arose, I'd be willing to fight for my ideas, my new comrades seemed poised for the literal fight. They perceived themselves as the ground troops, grunts and proud of it. Unlike them, I hadn't been brought up on war movies or played with guns as a child. I didn't have any desire to test myself in battle. Fresh from the New York suburbs, I was simultaneously more sophisticated and more naive than they...

My sense of humor grew damp and useless in that house. As mysterious as men were, those I had known ... had always seemed to make some space for me in their lives, even if it was superficial or momentary over the course of a conversation. These five members of the White Panther Party made it clear from the first that I had been imposed on them...

Pages 87-88 of Red Star Sister

I'm amused by her calling us a "swamp of male chauvinism." We were male, sure, except for random visitors like Seed staffers, and Tracy had been driven away, which left us a stag party until the free-spirited Kay and Barb showed up, but they drifted between the LaSalle house and their stomping grounds in Hyde Park. They may not have been around to meet Leslie when she woke up that first day.

"You guys need to humor Leslie," Bob said. "She'll attract more women to join her discussion groups." But Bob wasn't around that much, and devoted most of his time to his radio career.

To put this in perspective, seventeen-year-old Leslie was about the same age as Schmitty, Jeff, and Kay. I'd turned eighteen in late March and Bill was maybe a year or two older. We were all brimming with youthful arrogance, but she'd come straight from high school and a safe home, rather than an independent, if unpredictable, life on the streets. I recall trying to help her feel at home, but when we asked her to take her turn on the chore schedule and guard duty, I found her aloof and dismissive. Here's how Leslie saw it:

> They perceived our shared cooking and cleanup details, gun and fighting exercises, and officer-of-the-night duties as basic training. To me, the fight class felt like the burden of gym, and the kitchen duties were a direct attack on my feminism.
>
> "Why didn't you do the dishes?" Desperado asked, pointing out the sink infested with a towering, clotted mess.
>
> "Women have been doing dishes for thousands of years," I complained. "That's chick consciousness, and there's not going to be any chick consciousness around here."
>
> Ibid. Page 88

When Leslie stormed in, demanding everything revolve around her, I took that to mean she would *never* wash dishes, and I don't recall her doing any. It shouldn't have been such a big deal. Even when it wasn't my turn, I washed dishes, just to create some order in the chaos of communal living, but her fair share of household duties was beneath her exalted feminist status. She didn't volunteer and none of us 'male chauvinist' men forced her to do anything. While I tried to be sympathetic and agreed with most of her feminist concepts, I thought she was a spoiled middle class girl who overreacted and didn't pull her weight.

As she writes:

> These Midwesterners, ... were so much more absorbed by their emotions. They rushed around without getting anywhere and reacted immediately to whatever they felt. They never seemed to think before they spoke, no matter how ridiculous or insulting their opinions. Speech itself seemed a lost art. Not even the Professor, the house intellectual, had time to waste on a conversation lasting more than a few sentences, they concentrated all their vital energy on the coming battle.

Ibid. Page 88

There were some heated discussions, but we gave in, and I remember less animosity than she indicates. Imperfect as we were, I don't think we were the raging chauvinist pigs she claims. Leslie didn't remember any of our names besides Rudnick for her book. We needed women and Leslie, stomping around like a frustrated commissar, would have to do.

33

BEHIND THE WHEEL

Bob turned to me. "Have you got a driver's license? I'm in a hurry and need you to drop me and Bill somewhere."

"Sure," I said nervously, without mentioning that I needed glasses to make out distant objects like street signs and I'd never driven in Chicago traffic. Our only vehicle was a VW van, parked in the tight alley behind the house. Backing up to turn around, I gunned the engine too much and bumped the Telephone pole before I hit the brakes.

"Jesus!" Bob yelled from the back. "Are you sure you can drive?"

Bill, sitting in the front, stuck up for me. "The fender is already pretty dented up from your driving, Bob. He just needs practice, is all." The rest of the drive went well.

The day after this poor beginning, Bob took the van to the studio and rather than figure out the directions on the subway in this new city, Leslie insisted on being driven to her High School Organizing Conference. By luck, a visiting comrade from Ann Arbor offered us the use of his car.

"The gas gage is just stuck on empty," he said. "Just put in as much as you use."

Figuring out the vehicle situation gave them a late start and

Schmitty, who usually took the subway, decided he'd a ride with her to his Blimpworks meeting. Neither of them had licenses, so they told me to drive, and Schmitty gave me two dollars from our kitty, for emergencies.

I hoped the car had enough gas, as we set off without so much as a map. Without glasses, I had to squint hard to read the street signs.

"Look, Schmitty, I don't know the city like you. Maybe we should drop Leslie off first so you can show me the way."

"I'm just up the street," he said. "Let me off there and I'll explain." He ran over some hurried directions to get Leslie to her destination. "Just drop her off and go home. She can call when she needs to get picked up."

Leslie badgered me about my confusion over directions. It rattled me, and I took a few wrong turns until I managed to find her conference building.

"How long will you be?" I said.

She ran inside, shouting over her shoulder. "Maybe a few hours."

I should have parked and gone inside too, but from her mannerism I assumed I wasn't invited or welcome and I didn't want to give up the two dollars I had to pay for parking. It was a sweltering day, and I saw myself sitting in a hot car for hours before she'd be ready. So I gambled on getting back for some more cash first and drove off, but I didn't count on the heavier traffic snarls on the way back, which burned more of the gas. That's when I realized that I should have waited with the car in the boiling sun.

Deep in the Loop, the bowels of Chicago's downtown, where the urban canyons reached the sky and blocked the afternoon sun, I found myself jammed in bumper to bumper traffic. The engine conked out. I turned the key. It revved a few times. My heart raced when it restarted, but it ran ragged, moved a few more feet, and cut out for good.

I glided in neutral toward the only empty parking space but didn't quite make it. I got out to push, and the guy in the car behind me jumped out to help.

"Thanks man!" I said.

"Don't mention it, kid." He gave me the peace or V for victory sign and jumped back in his car to creep forward in the bumper-to-bumper traffic.

"Chicago people are my kind of people," I said to myself. Taking a deep breath to get myself together, I got out of the car, just in time to see a meter maid walk up.

"Please," I said, begging the older black lady. "I'm out of gas and don't have enough for the meter, too."

She listened, clicking her tongue with more sympathy than I expected. "Well, alright. I'll give you a grace period, but better get that car out of here before the parking lane opens to buses in an hour. The tow trucks will yank it out of here if you don't."

"Okay, that's no problem," I said. So far, my day had been jinxed.

I ran a few blocks to a gas station. "Can I borrow a gas can?"

The black attendant eyed me with suspicion. "No way, man. Too many of my cans get stolen."

"I'm just down the street, please. I'll bring it right back, honest!"

"Well, okay, if you leave me a buck-fifty deposit."

That meant I'd only have fifty cents left for gas. He wouldn't budge. I had no choice. So I paid, and ran back, remembering from my earlier experience starting a car that was bone-dry out of gas, to pour some down the throat of the carburetor and put the little remaining into the tank. It started. What a miracle! I rammed it into gear and pulled back into the terrible, slow traffic to the station. The attendant gave me my buck-fifty back, which I put in the tank and started back north.

"Come on, please..." I begged the invisible forces of destiny, but they failed me. About ten blocks shy of Division, the machine died again. I ran the rest of the way home. Jeff unbarred the door and let me in. Collapsing on a sofa, I caught my breath and explained my predicament to Jeff.

"There should be a gas can around here somewhere, Ron. I'll look for it."

While he looked, I went up to the third floor, where the cash box was hidden behind a panel in the wall and pulled out five from the twenty bucks I found. That should do it. Then Leslie popped in the house, fuming that I didn't wait for her.

"Shit," I said. "I wish the hell I had. But I can't undo what's done, can I? Give me a break. I already feel like shit." She finally cooled down as I explained the whole gas situation. "I need to go get the car now."

She looked at me with a tad more sympathy. "Alright, Ron, I'll go with you."

"Cool. Let's go." I was grateful for presence, my misery needed company. With all the worry filling my brain, I didn't even ask how her meeting went, or if she talked about it. I didn't register it. At least she had friends who'd driven her back, safe and sound. No matter how rough her day seemed, I was convinced mine was much rougher.

"How far is it?" she said, after we'd gone about six blocks.

"I didn't count the blocks. I just know it's down on the right, this side of the Chicago River." Then I recognized the place I'd parked, but not a single car was on the empty street. "They towed the goddamn thing already!"

We could only trudge back to the house again and call the City to find out where it was being held. The owner wasn't pleased. To add insult to injury, he had to pick it up and pay the fine and tow charge. It was no way to make allies in the community, although Bob may have reimbursed him for the towing charge. I didn't need another day like that, but I learned a valuable lesson. "Fill the gas tank before you fill your belly." A motto I tried to live by ever since.

34

SISTERHOOD

K ay returned after disappearing for a couple of days that seemed forever to me with a brash, high-born lady look. A black bowler hat a size too big rested on her ears, as if she was ready to ride off on a fox hunt. She'd brought her sidekick Barbara and a couple of high school chums from Hyde Park who intended building a network with us.

Leslie smiled a greeting. "I'm starting a women's group where we can rap about sisterhood. Do you want to join us?"

A few women I didn't know came and joined them from time to time. They met in a separate room away from us, while we attended our own ad hoc men's sessions to raise our political consciousness above the behavior our birth culture encoded in us.

To create a powerful sisterhood, women had to liberate themselves from passivity, rely on themselves and each other, rather than depending on men. Although the sessions weren't intended to turn them into man haters, they tended to gripe about us. I sometimes overheard loud exclamations coming from the room. "They're all sexist pigs!"

Even chivalry, the ingrained reflex of men to assist women, opening doors or lifting heavy objects, was lambasted as infringing upon their independence, unless requested, of course. Equality meant being able to do everything a man could do, but whether they wanted to do so was another matter. There were misgivings about these meetings that I kept to myself.

Women seemed to have it both ways as less and less was required or expected of them. Certainly not the dishes! They were still just women when it came to guns and guard duties, even though they demanded that we treat them as equal in all other respects. In some respects, they became the feminine "weak links" that scoffed and refused to accept any discipline or training. The rationale was that they were making up for centuries of sexual exploitation. They had to stamp out their own "chick consciousness" until the metamorphosis from chick into some kind of "super-woman" was complete.

Kay was a capable, strong woman, attractive to men. The way she wore men's clothes that didn't quite fit her accentuated her appearance of feminine vulnerability. Yet I knew she had ice in her veins, a femme fatale, and was the goddess I worshipped. She had insight into using her feminine psycho-sexual dynamics, a woman's superpower, however I wasn't sure if that represented "chick consciousness" to hard core feminists.

Comrade Leslie, no matter how she liked to portray herself, was like all of us except Righteous Bob, young and still figuring things out. After reading her book, I see that she wanted male attention and felt ignored by us, all except for the character she calls Buggy, who I think is Fuzzy.

At the time, I feared that we'd go too far in rooting out parts of our sexual behavior, the games that attract and bonded the sexes to each other. Women, whether instinctually or by training, often exhibit a demeanor of dependent, helplessness that attracts, or as some would say, ensnares men. Even knowing that as a ploy, it still had a profound effect on me and susceptible men in general. I questioned whether, in combating sexism, we had to destroy the ties that bind us in our beguiling dance of life.

35

SUMMERTIME BLUES

June 28th was the Fred Hampton Memorial Concert in Grant Park. We White Panthers hadn't forgotten our fallen comrade, and we swore to avenge him. Between speeches and songs, we shouted slogans: *STP! Stop the pig and serve the People! Seize the time! The time is now! Seize the time and off the swine!*

"Right on!" we shouted in response. *Off* meant kill, and *pigs* were the police, who surrounded us in the park, as in all rallies, and they could more easily turn their guns to *off* us, than the other way around. I wondered if any of us were ready for that profound step of offing anyone. Not yet. In any war detailed from the Bible on down, an enemy had to be dehumanized first, the soldiers had to work up enough hatred to kill and it could go too far and be turned against prisoners, the civilian population, or even their own group.

US troops chanted "Kill VC!" as they trained, doing push-ups, and jumping jack calisthenics in time to that murderous beat. Our boys called their enemy, and even their Asian ally's derisive names: Gooks and slopes, among other less complimentary terms.

The Nixon administration called us "loudmouths" and "effete snobs" for demonstrating against the war, but after closing college campuses across the nation and losing student lives at Kent State and elsewhere, we had helped accomplish something. On June 29th, the invading American troops were finally pulled out of Cambodia. But we knew that the CIA carried on clandestine activity against Cambodia and in Laos and Central and South America. Every day became a whirlwind of meetings, classes, marches, and speeches, exciting events that kept us on the go and we were getting stoned too, on reefer and Ripple wine with our brothers and sisters on the street, or back at the *Crib* on LaSalle, so a lot of events blurred together in my mind.

Each month, I had to send in form letters to my probation officer. I had to scrawl an invented job search on a form, or claim to have done some chores for neighbors, to convince whoever read them I was seeking employment and staying out of trouble. Where all those letters ended up, I didn't know, but if I forgot to send them, I might end up back in jail.

A lengthy article in the Seed by Bernie Cobb-Farber portrays the sentiments of that time in the alternative community of Chicago.

Summertime Blues

The end of June—the beginning of July. Summer begins. All of a sudden, it's upon us. It's hot; it's hard to concentrate. Mostly we want to relax—go to the beach, go to the park...

We want to be together. We want to share. We want to feel a sense of community---to break out of the little cubicles of city living, the paranoia of what's been aptly called "Fear City"---Chicago---to get out of the masks and ego-projections, the divisions and barriers that the system builds. Our lives feel restricted and tied down: jobs, school, with often nothing that could be termed a future...

And the first half of the first year of the 70's is over. Fred Hampton, murdered in his bed just before the decade began...

Summer 1970: as it begins, the Clark Theater dies, men demonstrate against Playboy, women's liberation and gay liberation start really getting it together, the right-wing Legion of Justice terrorists attack a movement office again, a non-bootlegged new Dylan album comes out, Bob Rudnick returns to radio. Free City

Exchange Switchboard becomes a reality. Alice's reopens. The Seed plans a benefit—and gets two threats, two days apart...

Yet thousands wave peace signs after Kent. Thousands applaud a statement at a Grant Park rock concert that "we're putting down the bricks and leaving that to the other guys... when they hit us, we're gonna grin... we're gonna have a hundred kids and raise them all right." Two years after the McCarthy fiasco, ever optimistic college students still talk about organizing a "Movement for a new Congress." After years of government lies and deceptions, after thousands of demonstrations and explanations, as Summer 1970 begins the Seed still gets an "open letter to the President" that ends:

"Please, Mr. Nixon, I'm your sister."

And we're really torn. Some movement heavies are into ego-trips about "picking up the gun." Others still search for the "correct" ideological stance without relating it to people's needs. Some of us see the valid need for self-defense groups. But lots of us still want to reason together with our opponents.

A lot of us look out into Amerika: and we must say it, we are frightened. The "Silent Majority" is probably more likely to be a "Powerful Minority" but for now, they do seem to have the power. Often this power is a stark and very evident physical reality.

Guns or flowers? Leaflets or discussions? An alternate lifestyle or trying to reach so-called "Middle America?"

Bernie Cobb-Farber in the Seed Vol. 5, number 7, p 2

This letter touches on so much of what was going on in our lives at the time. Under careful analysis, our situation appeared hopeless, but we had to *buck up*! It was counter-productive (read counter-revolutionary) for each of us to beat our chests and bemoan our own petty fates. We needed courage and confidence, not discouraging self-pity, which only played into the hands of our enemy, but no one wakes up full of raving confidence every day.

36

FRIENDS DROP IN

One day I came into the kitchen to find Marvin, the guy I suspected of being an undercover pig, sitting at the table between a glassy eyed Bob Rudnick and a worried looking Bill as he rolled a joint.

"Hi Ron," Marvin said with a smug smile. "I heard you were here. Try some of this dynamite weed."

I shot a worried look at Bill. "Ah, maybe later, Marvin."

Bill followed me out of the room, and I asked, "How the hell did he get here?"

"Bob brought him," Bill said. "He says he's okay, and he's sure got plenty of weed, but I'm not so sure where his head is at."

"Yeah," I said. "I don't trust him either; he always gets away with breaking the law and even talking back to the pigs. That's something none of us could do without getting busted and doing some time."

After Marvin left, we conferred with Bob, who was stoned, but seemed to agree with us.

"We'll just keep an eye on him," he said. "But meanwhile we can smoke his good shit."

There was no escaping Marvin. He kept turning up wherever he pleased and made himself at home, above suspicion, from the Waveland house to this Panther stronghold of the revolution. We all took turns on guard duty, but our tight security seemed like a joke if we let a probable police agent like Marvin wander in.

Foolproof security was hampered the more we tried to interact with the community, hold women's and consciousness raising classes and try to expand our membership. We all suspected that there were enemies among us. Deep cover infiltrators weren't as transparent as the middle aged Red Squad guys we got to know by their first names. It was well-known that Fred Hampton had been set up and drugged by an undercover agent who'd become a trusted member of the Black Panthers.

Some long-haired, *freaky* dudes walked among us, spouting all the slogans of the counterculture, but who could just as well be pigs. Fuzzy came up with the idea of using a prearranged password, but that became a joke when none of us remembered it and as more visitors dropped in from out of town, they often arriving unexpectedly late at night, so we gave it up.

A day later, Schmitty walked into the kitchen to find the back door wide open and Marvin poking around the kitchen on his own. "How the hell did you get in here?" he said.

Marvin leered at him and said, "I used my sorcery. Spooky, huh?"

Schmitty confronted Jeff, who'd been on guard. "Why was the door left open? They're supposed to be locked and always barred."

"I didn't open the door. It was secure the last time I checked."

Everyone in the house claimed the doors *had* been locked and the cross beams in place, and no one admitted to letting Marvin in. I wondered if Marvin was trained on CIA spy craft. He relished our confusion, and this event helped convince the others that he was an agent of the pigs, but Bob kept letting him and his high-quality drugs back in.

For all his radical sermonizing, Bob was more interested in getting high than screening out a guy like Marvin.

The saying went, "You are either *with* us or *against* us." You were either, "A part of the problem, or a part of the solution." But by the time you have convincing proof that someone is an enemy agent, it's probably too late, as Linda Evans found out.

One day I answered the phone to hear, "Hello, this is Linda Evans."

I knew the name from the news. She was one of the first members of the underground Weathermen to get caught in the massive FBI manhunt. We chatted for almost an hour.

"I'm just so happy to talk with a brother who understands what I'm going through," she said, sounding wistful and lonely after being almost three months in jail. And I gave her all the sympathy I could to boost her spirits.

Linda hailed from Ft. Dodge, Iowa, an ultra conservative area. In 1969, she had been twenty-two when she was arrested in the same *Bring The War Home* riot that I too was arrested in, so we had that in common. I told her about my time with the Weatherman in jail, and I remembered her name coming up a few times.

She'd gotten the usual charges we all did, aggravated battery, mob action and resisting arrest. She jumped her $35,000 bail to join the Weather Underground and manufacture bombs, but she'd been captured on April 15th along with Diane, another Weatherwoman, because of an undercover agent.

Larry Grathwohl was the infiltrator who'd engineered her arrest. Linda had this to say about him in the Ann Arbor Argus, a lesson for all of us.

> ...Diane and I were busted by a single clever infiltrator who had survived living in one of our collectives for six months, suffering incredible sexual-social traumas without flinching, even made it through a two-day acid epic test because people suspected him of being a pig. They got me because of our bad security in the past (while we were an open organization), and because I was careless, trusting other people's evaluations of this motherfucker, rather than following my own head...

"Linda Evans" in Ann Arbor Argus
page 13, number 25, July 22 to the 29th.

Before she hung up, Linda said she was being held in Chicago at
the time and promised to stop by our LaSalle house if she got
released or bailed out. That turned out to be wishful thinking,
because with her heavy charges and having jumped bail once
already, that wasn't in the stars.

Another call came from a distraught guy who sounded like he
was crying. "I'm up in Bismarck North Dakota, where I'm trying to
organize some kind of anti-war movement. You can't imagine how
lonely I feel up here. I'm surviving in a hostile conservative
environment. Could the White Panther help me set up a new chapter
here?"

The thought of expanding our Woodstock Nation to turn on more
areas of the country to our values excited me, and per instructions
from Chairman Bob, I could only encourage him and advise him to
get in touch with the Ann Arbor head office.

He never called back, and I wondered what became of him and
whether he had any success, or if the call was some kind of a ruse. We
had to open up and trust people, even though we knew not everyone
was on the level.

Our Chicago Collective was a small, struggling band that needed
to grow if we were going to have any lasting influence. I invited my
friends from the Waveland house and Chris from the West End in
Bensenville to check out the White Panther scene. While they
seemed impressed with our pad on LaSalle Street, they didn't move
into our collective, or stay long. The Doan brothers had their own
small organization in Elmhurst, and we all kept connected like one
big, happy, extended family.

On another front in the culture war, our West End friend Lee
Swanson persevered with his music agenda, elbowing rock and roll
into the conservative town of Elmhurst despite the anxieties of the
city council. He opened with some well-known bands. The July 8th,

1970, edition of the Elmhurst Press mentioned that Paul Revere and the Raiders and REO Speedwagon were slated to play the next day at his Wild Goose dance club. That became another place for us to leaflet and canvass for donations and recruits, but our core group remained small.

37

VOICES IN THE NIGHT

Despite our inauspicious beginning, my relationship with Leslie grew warmer over time. We found ourselves wandering together, a little lost in the night, as we returned from a rally, and stepped into the foyer of an apartment building with high ceilings, lit by an ornate chandelier. The door thudded shut behind us and I felt more than heard the acoustics ripple through my body.

"Wow," I said. "That was trippy. Listen to this." I began chanting "OM."

That got Leslie laughing. "Do you know any Gregorian chants, Ron?"

"No, but I can fake it." And for the absolute hell of it, I gave voice to hallelujah and the few Latin or Greek words I knew. Despite growing up Jewish, Leslie knew others, and we filled the air with Ave Maria and Kyrie Eleison.

"Let's try Hare Krishna," I said, and after we did it, I asked her, "Can you feel that vibrating your chakras?"

We added other mantra sounds, enjoying some playful harmonizing together on that warm summer night. It sparked a brief conversation about the effect of sound and vibration in arousing our spirit force. Even hard core Marxists can agree with that, if you use the right terminology. For a moment we weren't the serious, one-dimensional radicals we'd been before. Leslie seemed more real, a natural woman, and I could have gone for her if Kay, who'd vanished again, wasn't uppermost on my mind.

A day or two later, Bob, accompanied by Marvin, came home from toiling on the radio and gathered us together. "Who wants to speak on the radio? There's an open spot on an interview program, and I need a couple of you to rap about the White Panther agenda."

Our response was not as enthusiastic as he expected. "Come on, guys! If no one goes, I'll have to cancel the damned thing."

"No," I said. "Don't do that. It would be a wasted opportunity to spread the word."

I don't remember which station it was, whether Bob's WEAW or his old WGLD. Chewing it over around the kitchen table, Schmitty, Jeff, and Bill pleaded that they had other plans and recommended cancellation. Only Leslie and I had nothing scheduled and, as both of us were the newest members, it would be an opportunity to prove ourselves. Neither of us had been on air before and I worried that speaking for the whole movement was a big responsibility.

"What should we talk about, Bob?" I said.

"Just rap about the Revolution, man. Talk about your reasons for dropping out of high school, joining the Panthers, and tell them what we're all about. It will come to you."

Leslie and I were suddenly spokespersons for the White Panther Party. There was no time to prepare for whatever interview questions we would be asked, or how hostile the host might be. There was a lot of trash talk over the airwaves anyway, so whatever we said couldn't hurt and might even help the cause.

"How're we getting there?" we asked.

"Marvin will bring you. Right Marvin?"

"You bet!" he said. "Here, let's fire up a dobby before we go."

Right away, I had doubts about getting high before we got there, but against my better instincts, I inhaled to feel an instant buzz. Marvin kept the joints coming after we got in the car. Leslie began laughing and looking into her glazed eyes. I knew she was as stoned as me. It was stupid of us to start our mission already fucked up on his shit, but it was too late. All we could do was surrender to the experience and hope for the best.

It was an article of faith among the White Panthers that smoking marijuana was our sacrament for expanded consciousness. However, my consciousness was already too expanded to focus, and it made me paranoid. Like a zombie, I followed Marvin and a giggling Leslie out of the car and into a waiting room where a heavyset, middle-aged guy met us. His hard, probing eyes were filled with what I saw as unconcealed contempt as he ushered us into his cozy little studio. His deep voice introduced us with a colossal buildup.

"The Radical New Left has been making waves in the news lately, from the underground Weatherman bombing statues and government buildings to anti-war groups destroying draft card files. The White Panther party, based in Ann Arbor Michigan, whose self-styled guru John Sinclair is serving a ten-year sentence for possession of marijuana, has a chapter right here in Chicago..."

My mind left the room to wander into distant dimensions as his words swirled around me. Leslie continued giggling. The Weed was probably laced with something, and I wondered if we were Marvin's Guinea pigs in a plot to screw with our minds. Maybe he'd brought us on the air to prove we were weirdoes, oddballs to be humiliated for a little comic relief.

He remained outside the studio, but I have a hazy recollection of his face popping in on us from time to time, his lips curled in a mischievous smile as if to check the status of his experiment. Our interviewer seemed to be another pig and his talk show's purpose was probably to demolish us and our sacred cause. He flipped a switch and turned to us.

"Okay, we're at commercial now. When the light flashes green, we'll be back on the air. Be ready." He looked at Leslie. "Try not to laugh so much, dear."

I had to clear my head. It seemed that I was looking through a long tunnel that muffled sound and slowed everything down. Voices, my own included, come through a delayed response to me, and I lost the thread of what had been said a moment before. The green light lit up, and we were back on the air.

Our host announced us. "I have a couple of guests here from the radical White Panther organization." He stopped a moment, positioned the mike before Leslie, and continued.

"The White Panthers, who are they, and what are they all about? Let's hear it from them."

"Hi, I'm Leslie Brody, a former high school student from a suburb of New York city..." She launched a tirade against the exploitive system of sexism and repression of America's youth, punctuated by giggles. "We are robbed of our individuality, molded into compliant cogs, playthings of a dehumanizing system..."

The announcer interjected and said, "It sounds like you're just another kid from New York City, Leslie. You're not one of our home-grown Chicago kids. In fact, you fit the bill of an outside agitator. What brought you to Chicago?"

I winced at his painting us as outsiders. Since Leslie used her real name, so would I. I'd let it all hang out, set them straight with full disclosure. The announcer gestured to me, and I swallowed my misgivings and spoke up.

"My name is Ron Schulz. I'm eighteen, a home-grown Midwestern guy from Wood Dale on the West Side of Chicago." I tried to fight the stereotype that radicals came from outside. "The *contradictions* of our society are what has spawned us radicals in the *Belly of the Beast.*"

I rambled on, telling the listeners I was a former student at Fenton high school before I dropped out to join the revolution.

"We are not just about the dress codes and loud music! We're against the imperialist war at home and abroad. What else can we do but advocate armed struggle and pick up the gun in armed self-defense as the inevitable answer to the oppression our country lays on Third World countries."

The telephone rang as a call came in. The caller gave his name, but the letters seemed to float in the air, and I couldn't grab and put them together into a name. I asked him *who*, and he repeated it, but I still couldn't grasp it.

"I'm from Bensenville too," he said, his voice dripping with menace. "And I knew you in Fenton."

"Really," I said. "I don't remember you at all."

"You may not remember me, *he-he*, but I remember *you* very well."

I pegged him as a hostile interrogator, no friend of mine. I was so damned stoned I could feel his hot breath coming through the wires as he grilled me about my statement that it was time for an armed struggle and assured me that, as a former classmate, he could reveal embarrassing details from my childhood. That made me blush. But then I wondered if he even be Marvin, calling in from another phone in the building. I wasn't sure about anything, like there was no ground under my feet.

Leslie, still breaking up into stoned giggles beside me, offered no help. I had to keep it together and not flinch, because this whole *scene,* maybe even the caller, was stage-managed by Marvin or his pig handlers to wreck our credibility. We were outcastes anyway, and as Marx put it, we had nothing to lose but our chains. I sat up straight, screamed a silent inner war cry, and tried to turn the tables.

"Ah, yes, my childhood of continual humiliation. So, you remember me, huh? Good for you. No, I don't need to be reminded of that."

"You were nobody, Ron," he said. "A complete loser and a wimp."

That pissed me off. "Yes, I was a loser. How about you? Were you a greaser, a jock? You don't sound like one, more like a little nerd, or a pimple-faced honor student who couldn't get a date to the prom. It doesn't matter to me because school is only a factory to turn us into cogs in the war machine. Get your head together, brother, and drop out. Be someone who stands for something."

The session ended and Marvin, our dubious ally, drove us back to our fortress on LaSalle. We were back among friends.

"You did okay for your first time on the radio," Bob said. But I didn't feel too positive about our performance.

Decades later, when I emailed her, Leslie claimed that she didn't even remember this radio episode of our lives. It is a hazy drug infused memory in my mind too, and I wonder if it's archived somewhere, or else it is just more hot air lost to time and history.

38

FRANK ZAPPA AND MAD MARVIN AT THE WHEEL

I t was the first of July, a fine summer day. Marvin sat at the kitchen table rolling a dooby with *Righteous* Bob, Jeff and Schmitty. There was no escaping him.

Bob looked at me with bloodshot eyes. "Did you hear? The Mothers of Invention are playing tonight up north in Highland Park. Marvin is offering to take whoever wants to go. Leslie's going."

I swallowed my misgivings. "Yeah, sure, I think my buddy Chris will be there."

Chris introduced me to the Mothers of Invention back in the summer of 1968. Their album *We're only in it for the Money* satirized plastic hip and straight attitudes. He had moved into a huge three-story house where Grand Avenue emptied into Lake Street, house sitting for the summer while the owners were away, with a couple of giant Irish Wolfhounds for companionship. Those dogs were almost as big as horses, but friendly.

"There are only six hundred of these wolfhounds in the whole world," he said.

"No wonder, Chris. I bet they eat ten times more than a regular dog."

Chris played Mothers of Invention albums exclusively on a

continuous loop. We'd grown up reading Mad Magazine, so the iconoclastic Mothers, by not trying to be in step with anyone, became the out of lockstep "different drummer" of legend. Lead guitarist Frank Zappa soon became a leading spokesman of the cultural scene, but my fascination never matched Chris's. He seemed to be turning into Frank Zappa, little goatee, and all.

"Let's get some of the Waveland bunch," Marvin said. "I'll change my clothes and pick up a stash of pot on the way."

He parked along Lincoln Avenue, south of Halstead. While we waited in the car, he ran around back and opened the trunk and proceeded to take off his shirt and pants and then perform a flamboyant striptease, gyrating his hips as he twirled his briefs on a finger, showing off his hairy behind in full view of passing traffic. Some startled drivers honked and old ladies on the sidewalk gasped in astonishment.

I couldn't believe what he was doing, and called out, "What the fuck, man! We don't need any attention from the pigs right now with all your pot in the car."

That only inspired Marvin to more outrageous acts. He ran bare ass naked around the car several times before he leisurely put on a fresh set of clothes from the trunk, as if he had all the time in the world. I had put on a few shows of my own and could appreciate some wild comic theater as well as the next guy, but I was on probation, and we had too much dope in the car to risk it. With the initial offence of "obstructing traffic" and "lewd behavior," the pigs would have reason to search the car and add "possession of narcotics" to our charges.

At the very moment he finished fastening his belt buckle and slammed the trunk, a patrol car drove by with two cops in the front seat, oblivious to the show they'd missed. Marvin, true to form, even flashed them his middle finger, but they didn't turn around. That was too much. As Marvin, with a smug smile on his face, got back in the driver's seat, I yelled, "Are you trying to get us busted?"

If he wanted to impress us with his daring, it had the opposite effect. Leslie sat wide-eyed the whole time, as if she was in shock, which was just as well, for we were a captive audience along for the ride.

With Chris and Weed from the Waveland house, we had a full car. It was good to rap with them about the events happening in our fast-paced life. I no longer cared who'd taken my money on that night that already seemed so long ago.

Ravinia Park was a pleasant green oasis of trees and fields, but I didn't have the entry fee. Chris and I circled around to find an unguarded place in the chain-link fence, climbed over, and dropped to the other side.

A harsh voice yelled. "Hey you damn kids!" We looked up to see a couple of uniformed men running toward us, but we were in better shape and lost ourselves in the crowd. We heard the rumor that the security guards and police were searching all the freaks for dope as they came through the gate, all except Marvin, of course. I evaded him until closing time. He was our ride, and it was a long, unfamiliar way back for me.

The sound system wasn't working at first, treating us to a lot of noisy static, but I didn't care. Chris and I wandered through the crowd, sharing the wine and weed that had gotten smuggled in despite the efforts of the *Man* to prevent our good times.

As the Chicago Tribune described it, "7,000 frenetic, energetic fans" whooped it up in the park. The Mothers eventually got the sound system working and serenaded us with their musical sarcasm, including *Ask Any Vegetable*, among other hits.

Leaving the park, we again had to pass through a cordon of both uniformed and plainclothes cops at the gate. The plainclothes guys, toting walkie-talkies with dark sunglasses hiding their eyes, looked bored and tired. Marvin jeered at them.

"*Oink, oink, oink,* I smell bacon! Hey, pigs. Are you real pigs or rent-a-pigs?"

It had been a long evening for them and maybe that's why they ignored Marvin's obnoxious comments, or maybe they knew he was one of them. I thought I saw a flash of recognition on some of their faces, or an appreciation for the inside joke he was pulling by pretending to be one of us.

As he drove away, he shouted a last round of verbal abuse out the window, honking his horn and screeching his tires, focusing all the attention on himself. He didn't take the direct route home. Instead, he sped around semi-rural, suburban two-lane roads and side streets, running stoplights and cutting off other cars. It was as if he was protected by some satanic force that protected him from the consequences of his actions.

Everyone else was silent, either stoned or in shock.

Marvin laughed and slammed his palm on the dashboard. "I'm just blowing their *straight* little minds, that's all! This is my street theater. Sit back and enjoy the ride."

His driving got ever crazier. He veered off the road and charged full throttle across a manicured lawn, revving his engine as if in a drag race. He tore through flower beds and cut *donuts* and *figure 8s* into unoffending lawns.

A light flashed on in an open doorway. The faces of a wrinkled old couple, who had to be somebody's grandparents, were framed in the golden halo of the porch light. They reminded me of the famous painting, American Gothic, except without a pitchfork. They could only watch in helpless terror as Marvin tore up their yard, flowers, and all.

There was nothing revolutionary about terrorizing helpless old people, and this was far from my idea of progressive street theater. Whether or not Marvin was a narc, he was a cruel maniac, and we shouldn't be associated with him. But I had to think of Leslie and the others with us in the car, and what else could we do besides jump out of the car and run. I was contemplating such a drastic move when Marvin at last seemed to have gotten his nastiness out of his system and drove back into the city and dropped us off.

I explained the bizarre circumstances surrounding Marvin's lucky brushes with the Law to Bob Rudnick. "He's pure trouble, a fascist pig if I ever saw one."

Following the Zappa concert, Marvin vanished. Maybe he

realized his cover was blown, and we didn't trust him. And maybe he was even afraid that we'd "off" him as a pig spy. Despite all our boastful talk, whether we had the *balls* to execute him, like the Black Panthers were accused of doing to some of their suspected informers, is doubtful. We hadn't reached that level of murderous combat readiness yet, and it would only land us all in the slammer.

39

A NEW VENCERAMOS!

Our righteous cause was always short of money. Schmitty complained that people weren't writing down what they put in or took out of the cash box. Our economy ran on an honor system. To keep us in burgers and fries, I was passing out flyers and asking for donations in Lincoln Park when I heard a familiar voice.

"Hey, Ron!" I turned to see Sandy from Elmhurst stroll into view with a couple of greasers in tee-shirts and baggy gray pants. She ran up and gave me a hug as if she meant it. "Wow, Ron, I'm in Rising Up Angry now! Can you dig it?"

I still had a crush on her and hoped that with Kay coming and going without telling me where or for how long, I could get together with her to fill the void.

She put her mouth to my ear; I held my breath and waited with great hope for either her wet tongue or sweet seductive words, but got something else.

"I just got the word," she said. "There's another Venceramos Brigade forming." She glanced around to be sure no one was listening. "It's still being talked about in secret to prevent the pigs from interfering. Each organization gets a few spots on the list, and I understand you White Panthers aren't filling yours."

"Maybe we can't spare anyone now. There are only five of us guys and a couple of women. Anyway, I'm starving. Do you wanna grab a burger or something?"

"Not now, Ron. I gotta run. See ya around, man." She linked arms with her greaser pals and slipped out of view. It looked like we'd never get closer than a comradely hug.

Another hour went by. I'd made about eight bucks and was ready to give up when some tinkling laughter broke into my ruminations and Kay ran up to embrace me with a kiss fervent enough to push Sandy out of my head.

"Oh, Ron. I've been so busy, sorry, but listen to this. I signed up on the next Venceramos Brigade to Cuba! What do you think about that? We leave in a week or two."

I was blown away and took a moment to catch my breath. "So soon?"

"Yes, isn't it exciting? Come with me Ron, there's still time to sign up if you make the last meeting."

"Let's wait for the next brigade, Kay. Our first duty is *here* in the streets of Chicago, not basking in the sun on some Caribbean Isle."

Temped as I was, I'd been trying to reign in my rash impulse to jump into things, which had gotten me busted the year before, and I decided to take a slower, more calculated approach instead of jumping off, half cocked.

"Oh, don't be such a wet blanket, Ron. We'll be working in the fields and meet Cuban and Vietnamese comrades. *Real* revolutionaries! Come with me to the next meeting."

I remembered Judge Epton looking over his glasses at me and pronouncing, "The terms of your probation are to be served in the State of Illinois. You're not to leave the State," and with Mori Daly and the Red Squad keeping tabs on me, I'd probably get arrested and sent back to jail. Even so, I'd be a fool not to go with Kay. My mind scrambled to find an excuse.

"Our Panther membership isn't growing, Kay. Fuzzy is talking about going back to Michigan and Bob told me the LaSalle house is slated to be torn down or renovated any day now. We'll have to find a new place. Things should stabilize in a few weeks and by that time there will probably be another Venceramos."

"Just go to Cuba," Bob Rudnick said later that day. "They'll manage here somehow."

I noticed that he'd said *they'll* instead of *we'll* manage and wondered if Bob had another radio gig planned for elsewhere.

But I missed the deadline to sign up for the Venceramos Brigade on June thirtieth. Kay was upset, but she insisted that they could *shoe* me in any way, but so many things happening at the same time, putting head in a whirlwind and I never found the address of where I had to go sign up.

Kay was miffed. I'd blown it. She didn't even say adios before she left. Cuba was a lost opportunity that I soon regretted. My usual thirst for adventure failed me. Writing with the hindsight of fifty-two years, I'm shocked at how inept and passive I had been to lose both Kay and a chance to see Cuba up close.

40

THE DESERTER

Bob came in late one night and rocked the house with his deep bellied laugh.

"Hey, everybody, wake up. We've got a special guest, a new Marine recruit into Uncle Sam's lean-green fighting machine!"

He didn't look the part. I saw a terrified kid on the verge of tears, still wearing his dress uniform; his close-cropped head marked him as a *Jar head*, what the Navy called their Marines.

"We found this poor guy wandering the streets of downtown Chicago," Bob said. "He was pleading for help from every longhair he saw. And to top it off, he can hardly speak English. Turns out he's from Hungary. They promised him quick citizenship if he signed up. This brother wants to desert to Canada and start life over in a country where he'd be safe from getting lassoed by the MPs."

"I go Canada. How I go?" he said, over and over. His limited English failed him in his distress. I couldn't imagine how he managed to follow the commands of his drill instructors. He knew he was bound for the Southeast Asian War and decided to make a run for it. We were duty bound to assist him to subtract one more body from the gluttonous war machine.

Bob got on the phone and arranged a predawn ride for him to the

Canadian border. Crossing over, he said, was a snap, but if he was caught on this side he could wind up locked in the brig with a serious charge of desertion and whoever helped him could get an aiding and abetting charge. We replaced his uniform with whatever civilian attire we could scrounge and a hat to hide his sheared head to help him blend in better.

If the Chicago White Panthers never did anything else, at least we got this one lonesome deserter up to Canada. It was a good, truly revolutionary deed that removed one more guy from the firing line a statistic that made the nation's ill-conceived war untenable.

Chicago's lefty newspaper, Second City, posted this article about the growing desertion movement.

Support Our Boys in Canada

The American Deserters Committee of Montreal has refuted the Pentagon's recent statement indicating that there are "576 American deserters in Canada."

In Montreal, the ADC has received approximately 650 deserters in 1969. Deserters continue to arrive at the ADC office at the rate of 20 per week. Deserters who are qualified spokesmen for the American Deserters Committee estimate that there are between 800 and 1200 deserters in Montreal.

"For every deserter the ADC receives and assists, there is one we never see," says Jim Weeks, a deserter who arrived in late 1968... Three thousand to six thousand deserters in Canada is a more reasonable estimate.

...Anti-war groups across Canada report that they are now receiving more deserters than draft-resisters...

...We have found... something very wrong and very sick in the country we were trained to defend and honor. With this new awareness, we have decided that to serve the war machine is to dishonor the name of America.

Chicago's Second City, Vol. 2, number 5, page 3

41

YOUNG LOVE

Too late, I awoke to the folly of letting my cherished Kay slip away to Cuba without me. I was lonely without her and berated myself and moped around, awaiting her return. No other woman could replace her in my heart, or so I imagined, as I nursed my pain in secret. I could and should have risked going back to jail and gone with her. Instead, I'd blown it with love yet again.

A buxom blond named Sue and a slimmer brunette whose name I forget came to Leslie's meetings and immediately moved in with us. Both were cute and flirtatious teen girls, becoming liberated women under Leslie's tutelage. I didn't respond to their coy advances, finding them too immature for my taste, too unlike my vanished Kay. After a couple of days living with us, Sue made a bold announcement in front of all of us.

"I'm still a virgin, but I want to lose my cherry."

She'd expected that desire to be fulfilled much sooner in our radical collective, with our reputation for "free love," but our cerebral approach to the sexual revolution and female empowerment that had been ramped up since Leslie arrived, meant that if a girl wanted to get herself "deflowered" she almost had to demand it, and so she did.

Sue took a breath, mustered her courage, and focused her gaze on Bill as she spoke.

"Which one of you guys wants to be my first time?"

"Ahem." Bill glanced around, nervous, as he cleared his throat. "Ah, I guess I can."

I was glad that he obliged her, rather than shrugging off her less obvious advance as I had. Like a shy honeymoon couple holding hands for the first time, they withdrew to one of the bedrooms. After half an hour, Sue emerged exultant.

"Wow, I'm a woman now! Thanks Bill, I finally got fucked, and it feels great!"

Bill came out behind her with a sheepish grin on his face, to our boisterous applause for a job well done.

Sue's friend called out, "Let's party!"

Thus inspired, we trooped down to the kitchen for a late-night celebration of their *cherry popping* experience. Bill and Sue gravitated into a couple, and I was happy for them. Bill was a quiet, low-key guy who seemed willing to let Sue call the shots in their relationship. Whether or not they remained exclusive, I can't say, but the way this romance began struck me as remarkable and unique to our White Panther experience.

42

THE BLACK PANTHERS AND SOLDIER BLUE

Odinga was our principal contact with the Black Panther Party. The first time I saw him, he seemed wary and on edge. A comrade came with him as a bodyguard who climbed up to our observation nest above the front door and studied the street the whole time they were there, a reflection on their tight discipline, while Odinga palavered with the rest of us at the kitchen table. They had lost too many leaders to police assassination, most notably Fred Hampton and Mark Clark the previous December, and needed to be cautious and prepared for an ambush, especially when they were away from their familiar turf.

On later visits to our LaSalle house, he appeared more relaxed and brought a couple of Black Panther *sisters,* who seemed less anxious or concerned with security. They wore the dark dress and black leather jackets that had become their trademark even in summer, whereas White Panthers had no uniform beyond a penchant for long hair and tie-dyed shirts in line with our hippie roots.

Odinga was a good conversationalist with a sense of humor who entertained us with stories about the moral corruption and hypocrisy of the rich. One of his stories dealt with sex and gender.

"There was this poor little rich girl, spoiled rotten by her wealthy family, and what she really craved was a big black dick. Her old husband didn't mind, he even liked to watch sometimes. Unfortunately, the young lady died suddenly and the true cause of death, choking on a long black cock, was not noted on her death certificate. The whole affair was hushed up, of course, by the family's connections."

I wasn't sure what the point of that story was, as he seemed to be blaming the girl who I saw as a victim rather than a spoiled, cock hungry girl, who deserved what she got. And what about the black guy who apparently lost control and choked her? I was probably trying to read too much into it; a story doesn't need to have a moral. Life just happens and we fools try to make sense of what is by nature irrational.

It was always a pleasure to rap with Odinga. We even delved into Taoist and other Eastern philosophies. One day in July, I'd returned early from selling papers to find Odinga at the kitchen table.

"I just saw a terrific new movie," he said. "You'd better take some of that change you made today and go see it, too."

"Think so? I rarely see movies."

He laughed. "Well, you should. The entertainment media indoctrinates us with propaganda to perpetuate class and racial stereotypes. A good movie raises your morale and political consciousness. And get some popcorn. Revolutionaries like us should learn to relax and have a good time, too."

That was all the encouragement I needed. I grabbed a few dollars from my day's take, turned the rest over to our common cashbox and walked down to the Loop alone.

Soldier Blue, starring Candice Bergen and Peter Strauss, was playing at the State Street Theater. Westerns had come a long way from the jingoistic morality play where the always clean-cut good guy *White hats* beat the scruffier *Black hat* villains and mowed down surly *hostile* Indians by the dozen. Straight-shooting heroes dispatched villains, Indians and sometimes Mexicans, who expired without blood and gore, their deaths almost sanitary, however the good main characters had time for brave last words to encourage the faith in an inevitable manifest destiny.

While Soldier Blue did not attempt perfect historical accuracy, it was based on a true story and switched the stereotypes around. The evil Colonel Chivington, who led the Colorado volunteers, was depicted as the racist murderer he was, with his statement that "nits make lice" used to justify the extermination of a whole Cheyenne village. I knew that story, but witnessing the cinematic events come to life on the silver screen fired my blood to exact retribution.

Conquest and genocide gave the descendants of the perpetrators this land and the tradition continued under the guise of the neo-colonial economic takeover of countries that included Viet Nam.

By the time I left the theater, my indignation had risen. I spoiled for a fight to even the score, for justice for the people against the pigs that trampled us into the dust. Stiff as a soldier, I walked down the street, and halted at a stoplight. As the cross traffic began to pass from my left, I saw an armored car go by and the blue uniformed passenger riding shotgun smiled a toothy grin and flashed the V fingered peace sign at me.

He seemed to be mocking me with contempt for me and *my* people, so I reacted with hot anger by raising high my middle finger as a *peace* sign of my own, and roared my self-righteous wrath as the Brinks' car drove on.

"Fuck you, pig!" I said and congratulated myself. I'd shown the pig that although I was a long haired hippie, I stood for justice, not some cop-out peace at any price.

The light changed, and I marched across the street. But as I went; I analyzed the event with a cooler head that made me doubt my action. For although the guard's uniform and hat were soldier blue, and he rode armed protection on the *fat man's* money, the *dude* was not a cop, just another working stiff in our capitalist economy. One who only meant to convey some fellow felling and perhaps even comradeship with me.

The next day in Lincoln Park, I hawked our underground papers and, shaking change in a coke can, asked for donations to the cause.

A pair of old ladies walked up who spoke with a distinct Eastern European accent, asking me what I represented. I laid my rap on them, telling them that we opposed fascism.

She studied me, peering over her bifocals. "Your long hair aside, you seem like a nice young man, not like those hippie radicals who smashed bank windows last October. They reminded me of the Storm troopers I saw back when Hitler came to power in Germany."

If she only knew that I was one of those who smashed bank windows last October.

Her friend put up her hand to interrupt. "But this young man is way too young to remember that long ago time! We had to leave Europe for America and were lucky. Most of our friends and family didn't make it and are dead."

"But," I said. "I do remember from my reading of that time. The *Night of Broken Glass* was made to look like a spontaneous uprising against Jewish control of the economy. The police protected the rioters, not the victims. History is repeating, but America's Right Wing is the new danger. We are not the Storm troopers. No way. We are trying to stop an immoral war."

They clucked their tongues and shook their heads. I knew that arguing with sweet old ladies would be futile. They'd been saved by American entry into the war against Nazi Germany and couldn't imagine that this government could do anything wrong. I tried to understand how hard it was for those raised on the propaganda in movies and other media to understand. The good guy today may be the bad one tomorrow. American society was polarizing more into antagonistic adversaries with little enough room for dialog or to see the humanity in each other.

ANGRY RED DEVIL Rides with the REVOLUTION!
55th STREET POINT
July 4th there was a rally at the point to protest the hassling and brutality against black people at the rocks there and also the 55th St. Nike base there.
A bunch of liberal peaceniks spoke and then the revolutionaries

came on. The Panther Defense Committee took over the stage to talk about the pigs beating on the brothers and sisters for playing congo drums on the point. The pigs had set up police lines across the base, and were using shotguns and .357 magnums to intimidate the people there.

Angry sister Nori got up and rapped about the revolution, and she told the GI's at the base that, "We don't consider you pigs. We know that some of you are in the revolution and that you are our brothers. All power to the revolutionary GI's!" Right on! Then Red Devil from Rising Up Angry and Hyde Park did his thing. He said, "I'm Red Devil and I ride with the revolution." So we'll be back people, to kick the pigs and the missile base off the point. Power to the People!
Vol. 2 # 2 issue of *Rising Up Angry*

Our White Panther group joined that lakefront Independence Day rally. We sold our papers and rapped on the revolution with our brothers and sisters, as was ever our wont. This was my first meeting with Red Devil, whose trademark look included beatnik style black sunglasses, fiery red hair frizzed into an Afro and a denim vest opened over his bare chest and arms, like one of the Furry Freak Brothers popularized in Underground Comics. Although he was a boisterous, exhibitionist character, we chatted in a relaxed manner. It surprised me when only a few days later Schmitty, who always had the latest gossip, told me that Red Devil was "a slimy motherfucker" and had been kicked out of Angry. Then I heard it from others. Red Devil was no longer to be trusted. The next issue of RUA ran another piece on his fall from grace.

RED DEVIL IS NOT CONNECTED WITH RISING UP ANGRY IN ANY WAY WHAT-SO EVER!

Rising Up Angry, being a revolutionary organization serving the people, recognizes the need for revolutionary discipline. Members of the Central Staff and all Angry Cadre study together, work together, and understand very well that without tying our lives together in a revolutionary, collective and disciplined fashion, we would be doing a disservice to the American and World revolutionary movement. Hence we recognize that the individual is subordinate to the group, to the revolutionary organization. To make the revolution we must practice revolutionary discipline. A bunch of individuals, running amok doing their own thing, Play into the hands of the pigs.

Red Devil started to come around Angry and sell papers. As the organization grew and developed to a higher level, he wanted to be a member of the Angry Cadre group. He attended education sessions, participated in mass work, and was involved in other organizational functions. But Red Devil could not make the break with an individualistic past, even though he wanted to be a revolutionary and work with others. He interfered with the revolutionary work being carried out by other brothers and sisters, and in general became a drain on the organization, demanding attention for personal matters that cannot take precedence over the higher revolutionary duties of all Angry Cadre.

Red Devil was suspended from all organizational responsibilities for a period of time and told to engage in activities that would lead to self-improvement. He failed and weeks later came to a Cadre meeting saying he had been suspended because he was a gay brother. People explained that this was not true, that he was welcome in the organization if he would accept the organization's discipline and act in a revolutionary manner. He failed.

Since that time he has spread many lies about Angry. Let it be known across the land, that Rising Up Angry has met with the Gay Liberation movement in Chicago, that we recognize that gays are an oppressed group, and that we support and consider revolutionary gay brothers and sisters to be an important part of the total revolutionary struggle. Our expulsion of Red Devil is in no way connected to Angry's position on the Gay Liberation movement.

Red Devil is no longer connected with the Rising Up Angry revolutionary organization in any way. Red Devil is a Liar.

RUA Volume 2, no. 4 "Early Winter" on page 19, 1970

Immediately under this ran a picture of a very pensive Red Devil and under it the caption: "KICKED OUT OF ANGRY."

I ran into Red Devil on the street. He seemed more subdued, less effusive than he'd been the first time I'd met him. I asked him about his problems with the Angry organization and how he was doing otherwise.

"Oh, I'm doing okay; I'm still affiliated with Angry but on probation with them. They are trying to help me get my act together, so don't worry about me." But, as he said this, he slumped a little, and I thought his body language seemed to belie his words.

Before he walked away, he said, "Don't forget, Ron. We all still have a life outside the organization."

43

THE COMMUNAL WORKSHOP

I had almost finished my stint on guard duty one afternoon when Bob Rudnick bounced into the house. "Ron, how'd you like to be an observer representing us at Lincoln Park's first workshop on communal living?"

"Sure, Bob, tell me about it.

"More people are looking into communal living in Chicago, and the successful groups have decided to build an interactive panel to share ideas, like what to do about legal hassles with the pigs and establish cooperation and backup from within the alternative community. This initial meeting is just to get acquainted and brainstorm ideas. Tell 'em about our revolutionary White Panther collective too."

"Where do I go?"

"It's at a commune called the Other Cheek, west of Alice's and the Seed offices on the southwest corner of Wrightwood and Halstead, just passed the Laundromat."

From the name, I imagined the Other Cheek commune had a "Jesus Freak" orientation, which put me on guard. I had found that Jesus Freaks could be as intolerant as straight-laced Bible-thumping

Christians and I wondered if this would turn into a 'come to Jesus' ambush.

Alice's Restaurant Revisited was an old haunt of mine, only a short ride on the El train from our Lasalle house, but Bob insisted that I use the bicycle some visitor offered us, and it was a nice warm July evening. My cut-off jeans, sandals and a tee shirt tie-dyed with the White Panther logo were all I wore, as I peddled up Wells Street through Old Town before angling northwest along Lincoln to Wrightwood.

I found a large, two-story house with a handmade wooden sign engraved with "Other Cheek" hanging over the well-lit porch. People were congregating outside before going in, but we were not alone. A familiar voice greeted me as I parked the bike beside the porch.

"Good evening, Mr. Schulz." I looked over to see a grinning Mori Daley, my Red Squad shadow. "We've still got our eyes on you, don't forget. Better be careful or you could be back in a nice, warm cell soon."

With my face frozen to hide my surprise, I ran up the wooden steps where a long-haired Freak greeted me with a warm handshake. "Don't let that pig blow your cool, man. Let me show you around." He ushered me inside as Morey shouted a parting *back to jail* wisecrack at me.

My guide led me through the living room to the kitchen and said, "Want some herbal tea, man?"

"Sure, don't mind if I do."

Someone handed me a mug, which I sipped as he led me around, showing off new features of the house, where they'd fixed a wall or put in a doorway since moving in, then, with evident pride, he led me through each of the bedrooms.

"To create more efficient use of our sleeping space, we built loft beds with ladders." Everywhere he pointed out tables and other furniture they'd built. They all seemed to be carpenters, and handy with tools. I'd noticed a common accent, or lilt in their speech, that reminded me of the Bubble man, Lawrence Welk, who hailed from

North Dakota, and whose music show was still popular on TV. Later, I learned that these *other cheek* communards were Mennonites from small farming communities around Menno in South Dakota. At a time when urban hippies were rapping about starting communes on the land, here was evidence of a reverse flow from the country to the city.

They were long haired, heavily bearded hippies, most of them in their twenties, who despite, or maybe because of their religious background, shied away from deep metaphysical discussions, which were popular among other Freaks, preferring to rap about practical concerns on the anti-war, racial equality and social justice agendas. Over the next few years I'd get to know some of these interesting folks, like the earnest dark-haired Virginia, who was active in the woman's movements.

Other members of the alternative community were there as well, and the meeting wound on as meetings do, with everyone promising to add more to the next session, and we closed on an upbeat note long after dark. The meeting recharged me with confidence that our efforts in building an alternative *hip* community were paying off. We were changing the culture of this city and the nation, making it more humane.

One of the non-Mennonite speakers raised his fist in the air and said, "We're building a new, utopian society that can challenge the money-grubbing culture of death that surrounds us!"

On my borrowed bicycle, I decided to enjoy the cool evening and explore another route home than the diagonally direct Lincoln Avenue. Instead, I rode south along Halstead to Division Street. Although it sliced through a section of the ghetto, and I knew my white face made me a potential target, I sped along the road at a good clip and didn't see anyone who could give me trouble.

When I reached Division, I turned east, whizzing by the few slouching pedestrians sprinkled around the street at that hour. It was an enjoyable ride, and I felt at ease with the world. Crossing Wells, I was back, safe in the familiar territory of Old Town, and I relaxed my guard. With my mind occupied with events of the day, I considered how I'd recommend these Mennonites to Rudnick as good comrades we Panthers could work with.

"Hey, man, wait a minute!"

I glanced back at the two black guys I'd passed who began running after me, yelling something. I supposed they needed directions, and it wouldn't hurt to help, so I stopped, half turned while still astride the bike and watched the first one catch up.

Wheezing hard from the exertion of his block-long sprint, the teenager called out something I couldn't catch. I was across from our L shaped alley, only a few feet from Lasalle, almost home, and in an expansive mood, ready to share my evening's joy with anybody.

"What's the matter, man?" I said.

His babbled reply didn't make sense to me. I let him catch his breath as his friend drew up close behind me. He looked older than the teenager in front of me and I hoped I'd understand him better, so I twisted around to face him.

He pulled something out of his pocket, and I looked to see if it was an address as he blurted a long string of run together words.

"Gimme you money you honkey mother fucker!"

"Huh?" It took me a moment to process, so I said, "Are you guys lost or something?"

Then in the dim streetlight I recognized the glint of a knife blade in his hand. He held the five-inch blade level with my kidneys. Glancing back around, I saw the younger guy also held a knife pointed at my stomach. The younger man kept his gaze down and shuffled his feet, as if he was less sure of himself, as his knife traced little circles in the air.

I was being held up, but it seemed so absurd that I almost laughed. These were my black brothers, and we were in a common struggle against pig oppression. The second guy had a trim mustache and wore a thin tee shirt and shorts like I did on this hot city night. I looked him in the eye, while keeping aware of the other guy's knife.

"What's the deal, man? I've got no money!"

My brain raced over the martial art moves I'd practiced. This was my chance to prove my skills. Maybe I could quick grab both knives, but still astride the bicycle I'd be hampered in making any simultaneous judo moves on both sides of me, and a single stab or slash from one of these blades could fuck me up more than it was worth. I only had about a dollar in my pocket, but it was my masculine pride at stake.

The man behind shouted, "I will fuck you up! Get off the *goddamn* bike! Move!"

I moved slowly, still arguing with myself whether to resist. After I swung my leg over, he grabbed the handlebars and wrenched them away, jumped on and sped away with the other guy running after him, back whence they'd come. I'd been prepared to hand over my dollar in change, but hadn't expected them to take the bike.

No sooner had they charged off than the sound of screeching of tires made me whirl around in time to see a blue and white squad car come squealing around the corner from south La Salle toward me. By instinct, I raised my arms to signal the cop before I remembered who I was. I was a radical at war with the police, the pigs who were oppressing the *people*.

I dropped my arms down at my sides and stepped back up on the curb as the cop whizzed by, lights flashing. Whether he was after the two guys who'd taken my bike, or it was a coincidence, and he was after someone else, I couldn't tell. They were out of sight.

As a radial, how could I expect the pigs to help me? In my paranoia, I even wondered if this robbery was a setup staged to embarrass us. We knew we were under surveillance, but we weren't sure how extensive it was. Whites were, in our *true analysis* of the situation, on the same side, class comrades, with our black brothers and sisters. We were both under the heel of the same puppet masters, the capitalists who conquered by dividing us. I shouldn't cooperate with the *Man* against my black brothers who were misguided by their oppression. Therefore, I would consider the bike as a gift to my class brothers.

As I walked across Division, and through the dark alley, the empty broken windows stared at me like hollow eyes, accusing me of incompetence for letting my guard down. I knocked at the back door and ignored the giddy greetings of my comrades to sit at the kitchen table, where our merry band was carousing over a great bottle of sweet Bali Hai wine. Bob noticed my uncharacteristic mood.

"What's wrong, Ron?"

Before answering, I grabbed the neck of the bottle and gulped a long swig before launching into a detailed explanation of the lost bicycle.

"Oh, man!" Fuzzy said. "You wimped out and just gave it to them? First the car and now the bike, you failed another test. Can't you do anything right?"

"Maybe I should have fought back, but they were on both sides of me and I could have been chopped up and lost a kidney just as easily."

Fuzzy insisted that *he* wouldn't let them get the bike under any circumstances. But Bob agreed I'd done the right thing and it would have been *wrong* for me to turn to the pigs for help, but that didn't help much. My mood nose-dived from euphoria into self-recrimination at how I'd handled the hold up. I hadn't proven my mettle, but could Fuzzy, or any of us, have done any better?

Ambush at Cabrini Green

On July 18th, two pigs were "offed" as they crossed the courtyard of the nearby Cabrini Green public housing development, a place even the straight press likened to a high-rise concentration camp for low-income Blacks. Four skinny young boys were arrested and paraded before the TV media. The war of words had evolved into a shooting war.

"They've got the wrong guys, that's for sure," Odinga said. "Neither of them looks big enough to hold, much less aim and fire the heavy weapon that supposedly did the job."

Our radical newspapers filled in where the official media left off. Rising Up Angry put out this take on it.

Cabrini

A PIG

IS A PIG

IS A PIG

Cabrini Green - little boxes in buildings 20 stories high. A tiny swimming pool stands in the middle, a mockery to the thousands of children who live in this concrete jungle. Silence and calm is unreality - the nights are shattered by sirens and guns. And the pig is always on the prowl, forever trying to destroy his enemy - and to him, all that is black is the enemy. On July 18th, the pattern is broken. Out of a sixth floor window, two shots are fired. The aim is right - two pigs, Severin and Rizzatto, are dead. Three attempts later, the bodies are picked up. It took three because people all over the projects were firing back.

Today four Cabrini brothers are facing murder charges - one a fourteen-year-old 90 pounder. The evidence is slim and full of holes. But the pigs need to blame someone. When in doubt, they always pick someone they're after.

And people everywhere are going through heavy changes, figuring out how they feel about it. Some say, "Wow. Like I don't dig pigs but those were good guys. All they wanted to do was play baseball and maybe hang around."

Even with smiles on their faces, and baseballs in their hands, Severin and Rizatto were pigs. And nice guy pigs are even worse than pig pigs. At least it's clear when most pigs are cracking you on the head and shooting at you that they are the enemy - that are protecting the rich chumps who run it at the cost of the people. But, a 'nice guy' pig tries to make you love the enemy. A pig is a pig is a pig! He only stops being a pig when he quits his job as a member of the armed force against the people. As a brother at Cabrini said, "If there's anything I can't stand, it's a pig who tries to come off nice. Like, he's frisking you and shoving you around, and then when he digs up on his mistake, he tells you to 'take it cool.' And then he drives away in his 'serve and protect' blue bubble. Serve and protect who? No pig ever asked me what I wanted or served my little sister free breakfast. But he's telling me to be cool."

Whether those kids were the actual killers or not, they were on *our* side and the victims were our enemies. Their loss was our gain, their deaths a small victory to tally up in this ugly civil war of attrition. But as in any civil war, like Vietnam, the lines between us and them blurred with friends and relatives on either side.

The White Panthers, Rising Up Angry and other parties stood in alliance with all oppressed racial groups, but not all black and brown gangs, mired in their own hopeless endemic poverty, saw it that way. White society only represented their oppressor, and so long as your face was white, they didn't care if your hair was long, or what politics you espoused. Cabrini Green was a short walk from our Panther lair on LaSalle, but due to the color line, it felt a world away.

Soon after this, Fuzzy needed to go back to Ann Arbor to appear in court on a trumped-up charge dating back to February. He and Leslie, in buoyant spirits on a beautiful summer day, decided to hitchhike there together. After withdrawing some expense money from our cashbox, they waved me a cheery goodbye as I let them out.

"Wait a minute!" I called out after them. "How are you getting to the expressway?"

"We'll walk. It's just a few blocks west on Division to the on ramp."

"You'll have to pass Cabrini Green, and with your white faces, I promise you'll get robbed along the way. It'll be cheaper to take a bus or even a taxi to the expressway."

Fuzzy snickered, "I'm no honkey, man. Blacks are my brothers, united in the same struggle."

"This is Chicago, man, not some middle-class suburb like Ann Arbor. The racial shit gets real and cuts both ways. All that matters to those thugs is whether you're white, not your politics or the length of your hair. In our fair city, you could get stabbed or shot and I gestured to Leslie. A girl could get raped."

But it was such a cheery summer day. Brimming with smug confidence, pale faced Fuzzy refused to heed my warning. He and Leslie skipped off on their way to a road adventure. I barred the door of our little fortress behind them, wondering if maybe he was right and, due to my recent experience, I was too cautious.

Twenty minutes later I answered a knock on the door to find a grim and sullen Fuzzy, who rushed past me without a word and raced upstairs to the cashbox, where Schmitty cornered him as he took out more money. I listened in from a distance.

"Jesus, Fuzzy. Did you spend all that dough already?"

"We got held up, right in front of Cabrini Green."

"Where's Leslie? Is she okay?"

"Yeah, she's waiting at the corner. She didn't want to hear any *I told you so's* from Ron."

I let him back out and from my perch above watched him race to the corner where Leslie waited. The rest of their journey to Michigan must have gone well. I ran across this article in the Argus that explains his case.

Judge say's "Oink" to Fuzzy

Today I witnessed pig justice in action when I went to brother Fuzzy's trail, and the charge was malicious destruction. At 12:00 on the night of February 15 at the Union Ballroom in Ypsi. (*Ypsilanti near Ann Arbor*) a benefit held for Huey P. Newton. While the light show was still going on and the band was still playing the pigs came in and told everyone they had to split because the benefit was over. The light show was packing up equipment when the pigs told them to get out, which they did. The light show was Trans Love' and Fuzzy Backus, Skip Taube, Peggy Taube, Doug Connely, Darlene Pond, Terry Taube, and Hiawatha Baily were running it. It was really cold outside so they were waiting for their ride inside the Union when they were shoved outside by the pigs. They were outside when Gary who was inside opened the door to let some of the heat out. A pig came up in back of Gary, so he split and the pig tried to shut the glass door but Skip Taube's shoulder was in the way. The pig tried again, and he pulled the door so hard that it shattered on his knee. Hearing the glass shatter the pig grabbed brother Fuzzy and arrested him.

In court the pig that arrested Fuzzy claimed to have been the one at the door, but he was actually about 20 ft. away and could not possibly have seen anything. The judge ruled brother Fuzzy guilty, even after 3 people testified that the door had shattered on the pigs knee. Will the injustice never end?

Ann Arbor Argus, number 25, page 9, July 22 to July 29, 1970

Life is an adventure we must not shrink from. The best teacher is our own experience and blind luck plays a part in that. Sometimes we can get by on a naïve sense of brotherhood to create empathy with an adversary, and sometimes we find no pity in this world. Either way, we need to find out for ourselves.

44

WHITE PANTHER NEWS ITEMS

PUN PLAMONDON

Prisoner of War

Our Brother Pun Plamondon, White Panther Party Minister of Defense, was kidnapped by the pigs on July 23, in upper Michigan. Pun had been on the FBI's 10 Most Wanted List for 9 months—supposed crime, blowing up CIA buildings. He went underground to show brothers and sisters that we can live underground as revolutionaries. He showed us that the man isn't as together as he wants us to believe. He showed us that we fuck with the pig and still get away. Pun was caught, but there are MANY who are still free. When a brother or sister is underground, we must do everything to help them and if they are caught, WE MUST FREE THEM!

Our underground is still secure. You can jail the Revolutionary, but you can't jail the Revolution!

RUA Vol. 2, page 9

Pun's wife, Genie Plamondon, "Minister of International Affairs," wrote the following, more moving, passage for the Argus:

WHITE PANTHER COMMUNITY NEWS SERVICE

30 July 1970

Second year of Zenta

On 23 July 1970, the day the Sun went into Leo, Pun Plumondon, Minister of Defense for the white Panther Party, beautiful FREEK of the universe, honored with being one of the 10-Most Wanted men by the FBI here in the asshole of the octopus, was captured... because beer cans were thrown out the window of the car he was riding in, a stupid mistake with enormous repercussions we should all learn from. It's true that it has caused a crisis in the White Panther Party (Skip Taube, Minister of the Interior, and Jack Forrest, Detroit Regional Minister of Education, were captured with him), but we have gone through many before this, and will no doubt go through many more before achieving final victory for the life culture of Woodstock Nation over the death culture of Pig Nation now in power.

This is not a time of sorrow. It is through struggle that we come together... Pun has been my partner, my other half, for three years now. As we both became more and more revolutionary, our personal lives meant less and less to us. We have been separated for ten months now, ever since he was forced underground with the CIA conspiracy indictment handed down last year on my birthday, October 7, 1969. As we become more revolutionary we learn more of the true meaning of love---Pun is my other half, a true revolutionary brother...

...I have defined my life as a Red Star Sister of the White Panther Party and it is not desirable to act as a tearful wife... Women have had our lives defined to us in a bullshit role too long---I refuse to accept that pig definition...

We must begin to define our lives. In order to do that we must struggle diligently, overcome any hardships we may face, and move forward to victory, to self-determination for all peoples. The White Panther Party is strong and becoming stringer with each new struggle before us. ---WE WILL NOT BE FUCKED WITH!

...

The East is Red Genie. It's the glow of the sunrise of the new age. Sometimes you can't hardly see it for the clouds, but it always breaks on through to that other side. And I know that sometime that sun will shine on all of us; on Pun, on John, on Huey, on Bobby, on you and me. Be strong! Be brave! Be beautiful!

Right on Sisters and Brothers!

ALL POWER TO ALL THE PEOPLE!

REVOLUTION IS THE WAY TO LIFE!

Genie Plamondon

Minister of International Affairs

Argus # 26, page 2

The John is John Sinclair, and Huey Newton and Bobby Seale were leaders of the Black Panthers. Red Star Sisters was a new creation focusing on feminism, and Leslie Brody soon rose to prominence with that sister's organization in Ann Arbor.

On July 26th, there was a Young Lords rally at People's Park, and we all came down to hang out together, *grooving* on a summer afternoon. I liked these Puerto Rican guys and envied them a little too. They seemed to be under less constraint than we were.

Male White Panthers had to confront our sexism under the tutelage of the burgeoning women's movement. All our chivalrous impulses, even kindness and simple courtesy, became suspect as signs of paternalism. Calling females *chicks* became frowned upon, which was okay by me, but a brother could get lambasted just for holding a door open for a sister and I saw that as overkill that could destroy the intricate magic that bound the sexes together.

With Kay gone from my life, I looked for echoes of her in other women. The best of them reminded me of her, but not completely. The catlike way her eyes smiled and the whoosh of her long black hair when she tossed her head, inconsequential yet emotionally attractive things that I pined for. Sometimes I saw a reflection of her in the demeanor of one or another of these honeys. But it was getting to the point where I couldn't say the word "honey" out loud, at least not around Leslie, as it was a sure sign of paternalism. Such language had to be replaced by "sister" or "comrade" but such reeducation takes time, even generations.

There were some *killer* gorgeous chicks at the Young Lord's rallies, too. The best-looking were clinging tight to their guys, but here and there I caught a sharp glance as if maybe some luscious honey was checking out my gringo ass. Maybe that appraising look was what I most missed about Kay.

And I still held onto the forlorn hope that I'd run into my little Puerto Rican, *almost* girlfriend Maria, from the Waveland party. There was a good chance to find her hanging around with the Lords. I tried to work out what I'd say to her, something that didn't make me out to be as much of a stupid loser as I felt. That enchanted night, however, was long gone. I'd blown it.

The Latin Kings had problems too. They may have been riddled with punks or double agents who were moving the organization away from a progressive social stance and back into the mere street gang they had been.

THE DAYTON STREET LATIN KINGS AND THE CORP

We are sad to relay this information:

The Dayton Street Latin Kings and the CORP are still going at each other. At this time last year they had just cooled things out (see RUA vol. 1 July, 1969). Things went ok for a while. Then in the late spring, some shit started up. There was a meeting to try and work it out. Some of the revolutionary Kings from out on Division St., rapped with some of the CORP. It was cool, but after the meeting, at the old red hot stand on Halsted and Dickens, they got into it. The Kings involved had not been to the meeting. A brother from CORP got messed up pretty bad. For a while there were only minor hassles, and at one point the pigs sent some dudes in to stir up trouble. Recently there have been mutual beatings and shootings. The pigs play one group off against the other, and then are heavy on both groups. In each group there are people hip to the revolution who've tried cool it out; in both groups there are brothers hiding from the problems of starting to build something new and a billion others trying to cop their super buzzes.

The pigs are digging it because brothers are fighting potential friends instead of enemies; looking to the west when they should be looking to the east. We dig brothers in both the Dayton St. Latin Kings and the CORP. It's clear that they both have some chumps. Both the Kings and the CORP have Latin brothers and white brothers. Both have people who will be fighting in the same guerilla units if they don't kill each other off first. Meanwhile, the neighborhood gets torn down by urban renewal and the notoriously vicious 18th district pigs vamp on the people!

RUA Vol. 2, number 2, page 9, under "STP Stop The Pig Serve The People"

45

THE CONCERT THAT NEVER WAS

The afternoon of July 27th felt like 90 degrees in the Sun. It prompted me to strip off my shirt, which I hung from the back pocket of my shorts and despite the tiny bits of broken glass scattered on the sidewalks; I walked barefoot beside Schmitty. We headed down Michigan Avenue to Grant Park, where the free Rock Concert featuring Sly and the Family Stone was scheduled to begin.

The mixed white and black crowd was already spilling over the wooden slatted snow fences meant to keep them in, breaking it down. Uniformed Andy Frain ushers were losing the struggle to keep a buffer zone of no-man's-land between the double fence lines. We could hear the music from the warm-up group begin as we circled the fence to find a way in, selling copies of Angry, the Seed and the White Panther Party's new, more colorful paper, Sun Dance.

Then the music stopped. We heard screaming from a confused tussle of bodies up on the stage and police with dogs hurried around us to the rear band shell, forcing their way in and clearing the stage.

"Pig! Pig!" the crowd shouted at them as they fell back. Other cops reinforced the ushers who stood by the broken places in the snow fence, forcing the crowd back amid shrill cries from people being trampled. Then the police pulled back. It took a while for word of what was going on to filter our way and it was impossible to distinguish fact from unfounded rumor.

"The pigs won't let 'em play," someone said.

"Who?" I asked.

"Sly and the Family Stone, man. Mayor Daley refuses to let 'em come on!"

"We ain't gonna take this shit lying down! The pigs got them and they're laughing at us!" someone called out.

The mood got ugly. Rumors circulated that Sly's band was under house arrest, and the Daley machine wouldn't let them play. Filled with righteous indignation, people blamed the *system* run by our mayor Daley to crush the People's Music. This concert could be an elaborate set-up to take down more of our cultural leaders and put us under their *law-and-order* thumb. We had no reason to expect justice from the machine, which functioned as our enemy.

Some newsmen put the Grant Park crowd at 50,000 and the NY Times said 75,000, a much larger crowd than expected, snarling traffic in Chicago's Loop to a virtual standstill that delayed the flow of police reinforcements. The situation seemed tailor made for revolutionaries to shape this event and rally the righteous fury of the People against the ruling class.

Schmitty and I flowed with the crowd as it moved north onto the baseball field, interrupting at least one ballgame. Some of the players cursed, upset at the mob intrusion, but other players joined in, leaving most of their girlfriends to sit, glassy eyed with bewilderment, at the edge of the field. A sense of euphoria electrified the mostly male crowd.

Someone shouted, "This looks like the Democratic convention all over again!" Another called out, "We are WOODSTOCK NATION! We will not be ignored!"

The concert goers had transformed into an impromptu demonstration of popular anger, glorying in our numbers and strength of spirit that propelled us to confront *the man*, and to take our future away from him and back into our own hands. But it took a kind of craziness, an almost suicidal frenzy, to get up the nerve to do this. Mayor Daley's cops were trained to shoot to kill. The bottles of Ripple and Bali Hai wine being guzzled everywhere helped our spirit, although I was stone sober and saw plenty of worried, sober faces around me, and some of these, my comrades, had their teeth clenched in a determined grin. We could die, covered with blood and honor rather than live as weaklings under the raciest tyranny. It was.

I was pumped up, energized by the spirit around me. Maybe this would be the moment, the spark that would set off the great conflagration. The energy around me was electric with the mood of defiance. We were the future of this nation and ready to fight back against the pigs. In this, the heartland of America, we would ignite the new revolution.

Schmitty, however, glanced around with a worried look. He groaned. "This is weird, man! It can't be happening!"

"What's wrong?" I was surprised that he didn't share my elation.

"This doesn't feel right. There's no proper leadership. People will get hurt."

"Leadership?" I said. "That's us. We need to step up and seize the time. The masses are rising spontaneously." I grabbed his shoulder and squeezed so he could feel the intensity.

"Wake up, man! This is People's War! Our revolutionary cadre should lead from the front. We're here to inspire our brothers and sisters."

It was natural for him to feel afraid at his first real action. Schmitty hadn't been in a riot like I had and no sane person can ever be ready for a violent confrontation. At all the demonstrations we attended, he spouted the same rhetoric with the rest of us.

"Seize the Time and off the swine!" But that's just mumbo jumbo if not backed up by action.

At the far end of the ball field, a thin blue line of police formed, batons ready in their hands as their sergeants barked orders through bullhorns. On that sweltering day, most of them dressed in light blue short sleeved shirts and light-colored helmets with plastic face shields. Pinstripes ran down the outsides of their dark blue pants and they carried cans of pepper spray and holstered revolvers that bulged on the utility belts at their sides. This is what our martial arts class tried to prepare us for.

"Stay with me Schmitty," I said. "You are part of our White Panther cadre, and the people need direction from us."

"No," he said. "I'd better get back to report on this to Rudnick."

"Well, Schmitty, I'm staying here where I'm needed."

Perhaps I was a little dramatic, but I didn't want to miss the start of the revolution. He left me alone in the crowd, among comrades whose names I didn't know, but that electric moment, they felt like blood brothers.

Reporters mixed with the crowd, which led to cases of mistaken identity by both sides.

"Back off," the Police ordered. A Tribune reporter who got in their way was roughed up and arrested. Plenty of plainclothes pigs, Red Squad agents, pretended to be reporters, snapping pictures to update their files on us, and sometimes real reporters, also snapping pictures, were mistaken for them by members of the crowd.

The Red Squad knew my face, and their tactic was to move in slow, isolate a known radical, and then grab him. I had to be wary and watch for those guys on the fringe of the crowd.

"This concert is canceled," the police shouted over their megaphones, ordering us to disperse and go home, but the crowd roared back a resounding *NO* and as a blue line of cops came marching at us to clear the park, the crowd fought back.

Empty green ripple bottles flew overhead. Some spun like screws, making an eerie, whirring hum as they sailed overhead to land with a hard thump. Most of the cops didn't have padded protection. Here and there I saw a cop crumple and drop to his knees, out of action, and a uniformed compatriot helped him to the rear. Every cop assisting a wounded friend meant two less to stand against us. Our side was used to being on the receiving end of their fists and batons, but here, at last, we drew some blood.

A savage roar erupted from hundreds of throats, as long haired young men charged forward. The police line broke; they turned and ran before us. I almost couldn't believe it as I ran barefoot across the grass to catch up with the crest of the wave where I wanted to be.

We cheered our victory, but it was short-lived. At the front of our mass of warriors, many as bare-chested as I was, I heard the police commanders shout.

"Stay in line, men. Keep cool!"

The police reformed and tightened their ranks, standing shoulder to shoulder and flailed out at us with their clubs. Few of us had any clubs to match the police batons and our wave fell back, picking up unbroken Ripple bottles as we retreated.

Lumbering heavily and clanking with the weight of their weapons and protective gear, they shouted a hoarse war cry of their own as they came at us, clubs at the ready.

We threw another volley of bottles, so thick that they shaded the battlefield for timeless seconds, almost like a solar eclipse. I caught a glimpse of what the ancient bards sang of. In battles, like the Spartans at Thermopylae, the waves of arrows or javelins flew so thick over the battlefield that they darkened the sun, and I had seen a version of that in my own time.

At least three times we charged, and they fell back, recovered, and counterattacked. Charging across the field winded them, and each new line they formed was a little farther back from where they'd started. Although they were better armed and protected than us half naked Indians, they hadn't opened fire and the weapons weighed them down. They were losing men and losing ground. I heard someone sing, "They've got the guns, but we've got the numbers!"

On their advance, they smashed the bottles on the ground to prevent us from using them again, and I wondered that so many more bottles continued to appear from somewhere. We needed all the bottles and rocks we could muster to gain an advantage in this unequal contest. What gallons of wine must have been consumed to produce this ammunition? Only a few of us had baseball bats with which they struck at the police, but most of us were unarmed and throwing bottles was our most effective weapon. A few stragglers were pounced on by undercover officers and beaten into the dirt before being dragged away to a paddy wagon parked behind their lines. Several of our own wounded staggered to the rear, bleeding, but I wondered how our impromptu army would stand up under gunfire.

At the crest of our third charge, the cops assumed a firing stance, raising their service revolvers at us in both hands. Feeling naked, I debated whether to drop to the ground like an infantryman or stand tall like a proud Comanche warrior. Maybe we would die as martyrs for the cause in a massacre worse than Kent State. I chose to rely on my cosmic faith to shield myself, and so I stood erect before that firing squad.

Crack-crack-crack-ak-ak-ak-ak! The ragged volley erupted along the line in front of us. Individual shots continued to ring out from time to time, some fired by plainclothes cops at specific targets they wanted to neutralize. According to the newspaper accounts, the shooting occurred at 7:48 p.m. and over 100 shots were fired, but no more than three of us were hit and no one died.

Apart from moving around and taking cover, the fluid crowd remained in the field. This mass of Freaks had staying power. Then I heard *pop-pop-pop* as the cops began firing teargas canisters at us. They were the size of tin cans and sailed in an arch, leaving a puffy trail of white smoke as they came up and then down to land among us. People panicked and ran away from where they landed, however I knew we had to throw them back before we started to choke.

I raced over and grabbed the closest one. It was already getting hot from the pressured release of the gas, so the quicker we tossed them back, the better. I tossed it as high and as far as I could in the direction of the police and called out to my comrades to do the same, as I ran for another, tossing back at least three.

Tear gas chokes, making breathing so difficult you feel like you're suffocating, but our quick action in tossing the canisters back gave the police as big a dose of it as we got. They either ran out of gas canisters or had too much of their own medicine, and the police gave up trying to drive us out and pulled their depleted line back across Balboa Avenue. The field of battle was in our hands. We'd won.

I wandered over the field, chatting with people. Some told me they just wanted a little fun in the summer sun, only to find a riot. I tried to raise their political consciousness.

"We are making history here," I said. "Our untrained rabble has defied the police and pushed them off the field."

But I knew they could have slaughtered us if they wanted to. They aimed above our heads, except in a few cases. Most of us were white, not a mob of black kids, and their leaders had seen the uproar when white kids were shot at Kent State.

A few girls sat together on the grass, looking dejected and dazed. One complained that her boyfriend abandoned them to join the melee. I didn't see any women join in the battle. We had no Bernadine Dohrn, no Linda Evens, and no Angela Davis there, and I didn't succeed in getting those girls to see the virtue of participating in the riot. For every warrior who charged into this spontaneous uprising, there may have been two or three who just stood by and watched.

Three helicopters flew overhead, swooping low, trying to scare us off the field, which, along with the lingering smell of gun smoke and tear gas, gave this Chicago battlefield the look of a Viet Nam air assault. We shouted up at them and threw ineffective rocks and bottles, which heartened us, despite the futility. I imagined it must be as frustrating for the Viet Cong to use their homemade weapons against the latest in army technology.

At 8 pm, the loudspeaker on one of the choppers called out an order.

"In the name of the state of Illinois, I order you to disperse. This is an unruly mob..."

I climbed uphill to Balboa Drive, where the crowd was rocking a car. One of the guys turned to me and said, "This is an undercover pig car. Help us push it over."

We did a countdown. "One, two, three!" We pushed it onto its top, and someone lit it on fire. I'd never seen a car burn before and was in awe. A flaming front tire gave off heavy black smoke as it rotated like a lottery wheel. Then the guys began working on a second car.

Although I'd been told they were both unmarked police cars, I later read in the newspapers that one was a driving school car, making it a misidentified casualty of the battle.

A Paddy wagon suddenly raced through our scattered crowd, westbound along Balboa. We unleashed a barrage of rocks, and the windshield disintegrated into splinters. I saw the two cops in the front seat duck under the dashboard as the driver floored it and broke through the crowd, but in the second before they ducked, I saw sheer terror on their faces. While I felt some pity, I reminded myself that we were at war with them. We held Balboa and made them pay to break through our lines.

The battle wore on, intermittently hot and cold, for a total of five hours. Drizzle fell to cool us off, and I put my shirt back on. By 9 pm it was raining harder, and the crowd broke for the loop, trashing storefronts for booty as it went. Most of the looters seemed to be black, and most of the damage had been done by the time I got there. I saw a cop car parked at the curb on my side of the street, its occupants standing guard in front of broken shop windows across the street.

Lying on the sidewalk before me lay the arm of a dismembered mannequin. Seizing my opportunity to strike a blow against the fascist state, I grabbed the arm and threw it like a boomerang into the passenger side window of the cop car. The window smashed, disintegrating into small shards, which surprised me as had the earlier windshield. I'd imagined they had stronger shatterproof glass on their cars.

Although there was no immediate response from the cops across the street, I took no chances and ran downstairs into the nearby subway entrance. It seemed a strange anticlimax as I rode like any other commuter back to our Panther pad.

46

AFTER-ACTION ANALYSIS

"Thank goodness you're back," Schmitty said as he threw his arms around me. "I've been listening to the news on the radio, and it sounds like it's a massacre. How many people are dead or wounded?"

"Oh, no, Schmitty," I said. "It was a battle, all right. Believe it or not, we, the people, stood up to the pigs and pushed them off the field. You should have been there to see it. We won! But of course there were casualties. It's a war, man, but I think we wounded as many cops as we had."

Bob asked me to write up a report on the riot which may have influenced the full-page article that appeared in the next issue of RUA, however they left out what I wrote about it looking like the Zulu Wars, with our often shirtless almost unarmed warriors charging the well-armed police.

FREE ROCK

Free rock! Sly and the Family Stone! A dynamite time for everyone-- just what the people want. Right pig Daley? Wrong! The power of the people told the pigs, Monday night, just what they thought of Daley's free circus. After waiting more than 2 hours for a concert that didn't show, some brothers and sisters stormed the stage. As bottles and rocks began to fly, the pigs freaked and did their usual 'thing.' This time the people were together. Instead of running as they usually do, they stuck tight. Suddenly the pigs were uptight. They threw tear gas- the people threw it back. The people turned over and burned pig cars - smashing windows on others. As the pigs charged, the people split - as the pigs fell back, the people moved up. The people had a rock festival of their own. The bottles continued to fly as the people grouped and regrouped, charged and retreated. At one point, the pigs turned and fired a volley of several hundred shots at the people. Many were injured, but the fighting spirit grew stronger as the people faced the guns with rocks and bottles.

The best thing about this whole scene was it was a people's thing. This time they can't blame it on 'a small minority of violent dissidents.' This time it wasn't the people fighting each other. This time it was a large 'majority of violent dissidents' fighting side by side - with the combined anger of blacks and whites exploding against the enemy. It was really only touched off by the fact that people waited 2 hours for Sly. Face it pigs, the people are pissed off. They wanted an excuse to waste some pigs and they made one. That's really where it's at. People are getting hip to who's been fucking them around all this time. We wont fight our beautiful people - we want pigs blood. We got it, too!!

POWER TO THE BROTHERS AND SISTERS WHO FIGHT THE REAL ENEMY AND LOVE EACH OTHER!

The NY Times called the Sly Stone Riot the "Bloodiest confrontation since the 1968 Democratic Convention" with three rioters shot by the cops and one-hundred-forty-eight arrested. Fifty people, including twenty-eight cops, were injured. Six or seven of the injured cops were plainclothes members of the Red Squad. Chicago's Mayor Daley insisted that the riot was planned and orchestrated by the usual suspects, outside agitators.

But it looked spontaneous and not orchestrated. I didn't see anyone taking leadership roles in this affray, and didn't see any RUA or other radicals I knew among the crowd. True, I was an agitator, but a local one and much as I would have loved to take responsibly for starting it, I only joined in and encouraged the leaderless group. The riot was a spontaneous eruption of the people's militancy. But of course, it was a single incident without inciting a general uprising, making it only a footnote in the struggle for political and cultural change.

THE WAR, such as it was, is over, and we live in a new era in a new century. With the perspective of over fifty years, I can agree that we were then young and impetuous youth, but so were those hot headed young men who harassed armed British soldiers in 1775 until they opened fire in the riot that became known as the Boston massacre. That was a pivotal event in pushing public sentiment to full rebellion, generating the American Revolution. History proves that it always takes impatient, violent youth, such as we were then, to force a sea change in society's direction.

The Chicago cops exhibited a cooler restraint than usual and had guts on that hot summer day in 1970. That only three of our side were shot says a lot for the self-control of the police, who could easily have mown us down. They were our enemy, dehumanized by us as pigs, but in fairness, I will show some of what they experienced as reported in the newspapers of the time.

Under "NEWS *Briefs*" by Robert Davis in the Chicago Tribune on Wed. July 29, I read:

Injured Cop Aided by Son

Howard Pierson, police department deputy chief of patrol, was one of the many injured policemen during the riot in Grant Park Monday night, and when he was struck in the face and foot with thrown objects, the first person to come to his aid was his son, Howard Jr., a policeman from the Austin police District. "Dad, take my helmet, mine has a shield," the younger Pierson shouted at his father.

"It's too late," the father said.

In the column to the right is a longer article:

Policeman Hurt in Riot Tells brush with Death

By Robert Nolte

Patrolman Lee Dudeck yesterday told of his night of terror when gangs of rock throwing youths attacked police trying to hold a skirmish line in Grant Park.

While 40 policemen tried to hold the line, Dudeck grabbed a lighted flare tossed at him. He caught the torch and was bending to snuff it out when a chunk of pavement the size of a telephone crashed into his head.

Dudeck fell to the ground. The charging youths cheered, Policemen ran to Dudeck's aid.

Face a bloody pulp

"I didn't see who threw it," said Dudeck ...

Dudeck was one of 126 policemen injured Monday evening ... involving 500 police and thousands of concert fans.

Morale was low

The 23-year-old Austin district policeman said manpower and morale were pitifully low during the 5-hour clash.

"We kept moving across the ball field, then retreating," said Dudeck. To many of us, it didn't make much sense. Policemen don't like to retreat." ...

"It's the first time I've been knocked out," said Dudeck, who has seven department commendations for outstanding police work. "It was a hellish experience but more shocking than the injury was the terrible violence shown by the mob. They wanted to kill us."

Yes, maybe some of us did want to kill them. Ironically, this cop was the same age as many of his antagonists, but he was on the *other side* and wearing the enemy uniform. Our Woodstock Nation tribe was pissed off and more than a little paranoid, but if we were paranoid, we had damn good reason to be so. Our frustration built up over the years, years of having our voices ignored, our sentiments derided, years of watching our leaders killed or locked up, like Black Panther Bobby Seale, who was bound and gagged in the courtroom for demanding his right to council. The sentiment of "Peace and love" was dead, killed by official repression and police clubs and not only in Chicago.

That same day in Houston, Texas Carl Hampton, no relation to Chicago's Fred Hampton except that they were both black, chairman of the People's Party 2, a group very similar to the Black Panthers, was shot and killed by police following a rally. In Asbury Park, New Jersey, the same day, police shot over the heads of a large crowd of blacks who were pelting them with bottles and rocks. Sixteen were arrested, a policeman was shot, and several cars trashed. The main difference between what happened in New Jersey and in Chicago was the cooperation between black and white rioters, a historical first for an altercation of its size.

In Chicago, Weatherman rioter Russell Neufield was still in custody despite reduced bail for his part in the October Rage. The disenfranchised sought refuge in gangs and were continuing to wage their own gang wars over turf. The cops raided the white "Outlaw" motorcycle gang, who had managed to stockpile more weapons than the Weathermen and the Black Panthers combined, just to shoot up some rival gang in what seemed to us a petty internecine war. Meanwhile, out in California, the Manson trial was in full swing today with a weeping and shrieking Linda Kasabian describing the brutal murders at the Sharon Tate estate. And in Viet Nam the anonymous killing went on, remorselessly, on that day as every other day.

47

DEATH TO THE SHAH AND AN OLD PAL

One of the women who ran the People's Information Office on Halstead waved me up to her desk. "Ron, will you be joining our march against the Shah of Iran?"

"Sure, I'd love to." With Kay gone, she caught my eye as a potential lover.

Schmitty, standing beside me, rolled his eyes and pulled me aside. "Don't march with them. Those Iranian students are Trots."

I hadn't heard movement people derided as Trots since I was with the Weathermen and I'd found it divisive then. That was the contemptuous term Stalinists called Trotskyites. In my opinion it was all hypothetical claptrap, an ancient argument built on Stalin's "Revolution in one country" versus Trotsky's "Internationalism," personal jealousies meant to justify Stalin's Machiavellian power grab in Russia.

"So what, Schmitty?" I said. "Why let those long dead Russians rule us? It's not like we don't need all the help we can get to build a revolution. The Shah is America's puppet, like Marcos in the Philippines, and we should support each other with solidarity in a united front."

Schmitty countered that some of the Iranians were infected with conservative, Islamic values that didn't jibe with our more progressive equality between the sexes.

"Well, sure, the same could be said about the PLO, couldn't it?"

Although it claimed to be secular, the Palestine Liberation Organization fought Israel for an independent Palestinian Arab State, but I heard stories of religion rearing its head with Muslim repression against women, but we, including the Jews in our movement, still supported them.

Schmitty became agitated over the comparison and I laughed. "Lighten up, man. It's not like they're going to storm the Winter Palace and seize power! And shit, I'm only an observer."

The Iranians carried signs – "Down with the Shah" and gruesome color posters depicting injured and dead young people, victims of ferocious atrocities attributed to SAVAK, the Shah's secret police. Many of these marchers covered their faces and wore disguises, claiming that SAVAK agents sought to identify individuals from news photos who could then be arrested, tortured, and even executed upon their return to Iran.

I don't think these Iranian demonstrations made all that much of a dent in American public consciousness at that time. There was just too much else going on. The Shah of Iran was just one more dictator in America's employ.

We marched in ordered ranks through the downtown Loop, chanting our slogans, and attracting some mild interest and a few catcalls from bystanders when someone called my name.

"Ron!" I turned to see Mike Filamonich, my old friend from back in our hometown of Wood Dale. He grabbed my hand and shook it with vigor, like he was pumping oil. "Long time no see, bro!"

"Like *wow*, Mike, it's been a year or more." He'd been a classmate, but I'd only gotten to know him in the bittersweet summer of 1968, after he'd gotten released from the St. Charles reform school. He'd spent a couple of years there, and unbeknownst to me, had been corresponding with my sister, Darlene. Mike never explained what he'd done to get locked up there, but he had a speech impediment, caused, he claimed, by his always-angry father punishing him by hitting his head with a hammer. He warmed up to my dad, who was a saint compared to his own, almost adopting himself into my family.

My prim sister's infatuation with him soon ended. She'd only seen him as a charity case and had plenty of other guys on a string, but she let him down easily and I introduced him to my friends in the West End. For a while he was one of us, joining us on beer and plunder raids and camping several nights in the Tree Fort. We opened our souls to each other, describing our psychosexual yearnings, the hopes, and dreams of young and still virginal men, not yet free to pursue their ambitions, which we hoped would take an alternate course into adulthood than our staid, work obsessed fathers.

Mike left home about the same time I did in the spring of 1969. I'd gone traipsing around the communes of Colorado, New Mexico, and New York, but from the length of our hair to the clothing we wore, it was obvious that each of us had spun off in different directions.

My shoulder length hair hung over a tee-shirt featuring a crouching white panther. Mike's wavy blond hair was short, and he was dressed in a checkered suit of loud, almost fluorescent clashing colors, green and orange, with a little red thrown in, like a caricature of a Bohemian mobster. It almost made me laugh aloud as he fell in beside me, behind two Persian chicks holding aloft a long banner that proclaimed, DEATH TO THE SHAH and POWER TO THE PEOPLE.

The Information Center chick had been right beside me but was patrolling the line of the march, solving minor problems, doing her job as a marshal. Mike took her place beside me. When she came back, she stared at him, confusion on her face. This guy looked out of place in his flashy suit, the uniform of our class enemy. He could be an undercover pig, and I felt a hot flash of embarrassment to be seen with him, making me suspect in her eyes. Mike took no heed of my discomfiture. In a booming voice that could be heard above our chants, he filled me in on his life since I had last seen him.

"I got it made, man. Look at this!" He opened his jacket to give me a peek at the brown butt of a revolver, holstered snug against his chest. "They gave me my own *heat* man, a Smith and Wesson 38 Special! I'm in good with these guys, plenty of perks on the job, too. I mean, wait 'til you hear this. Remember how we used to talk about getting laid by some wild chicks? It seemed like an impossible dream then. We were still kids in that oak tree above the forest."

Hoping the chick didn't notice how intrigued I was, I gave him a curt nod. Mike couldn't be a cop, not dressed like he was. He had to be working for the Mafia or some other criminal enterprise, but I held off asking if he ever had to shoot someone. That would be an expected part of his job, or they wouldn't give him a gun.

"Well, Ron, that's my life now. I'm living it up; all my wildest fantasies have come true!" He shook his head, as if he didn't believe it either, and right there, surrounded by marchers chanting 'Down with imperialism and death to the Shah,' his lurid story came gushing out in a torrent of words that excited me as much as I tried to keep from showing it from those around us.

"The guys bring me to these *Outasight* whorehouses on the south side, you know, in the colored area. The guys call it Nigger town or Zululand."

"Shit, Mike! Where the hell do you think you are? Don't shout that *N* word around here."

Most of those in our section of the march were white, even the Persians, who were whiter than us, with a few Chicago blacks and Chicanos sprinkled in farther to the front and back of us. I wondered how they'd take the blathering of this friend of mine and, most important, how would it reflect on me?

"Ah, okay, Ron. Like, I'm not prejudiced. You dig?"

He came closer and lowered his voice. "I'd never even noticed how gorgeous and *stacked* black chicks could be until the guys took me to the whorehouse. I couldn't believe it. When we walked in the parlor this honey of a chick in a nightgown walked right up to me and striped it off, real slow, not caring that the other guys were watching, she dropped to her knees and unzipped me with a sweet little smile and a wink. I'm serious, man. Could she ever suck cock!"

I answered Mike's enthusiasm in monosyllables. Uh huh, yeah, and I hoped he would take a clue and shut the fuck up until we could continue this conversation in private, but more than the exertion of the march, his tale made me sweat and flush red. I pulled up my jeans to hide a spontaneous erection, and glanced around, nervous, praying that my feminist comrades wouldn't hear his details. No way could they miss my conspicuous partner in the loud suit, shouting to be heard above the slogans bashing sexism and male chauvinism along with the Shah.

Whose side was I on, anyway? I was no chauvinist. I loved women, considered myself a feminist, and yet the ever more strident feminism I was hearing of late was becoming too prim and puritanical. Mike and I were healthy, randy males, and almost brothers.

"Man alive, Ron. That gal is my angel, the most beautiful chick in the world. Who cares if she's black and a whore? You know what they say nowadays, black is beautiful. Right, man?"

"Yeah, sure, Mike. Black is beautiful alright. Too bad I never had a chance to check one out."

"Well, Ron, I'll show you around, give you a taste of the good life." He slapped my back, grinning like a coked up madman, and launched back into his story. "That chick, man, she looked up at me like I was her god or something and swallowed my cock like she was starving for it. When I *came,* right in her hot mouth, I was in heaven, totally forgot myself and I took that sweet black chick up off her knees and kissed her, tongue and all, I didn't care that her mouth was full of my juice."

Listening to this, I flashed on my heady experience with Kay. Mike and I were almost living parallel lives.

He dug his fingers into my shoulder and stared at me, wide-eyed. "I'm in love, man, but she ain't jealous and lets me try her friends, too. I've fallen in love at least a hundred times, but she's still the best."

He glanced around, as if he suddenly realized where he was. "Come with me, Ron. I'll introduce you to the guys and put in a word so you can join us. They'll help you get a gun and make some real dough, and then I'll take you to the whorehouse. My treat. I owe you, remember?"

The chick I'd been working on gave me a sideways glance, and I knew I'd be criticized. Maybe I'd already blown it with her. Although I was tempted to go meet his girls, I was leery of rubbing shoulders with Mike's gangster pals. Even though breaking laws that only served the rich and hurt the poor didn't bother me, gangsters were just greedy capitalists.

"Let's talk later," I said, then got close to whisper. "I'm working on that chick over there. See her?" She was eyeing us with tangible suspicion.

"Her? She ain't nothing, man. You'll see better where I'll take you. Let's scram away from here."

Maybe he was right, and I was curious to see what it was all about, at least. We had the same taste in women, came from the same fucked up background, but I worried about Mike shooting off his mouth around the wrong crowd, either mine or his. If he *yakked* too much and became a liability, the dudes who picked out that suit and gave him the gun might try to shut him up permanently. I had to shake him loose before my whole reputation in the Movement crumbled. He kept trying to convince me, but I finally cut him off.

"I can't split right now. You go ahead; because my, ah, my people are, like, counting on me here, see? I'll see *ya* later, man."

Mike, crestfallen like a whipped puppy, took the hint. He stepped out of the march and disappeared into the crowd along the sidewalk. To my great regret, I didn't get his phone number and never saw him again. After the passing of decades, I still wonder what became of him and his beautiful black girls. As for the woman I'd been working on, she kept her distance and I never got anywhere.

48

SOLICITING

Having run out of newspapers to hawk, I jangled a few coins in an empty pop can as I called for donations to the Revolution along North Clark Street, an upscale area full of well-dressed people. After an hour, I'd only made about seven dollars in change when a pretty woman, dolled up with lipstick and smartly dressed, approached me. All the hippie girls I knew didn't wear make-up, but she was about my age and I figured she never read anything but the fashion pages.

"Have you got change for a twenty?"

"Gee, let me see." I didn't, but wanted to stretch out my time with her and began shaking coins out of the can. That made her giggle.

"Looks like you don't have enough for me. How about a cigarette, then?"

"I don't smoke tobacco, but let's walk and talk. Maybe I can find us some weed."

She was giving me the eye like she dug me. "You'd look like a real stud if you cut your hair."

"No way, I'm a proud member of Woodstock Nation, into nature and living free."

"Oh, yeah? Tell me about this Woodstock thing."

We were in the same generation, but our life experiences were entirely different.

A couple of blue uniformed cops walked up behind me. My guard was down. It was too late to give them the slip. One grabbed my can, and I started to slip the rest of my change into my pocket.

"Hey, put the rest of it back in the can. Soliciting on the public streets without a license is against the law."

"Really? I didn't know that." I associated soliciting with prostitution, the only way I'd heard the word used.

"Ignorance of the law is no excuse, Buster. You'll have to go down to the precinct with us."

The woman backed off as the cops slapped handcuffs on me. Too bad. I'd have liked to get to know her. With my hands cuffed behind me, they led me to a squad car parked around the corner, tossed me into the back seat, and drove south on Clark toward Lincoln, where we got snarled in traffic. A long haired guy on a bicycle came alongside my window, half open on the torrid day.

"What's going on, brother?" he asked.

The driver, acting as the *bad* cop, called to the cyclist, "Get away from the car!"

Other members of the Freak community began congregating around the stalled car.

They approached my partly open window. "Are you alright?"

Another guy walked up beside him. "Do you need any help?"

My brothers and sisters were there for me, united against police oppression, which warmed my heart, proof that Lincoln Park was friendly, liberated territory.

"Move along now," the driver ordered, but the crowd grew and began rocking the car. Fingering their nightsticks and holstered guns, the cops looked scared. "Get the fuck away unless you want to join *him* in the back seat!"

"We're just doing our job, is all," the other cop said. "He's not going to jail. It's just a misdemeanor fine!" He turned back and assured me, "No big deal, fellow, you'll go home soon."

That was good news. Although gratified by this community

support, I didn't want anyone to get hurt on my behalf, so I called out the window. "I'll be okay, honest. Thanks for your concern. That's people power in action!"

The crowd opened as the traffic started to move and I was on my way to the local precinct cop shop, where I was fingerprinted and processed. They poured the contents of my pop can on a desk and counted it up, a little over seven dollars in a neat stack of change that represented a day's effort for me.

"Can I pay the fine with this now and get it over with?"

They laughed. "No, it's evidence."

Lucky for me, I'd stashed a couple of dollars in my watch pocket before they nabbed me and didn't check it when they frisked me. It was all I had to show for my day. They handed me a slip of paper with my court appearance date and turned me loose. I jammed it in my pocket, but in the disorganized state of my life at the time, I couldn't find it several days later and didn't know who to call to get it straightened out.

I told myself it didn't matter. They had my measly seven bucks, and unfamiliar with these things, I doubted that my fine could be much more.

49

OFF TO SEE THE WIZARD

Approaching the Panther Pad through the back alley, I saw a school bus, painted in wild psychedelic patterns, in the alley. Coming up the stoop, I met a new crew of hippies lounging in the shade on the back porch with Bill, Jeff, and Schmitty. They handed me a gallon jug of sweet Bali Hai wine by way of greeting. I needed a cool, refreshing swig after my day's ordeal and then sat down to listen to our guest's thrilling tale of adventures on the road. They were White Panthers returning to Ann Arbor from a trip along the West coast and Rocky Mountains, visiting the hippie enclaves of our new Rock and Roll Nation as well as some Native American tribes.

The apparent leader of this troupe was a Mamma Cass sized Earth Mother of a woman, dressed in a splotchy, multicolored tie-dyed dress. She often broke into a booming laugh as she monopolized the conversation.

A younger woman and a couple of dudes added a word or two, but more often nodded in agreement with her version of their Trans-American journey and kept passing the bottle around.

One of the guys had a pronounced potbelly that hung down over his jeans. Earth Mother curled her lips in a snarl when she referred to him as Pud, which I took to be his name, but it was a word I'd recently learned as a disparaging reference to a limp dick, a wimp, a pansy, a less than *manly* man. Guzzling wine as I listened, I confused the word Pud with Pun Plamondon, the name of the Party's Minister of Defense, wanted by the FBI and living underground. Pud didn't look anything like Pun's picture, but then I remembered Pun, the paragon of male virtue, had just been captured.

Pud was a term I'd come to hear often among the Ann Arbor White Panthers, and it confused me that this Pud seemed undisturbed by the subtle contempt of Earth Mother and the others heaped on him. Earth Mother moved the conversation around to her life. She'd been raised by Communist parents in the Old Left.

"We were always being infiltrated by the FBI," she said. "But we knew *exactly* who they were. We even welcomed them at our meetings."

"What?" Schmitty put down the jug, almost coughing on a mouthful of wine.

Earth Mother smiled at the reaction she'd caused. "Sure, strange as it sounds, the FBI agents were the only ones in the depths of the Depression who were able to pay their dues, and we needed the funds. So, in a way, you could say that J. Edgar Hoover helped finance the Communist Party!"

Everyone laughed, even though J. Edgar, ancient as he was, was still our boogeyman, repressing the New Left and Civil Rights movements. These hippies seemed down to earth supporters of the Cause, yet able to laugh about it, whereas our Chicago collective was getting hung up on towing party line with every breath. They intended spending a day or two visiting our urban oasis, before leaving for Ann Arbor.

Earth Mother leaned over and put her hand on my knee. "Why don't you come along with us?"

Bill nodded encouragement. "Go ahead, Ron. Chairman Bob wants us all to check out the Ann Arbor Headquarters. Fuzzy and Leslie are already out there, and you can take in the Rock Concert at Goose Lake on the way."

That settled it. I joined the pilgrim journey to Ann Arbor. Stepping into their psychedelic bus, I met a three-foot tall red lacquered statue next to the driver's seat. It was an obese wooden Buddha, standing with his arms stretched above him in the awakening pose. Some of the seats had been removed to make room for opulent boudoirs hung with India prints, pleasant nooks to chill out in and make love, smoke dope, or read in near privacy.

"Let's hit the concert before the rush starts," Earth Mother said. "We've been looking forward to this festival since leaving the Rocky Mountains."

Several simultaneous concerts were scheduled for that weekend of August seventh through the ninth. Besides Goose Lake, the concert at Mosport, Ontario, just across the border in Canada, was billed as the "Strawberry Fields Rock Festival," but also as a motorcycle race to evade certain town bylaws that stipulated where a rock concert could be held. And the Ann Arbor Blues Festival was to be held thirty miles from Goose Lake on the same weekend. About 10,000 mostly white fans made it to that non-profit event that featured both well-known and less commercial musicians.

Goose Lake was a 390-acre private park in Michigan. I wore shorts and chose to go barefoot in the heat, which I soon regretted. It had been raining, and the grounds were deep in mud, which oozing between my toes felt refreshing at first, but then I cut my foot on a jagged soda can.

I yelled, "Damn litterbugs!"

"What's the matter?" A concerned brother came to help me rinse the bottom of my foot and assess the damage. "Looks like a deep gash. You really ought to get bandaged up in the clinic."

"The clinic?" The thought of such a facility in this ad hoc hippie boomtown amazed me.

"It's over there." He pointed out the big red cross marked on a tent and led me limping to a cot inside. It was a well-run operation. Volunteer medics in white lab coats handled minor emergencies, dispensing aspirin, and sewing up minor wounds like mine.

The medic wore a little lamp on his forehead, like doctors use for looking down throats. After cleaning and bandaging my foot, he asked, "When was the last time you got a tetanus shot? You might not need one if it was recent enough."

"Gee, I don't know. It must've been back in junior high when I ripped open my knee on the gravel playground."

"How far back was that?"

Junior high seemed another lifetime ago. I began counting the summers backward on my fingers. "I guess it must have been about 1964 or '65, maybe six years ago."

"You better get another one."

He shot me up, and I was on my way, hopping on one foot to try to keep the bandages clean and dry, which put a damper on my exploration of the concert. For the duration, I kept close to the bus, less mobile than I wanted to be. Besides that, I was hungry and flat broke. I'd neglected to take as much cash from the kitty as Fuzzy and Leslie did, forcing me to rely on the hospitality of my new brothers and sisters. I got high with them more often than food came my way. Crashing on the bus, sleep eluded me too. Despite my best limping efforts, my bandaged foot became a muddy boot. I'd heard that American Indians and even animals soak open wounds in mud, which helps to heal faster and hoped it would work in my case.

Although I longed to find a girlfriend, I came alone, and I left alone. So, hungry and flat broke, I relied on the hospitality of my new brothers and sisters. Keeping close to the bus, and surrounded by loud, unceasing Rock and Roll, sleep eluded me too.

The New York Times and the Argus had a close agreement in their articles about the concert.

Rock Fetes Draw 250,000 to Ontario and Michigan Area.

By United Press International

More than 250,000 young people rocked along yesterday as the halfway point of the weekend rock festivals at Goose Lake, Mich., and Mosport Ont., passed with relatively few problems.

Forty-seven persons were arrested on a variety of charges while attempting to cross various United States-Canadian border points...

The American, Vietcong and Canadian flags were displayed at Goose Lake, where more than 2000,000 persons crowded into a 390-acre private park.

Drugs were being sold "like hotcakes," but only a few bad trips were reported, one of the attending physicians said. The authorities arrested about 50 persons outside the park on drug charges.

"Leave the young people alone," Sheriff Charles Southward of Jackson County said. "I don't care what they do once they're inside the private park."

The promoters, who expected about 60,000, said they were able to accommodate the extra 140,000 persons at the grassy amphitheater...

The New York Times, August 9, 1970, page 64 of section A

The Argus account was titled in lower case.

goose lake

Over 200,000 rock and roll maniacs came together at the Goose Lake Pop festival put on by Dick Songer and company last weekend in what was the biggest gathering of the people of Woodstock Nation ever held in Michigan. This was probably the most successful pop festival in our recent history: Although nearly 160 brothers and sisters got popped outside the park for dope, there were no pigs inside the park and hence no big mass arrests and beatings of the kind that happened at Cincinnati. All the bands came and played on time, there were no murders, no serious injuries, there was water to drink most of the time and food for those who could afford and eat it. In short, we survived Goose Lake.

...But there was no *magic* in the big rock and roll carnival at Goose Lake, no history made except that we had all been there in one place for a while and lived to tell of it. 200,000 of us together there for 3 or 4 days, but we really didn't do anything, we just sort of made it, we just sort of got blasted, and we just sort of went back home from our little vacation to keep on doing whatever it was we were doing before we left.

Musically, Goose Lake was nearly identical to every festival held anywhere else this year... the same "big bands" were featured... Jethro Tull, Mountain, the Small Faces, John Sebastian, Ten Years After, the New York Rock and Roll Ensemble, all came to do their little 45-minute shows of their big hits, pick up their $10,000 and $20,000 and $50,000 checks, and leave to play yet another pop festival someplace, anyplace, else. The local bands that did play at Goose Lake were whisked quickly on and off stage during the day so as to leave plenty of time for the big stars...

In short, we *(The White Panther organizations)* know how to deal with our own culture and our people in an efficient and meaningful way, we can do what Songer and Gibb don't know how to do and haven't done at Goose Lake.

We propose that a committee of people be set up by STP and the Tribal Council to deal with the Goose Lake situation. ... We are the only people who can do the job righteously and this must be acknowledged by Songer and his people...

"goose lake" in Ann Arbor Argus, August 17-31, number 27, page 15

50

THE ANN ARBOR SCENE

The bus arrived in Ann Arbor and parked at the White Panther "Trans-Love" commune on Hill Street. I met an exciting, adrenaline-fueled cast of freaks at the commune, full of grandiose ideas that they bounced around with high-flown Marxist slogans, sprinkled with quotes from revolutionary saints like Che. It reminded me of how Jesus Freaks used the Bible, except the quoted passages weren't from Psalms or Leviticus, but the Little Red Book of Chairman Mao. If the listener's eyes hadn't glazed over from the dense tangle of verbiage and pseudoscientific terminology, he'd become lost looking for the obscure point that the speaker was trying to make. I thought there was a lot of yakking going on, but little genuine communication.

The wound on my foot had been cleaned and re-bandaged, but it still hurt to hobble around on, thus curtailing me from getting around and souring my mood. Busy as they were, the commune residents ignored me anyway, and I felt out of place. Then a vivacious woman came up and took my hand.

"Hi there, you must be from the Chicago Collective. I'm Genie Plamondon, Pun's wife."

She gave me a welcoming hug that recharged my spirit. She

struck me as devoid of the phony airs some of the others displayed, despite her title as Minister of Foreign Affairs. There were no mere members in the Party, only generals. I didn't even remember what bombastic title Chairman Bob had christened me with, but I suppressed a giggle every time someone introduced themselves with one of the high-flown titles the Party bestowed on them. Genie was seven years older than me, an attractive woman, and I enjoyed listening to her rap.

"All the people struggling against oppression want the same thing, but each nation, or culture, or self-consciously perceived culture within a culture, needs its own political party to represent it within the broader struggle. Therefore, working class whites, blacks, Indians, lesbians, and gays need to preserve their identities while working together on common goals."

"Right on, Genie!" I said, punctuating her statement.

She smiled and continued. "Our White Panther Party is for Hippies or Freaks, most of whom identify as white, but any black, Indian, or Chinese who identifies more as a Freak than with his or her ethnic group, is free to join us, rather than the Black Panther, or the American Indian Movement. For example, we have a black member, Hiawatha, who's more into our Rock and Roll youth culture than with the bluesy ghetto culture of the Black Panthers."

Although I loved basking in the glow of Genie's sweet vibe, she noticed that I was red-eyed and drooping from exhaustion.

"You look like you need some rest, Ron. Hiawatha won't be back until later and he's someone you should meet. You can crash up in his room and get some peace and quiet. He won't mind."

Hiawatha's room at the top of the stairs was easy to spot. Like Genie implied, the walls were covered with Rock and Roll posters, that of Jimmy Hendricks being the most conspicuous. After a refreshing shower in the bathroom at the end of the hall, the first I'd had since leaving Chicago, I rinsed the mud out of my grungy clothes, wrung them out and hung them on a chair before collapsing on Hiawatha's king size mattress on the floor. I pulled the sheet over my head and fell into a deep sleep.

Something woke me, and I turned to face a black man sitting beside me with his warm hand on my thigh.

"Oh, hello, there. Ron, is it? I'm Hiawatha."

I started to rise.

"Don't get up. Genie told me you were up here. It's cool, go ahead and get some rest."

I rolled over and closed my eyes, conscious of Hiawatha's movement about the room. He stripped, folded his clothes, and climbed into bed on my right side. I felt it was incumbent on me to clarify my sexual orientation.

"No offence, man, but I'm not gay."

"Oh, that's okay, man. I won't bother you, I promise. I need some rest, too."

I took him at his word and closed my eyes. It was his bed, and I was grateful for the use of it, to catch up on some much-needed sleep. For a while he lay motionless, then he snuggled closer to me, stopped for a moment, and then his fingers began to creep up my thigh, working their way to my groin.

"Sorry, man," I said, sitting up. "Nothing personal, but like I said, I'm not into dudes." The thought of it made me nauseous, but to be polite, I didn't say that.

"No, please stay. I, ah, promise..."

I'd had enough similar experiences to know he wouldn't keep such a promise, and I didn't want to listen to his pleading.

"Sorry, I've just gotta go." I stumbled up, still groggy, and got dressed in my damp clothes before I went back down into the din of the communal house.

If I hadn't been in such bad shape, achy and tired, I might have stuck around and gotten to know Hiawatha better. He was four years older than me, born in Georgia, and later became part of the Punk music scene after doing prison time for possession of cocaine and psychedelic drugs.

Downstairs, I dodged from one corner to another, trying to find some peace and quiet. The layout of the house itself was attractive, decorated with psychedelic Hindu Yantras and pop art themes, tie-dyes and India prints alongside posters of Janis Joplin, John Sinclair rolling a joint, and other revolutionary heroes like Genie's husband Pun Plamondon. But I wasn't in my usual gregarious mood.

Then Fuzzy came in to brighten my day.

"Hey, Ron. I'm looking for someone to hitch back to Chicago with me."

"Sure!" I jumped at the chance. "Let's go."

51

HITCHING HOME

F uzzy and I stood at the freeway ramp bound for Chicago, sticking out our thumbs in the time-honored fashion each time a car whooshed by. Our hopes rose to giddy heights only to be dashed as, one by one, the vehicles sped into the horizon. The minutes dragged by as we slumped along the curb. Then a battered old VW bug slowed down, checking us out.

A hippie car! We jumped up, waved, and shouted, but our elation evaporated as they drove on past us. We'd noticed that the occupants were not hippies but two black men, and racial tensions being strong, they rarely stopped for whites. The car went some fifty feet beyond us before it stopped and began backing up. The young black man in the passenger seat rolled down the window and hollered, "We're only going to Chicago."

"That's terrific," I said. "So are we."

I was glad not to have any gear with me as we squeezed into the cramped back seat. Fuzzy held his small bundle on his lap.

"I'm Tyrone," the young man said. "This is my dad. He didn't want to stop for you guys, but I insisted. He's kind of conservative, even supports Nixon and the war."

Together with Tyrone, we set about explaining the necessity of bucking the system to his gray-haired father, rapping about the Black Panther Party's community programs, the evils of the Viet Nam War and our common cause to liberate all mankind from social and economic tyranny.

The father shook his head. "You boys seem like nice young men, but I've fought for this country. It isn't perfect by a long shot, but I don't want to lose all the rights and freedoms we've gained to encroaching communism. Those people over there don't have what we have, and I'm trying to keep my son out of trouble. You've got to admit that we need law and order for society to work."

"Come on, Dad," Tyron said. "Every day as a black man in this country you have to experience humiliation, like with the unequal pay you always complain about. I think we need the Black Power movement to set things right."

I felt sorry for dear old Dad. We ganged up on the old man for his own good, and it seemed he began to understand that his son wasn't alone in his 'crazy, radical' convictions. It was our duty to raise the red flag whenever possible, and we made some headway in opening the old man's mind and reinforce the black and proud views of his beleaguered son. After such a warm discussion, I was sad to leave our hosts. They dropped us at a subway station on the south side and we were home in a flash.

52

HOME RUN

Chairman Bob grabbed the van keys, tossed them to a radio friend of his, and waved to Bill and me. "Do you two guys need a lift home?"

"Sure," I said, and we piled into the back of the van with Bob's friend at the wheel.

Jeff and Schmitty were on home turf and didn't need a ride. They'd hop on the subway to the north side and we'd all rendezvous up there in a few days.

After many delays and false rumors, we'd finally arrived at the decisive moment, being evicted from our rent-free life at our LaSalle house. It was slated to be torn down or renovated, and we'd have to scoop up our meager possessions and find a new crib. Once we'd gotten our bearings, we'd reopen our collective in a new house-fortress, somewhere where we could buckle back down to the serious task of building our chapter of the White Panther Party into a serious part of the People's Revolution.

Rudnick suggested that we all take this opportunity to go back home and see our parents, something I'd not done since April. Despite his rabble rousing, he'd managed to stay close to his mom and recommended that we try to be more understanding of our family's middle-class experience, because capitalism hurts us all.

Driving up Lake Street to Bensenville, we dropped Bill off first. That's when I realized he lived across Fischer's Woods, so close to where I'd stayed with Chris. Then I directed us farther on Lake to Addison Road, where we turned right and drove two miles to pull into my parent's driveway in Wood Dale.

Rudnick stepped out wearing his loud dashiki and straggly Afro and gave me a hug. My parents stood in the doorway and, not recognizing me at first, gaped at the strange gang of hippies, probably wondering whether to call the police. Rudnick thought better of stepping up to the door with me to meet my wary folks. He got back in the van and gave me a curt wave before zooming off to God knows where.

Far from enthusiastic about reuniting with my folks, I walked up the stoop like a condemned man. It was bound to turn into a disaster; I wouldn't stay long. After my "Hello," Dad jumped in; upset at seeing the company I'd arrived with.

"Looks like my idiot son has returned to us, probably hooked on drugs." He shook his head with a frown. "Those goofballs looked more like ugly women than men."

All that hair and color was the very nemesis of the staid, button-down look of his middle class "Silent Majority." It didn't help matters that I wore a shirt emblazoned with a marijuana leaf and the radical slogan, "Seize the time," with "Power to the People!" on my back. It didn't take much self-expression to be controversial with Dad, and I'd long since passed the point of no return. I tried to divert him with some ordinary conversation.

"How's grandpa and grandma?"

Dad ignored that and continued making disparaging remarks about "shiftless hippies who don't support themselves and live on welfare or at their family's expense."

I winced at the comparison. "Come on Dad, you know I never asked for a dime from you."

"Well, I had to bail you out of jail last year, and insurance didn't cover all your expenses in the mental hospital."

"I told you not to. The SDS legal team would get around to it and despite what that doc says, I'm not crazy."

"You and your Commie friends again! You're just too stubborn and idiotic to see things from a realistic perspective."

"You mean the establishment view, right Dad? Order and hierarchy, huh? That what it's all about, just like Nixon and Agnew promoting fascism."

Dad knew nothing about the counterculture aside from the slander of right-wing media. I was duty bound to stand by my ideals and explain our cause and lifestyle. His remarks enraged me, and I wasn't prepared to let them slip by without a rebuttal. Mom arched her eyebrows with concern and tried to calm us down.

"Let's go into the kitchen for some coffeecake."

But it was too late. The only means left for Dad to uphold his parental authority over his wayward son was brute force. His face contorted, turning as livid red as the Soviet flag. He jumped on me like a clumsy bear, losing his balance as crashed into me and we hit the floor and tussled. I was rail thin and no match for his weight as he wrapped me up into a half Nelson package.

I peered around his bulk to see five-year-old Amy, the youngest of my five sisters. Her eyes bugged out with shock as she watched from behind Mom's skirts. What an embarrassing scene we made. For years I'd been around so little that I must have seemed like a bogeyman of a brother from far beyond her solar system.

My mind raced back to happier times, when I too was a kid. Dad and I would lie sprawled out on the living room floor together, side by side, exactly where we now wrestled, watching his favorite programs on our first black and white television. The stories on *Navy Log* and *Victory at Sea* were personal for Dad, who'd fought in many naval battles of the Pacific. His eyes would mist over as he recounted his exciting experiences as a gunner on a Fletcher class destroyer, from shooting down Jap dive bombers, to watching hula girls while on leave in Pearl Harbor. Feeling that connection with him inspired my love of history. Too bad we'd grown so far apart over the years. Dad just couldn't buck the system or see the effects of racism, which he made excuses for, but I hated to accept that we were irreconcilable enemies and didn't want to get into a physical fight with him.

Dad twisted me into a tight scissor lock with my head and right arm clamped tight between his legs. Unable to break free, I saw no other option than punching him in the nuts, something I was loath to do. I didn't want to hurt him, and gave dear Dad a light punch smack in the balls, but he still held me tight. I'd have to do it harder. Feeling sick about it, I grabbed his balls and squeezed with increasing pressure until he released me.

I jumped up and moved to the far side of the room, sputtering. "This is a fine way to greet your son! Ever wonder why we don't see each other? Goodbye, I'll never come home ever again."

This worried Mom, and she dragged me into the kitchen. "I know you don't really mean that, Ronnie. Why do you bring up things that upset him so? Give him more time to settle down, please, for me and your sister's sake."

I'd kept my mouth shut for years but could no longer bear hearing him berate the Youth Movement, my sacred cause, without a mummer.

Mom pulled me across the kitchen into my old bedroom. It then belonged to one of my sisters, and was festooned with the trappings of girlhood, the triumph of pink over the few relics of my boyhood yet remaining.

"Isn't there anything here you could take to remind you of your home and family, Ronnie?"

There was something I cherished, a knickknack from World War Two. Still hanging on the antlers of Grandpa's deer trophy, long serving as a hat-rack, was a yellow ceramic tile. This piece of folk art featured the ugly caricature of a bucktoothed "Jap." His gigantic, elephant-like ears spread out like Dumbo the elephant, as if to catch any sound, and his tiny, slanted eyes were squinted slits above his grotesque buck-toothed grin, making him an altogether horrible little fellow. Above the visor of his officer's cap was a rising sun, the insignia of the rising Japanese Empire. Above and below his face, in bold relief, was the slogan:

BE CAREFUL

THEY LISTEN.

I'd grown fond of this ugly heirloom, a time capsule that illustrated the attitude of my parent's generation. It was part of our collective, historical unconscious, a specimen of wartime propaganda which, from gazing at it since my early childhood, helped me understand how racial stereotypes focused hatred against an enemy. I found it relevant to the propaganda we used in Vietnam.

My father and his whole generation confused this war in Vietnam with the "Great Crusade" of their own generation. Their war was, for the most part, a good one, as wars go, even if some of the motives were not altogether pure.

With a brief, although stiff hug, I bade Mom and my baby sister farewell and slipped out the back door. I took my usual path through the small prairie at the rear of our yard and cut through unfriendly neighbors' lots and forest preserves to the far West End of Bensenville, my adopted neighborhood, where I was certain to receive a more convivial welcome. I needed to wander the woods again and refresh my psyche in a natural environment after being so long in the concrete jungles of Chicago.

53

TRUE CONFESSION

On the appointed day, Schmitty, Bill, Jeff, Chairman Bob, and I gathered in the cluttered basement of Schmitty's family home in Roger's Park. We were but a pitiful few remaining in the Chicago Chapter. Fuzzy had gone back to Ann Arbor, where Leslie remained with the Red Star Sisters. But I was confident from the prevailing attitude in the community that together with Rising Up Angry and the other progressive organizations, we could still contribute to the Revolution.

Waiting for others to arrive before we'd convene our meeting, Bob and I chatted. I didn't detect anything unusual about his attitude. It looked like we were back on track. I showed him my big eared propaganda plaque.

Bob took a big interest in it. "That's quite a souvenir, Ron. We'll have to figure out how to display it somehow."

I set it on one of the storage rack shelves that surrounded us and changed the subject to how I looked forward to our chapter's future. When everyone came in and settled down, with our expectant eyes upon him, Bob called us to order. But what he said next was most unexpected.

"I'm going to come right to the point." His eyes darted over us without lingering and then, clearing his throat, focused on the carpet we squatted on. "I'm back to shooting heroin again and I've blown all the collective's money on it. There's really nothing left for me to say at this point. I'm sorry; I've fucked up and failed you all."

Bob paused, waiting for anyone to respond. I glanced across the room at the blinking, open mouthed faces of Schmitty, Bill, and Jeff, my revolutionary brothers. A shocked silence hung over us all. Seconds before Bob called us to order, he'd seemed his jolly self, giving no sign of anything as serious as this. He shook his head and pronounced his final verdict.

"Well, I guess that's all we can say about it. I hereby dissolve the Chicago Chapter of the White Panther Party. Everyone is free to go his own way."

Free. Like spilled marbles, we scattered in all directions. This ending was too abrupt, too unexpected to register in my dazed head. Whether we shook hands and wished each other bon voyage, or stumbled wordlessly out into the bright afternoon sunshine, I cannot recall.

The Chicago collective had been my family all summer. We'd all worked so hard hawking underground newspapers and asking for donations, only for Rudnick to blow our earnings on *smack*. He had his own, unshared income as a DJ on Radio Free Chicago, and I supposed all that was gone too. Maybe I should have demanded that he fork over whatever dough he still had, but my brain was too numb to think.

The awareness of my surroundings only kicked back in when I found myself standing on the corner of Lincoln and Halstead. With only a couple dollars in my pocket, I was broke and homeless, and had to discover a new direction for my life on those city streets.

Later I realized that I'd left my big eared plaque at Schmitty's place, but I was too busy reorganizing my life and never went back for it. I guess that was another symbol of my past lost to time, unless it turns up some day on eBay.

The last mention of the White Panther collective is in the Chicago Seed's FREE CITY DIRECTORY, Vol. 5 Number 10, although by the time this hit the streets, the Chicago Panthers were already gone. The Seed's cover had an image of a green-faced Frankenstein leaning on the pyramidal John Hancock building.

> The White Panther Party is an organization in the white hip community parallel to the Black Panther Party. They put out free city news, distribute Sun/Dance, and offer free classes in political education and self-defense, call 787-1962 for more information.

I read that with wistful emotions tugging at me and thought how ironic it was that the phone number had finally gotten posted after it was all over. A couple of issues later, as fall brought its deep chill into our fair city; I read another Seed article that saddened me.

Under "Free City Gossip" I saw "there's no more rock and roll at the Aragon Ballroom." That was a big loss. After that came an article entitled "Arsenals," which stated that crime was up in the black community ever since the Black Panthers pulled out their neighborhood patrols under pressure from State's Attorney Hanrahan, the murderer of Fred Hampton and Mark Clark.

Here is a short blurb the Seed put out on Chairman Bob:

> Rudnick
>
> Stanley G. Rudnick, former head of the Kokaine Karma Kollective of Radio Free Chicago, has been appointed Professor of Communications and Media at Goddard College, Goddard Vermont. Prof. Rudnick is eminently qualified for the post, his radical views have gotten him thrown off the air at WGLD in Chicago, WABX in Detroit, and WFMU in New York. His presence on Radio Free Chicago (WEAW 105 FM) will be sorely missed.
>
> Seed, Vol. 5, # 12, page 1.

Whether or not he got clean or was *smacking* up on the sly, he'd gotten another gig beyond Chicago, a perfect exit strategy. I didn't have one. I made my way back to the streets of Old Town and Lincoln Park, looking for a place to crash. My life had made another full circle for me to wind up back on the street again, as broke and homeless as when I started my odyssey.

I had options. I thought about joining Angry, but I needed time to think things through and explore other alternatives, like getting back out in the country to check out some rural communes.

We still needed to fight the system. The news from Nam was hot that August. A Red Cross girl named Virginia Kirsch who'd just arrived the day before was found stabbed to death in her quarters on August 16th. The killer was almost certainly one of those she'd come to comfort, one of our "good guy" GIs. The Senate subcommittee hearings probed the increase in "fragging" incidents, in which soldiers (grunts) tried to kill their own officers. It was evidence of sagging morale in the Armed Forces. A Sergeant said that marijuana was being used everywhere by our troops even back in 1968. Seven military prisoners escaped the Army Stockade in Mannheim, Germany.

On the Home front, the shooting war heated up, and it was not always easy to tell criminal from *revolutionary* actions. From August 6 to the 7th, a black mob was on the rampage in Pompano Beach, Florida. One cop killed and seven wounded in an Omaha "bomb trap." Another bomb in the Minneapolis Federal building left one watchman hurt and $500,000 in damage. There were more firebombs set off in Atlanta, too. In Chicago on August 17th, Detective James Alfano died, having been shot by a sniper, a Black "P Stone" gang member, the previous Thursday. Jesse Jackson told the media that cops were "silent" about crime in the black community unless it was directed against cops.

Incongruously, the Charles F. Kettering Foundation was financing the Black P. Stone Nation's legal defense. On August 28 Mr. Kettering said, "I feel strongly that the Stones and, particularly (the leader) Hairston, have potential for great social impact... if we can keep them out of jail." (Chicago Tribune page 4, column 5)

Angela Davis made the FBI's Top Ten Most WANTED list. Blacks took hostages on the south side of Chicago after a failed robbery on August 20. A jury acquitted the Weatherman Flanagan; of charges stemming from Elrod's crippling during the October "Rage." Flanagan raised his clenched fist in the "power" salute and was quoted saying, "Law and order in Chicago is a farce. I just want to get back on the streets where I can fight" and "we fight side by side with the Viet Cong!"

There seemed to be a pall of death over everything. I wondered how ready I was to join the escalating war on the home front. Could I *plug* a cop and start my own body count? Did one more death really make a difference and bring victory in our People's War any closer? Maybe the best recourse was to forget about seizing political power outright and focus instead on generating positive social change at the grassroots and push public opinion to bring our brothers home from Vietnam before their hands were stained with blood and killing took over their lives.

From the Ann Arbor Argus, number 29, page 10:

CHAPTER CHANGES

Once upon a time there was a White Panther Party on the planet with a program: rock and roll, dope, and fucking in the streets. That time has been seized and political realities have thrown a petit bourgeois concept of revolution up against the wall. A new incarnation staggered to its feet, wearing the same shoes, but with a brick in each hand, one for building and one for throwing in self-defense, and announced in anger... that from now on "we will not be fucked with."

...We only wanted to be free; but you cannot successfully wield any tool or weapon for liberation, be it Marxist-Leninism or an M16, unless you first examine it, understand and know it, until you can break it down and piece it together again...

54

SISTERHOOD

Statement of the Red Star Sisters

Ann Arbor Sun, July 4th, 1970

The Red Star is a universal symbol of COMMUNISM, of living and working together, coming together, a symbol of righteous revolution and love for ALL of humanity. We, the sisters of the White Panther Party, take the Red Star as the symbol of our own liberation, and align I ourselves with all oppressed people on the planet.

In Vietnam, the spirit and determination of the women to free their people is as strong as the men's. In Vietnam, the members of the Vietnam Women's Union tell of how before 1930, before the Party was formed, there were two main tendencies among women's liberation. One tendency was bourgeois, which wanted equal rights with men and opposed the bonds of the feudal family (which were extremely oppressive), but didn't commit themselves to freeing ALL their people. Their aspirations were right, but they didn't see the root of the problem. The constituency of this tendency was mainly women from the cities.

The second tendency was revolutionary, influenced I by Marxism-Leninism. These women felt that only through the liberation of ALL the people could they achieve their liberation as women. They worked in many revolutionary groups, and only after the Party was formed did they form a separate women's organization, which then became an anti-imperialist women's organization, not an organization for the liberation of women. They knew they needed to give women a sense of confidence, and that through revolutionary activity, consciousness is raised to a higher level—through revolutionary struggle, people begin to see their own potential as human beings. The Chairman of the Vietnam Woman's Union is quoted as saying that making a revolution is like going to a celebration; it makes you younger. And she told of Minh Khai, a recent revolutionary sister who engraved on her wall in prison, "Revolution is the way to Life." It is through righteous revolutionary struggle to free all the people that each one of us will achieve our liberation, each one of us as individuals, each class, each ethnic minority, each nation, as women, men and youth. We will ALL be free.

We, the Red Star Sisters of the White Panther Party, are a cadre of sisters united and dedicated to serving the needs of the people with a specific purpose of educating and organizing more revolutionary sisters into The White Panther Party. We believe that women cannot be free until ALL the people are free and dedicate our lives to that principle. We believe that male and female are two halves which make up the most powerful whole on the planet, and that united as brothers and sisters we are UNSTOPPABLE! In the past the White Panther Party has been criticized for male chauvinism, and the objective reality shows that there are indeed more men than women in the Party. We recognized that sisters throughout the planet are subjected to specific kinds of sexual oppression in the roles that we have been expected to fulfill, and we are determined to rediscover our true roles as a whole people, as revolutionary women. We, the Red Star Sisters of the White Panther Party, believe that we can deal with this problem within the Party, and are doing so. We call on all revolutionary sisters to unite with us to make the White Panther Party a truly revolutionary Party dedicated to serving all the needs of all the people.

ALL POWER TO THE PEOPLE
POWER TO THE RED STAR SISTERS
REVOLUTION IS THE WAY TO LIFE

L eslie remained in Ann Arbor, where she became immersed in the White Panther's Red Star Sister organization. Here is a good run-down about the Sisters in the Ann Arbor Argus. The microfilmed copy I found was confused or out of order, so it is either issue number 29 or 30 at the top of page 14.

Rising in the East

... Red Star Sisters was conceived last July as a women's organization within the White Panther Party...

At the Plenary, Red Star Sisters agreed on opening up to all revolutionary women who identified with the youth culture and wish to work together with the White Panther Party... Since at this time, all women members of the White Panther Party are Red Star Sisters, local chapters, regional branches, and White Panther Party National Headquarters are being used as organizing localities. As more and more non-Party women become Red Star Sisters, organizing and leadership will perhaps by (sic) coming more and more from non-Party sisters...

The first national program called for by Red Star Sisters are for "Children's Community Schools" to be created in communities all over the country. These schools will be revolutionary extensions of day-care centers. They'll be community-controlled schools that seriously deal with the cubs education. The name "Children's Community School" is a suggestion coming from the school in which Diane Oughten worked with here in Ann Arbor before she died in the 11th St. townhouse fire, along with Fred Gold and Terry Robbins. The schools will continue Diane's practice---they'll educate and be whatever the cubs make them...

Leslie's involvement is mentioned at the end of this more extensive article.

...Any sisters in the Ann Arbor area interested in helping to formulate and further develop a firm ideology for the local revolutionary women's organization, should contact Leslie Brody, coordinator of the Red Star Sisters in Ann Arbor, at 708 Arch Street.

Sisterhood is Powerful!

Leslie was finding her place in the Women's Movement, although she didn't remain long in the Ann Arbor sisterhood. She later voiced her complaints in her book, Red Star Sister.

The very first Red Star Sisters national program, Libby told me, would be a network of community schools...

I confessed my disappointment. Nursery schools sounded like old fashioned women's work to me. I had hoped for more range. "I think I'd rather work on the newspaper."

The minister (Libby) shrugged. She had only so much patience, and it was dwindling. I never saw her much after that. She came to one Red Star Sisters meeting and we posed together for a photograph. She held her fist in the air, Vietcong souvenir rings on every finger.

Pages 105-106 of *Red Star Sister*

We all had our issues and imperfections. At the time, I considered Leslie a bit of an elitist, too good for the activities of daily life that the rest of us, male or female, had to do. People can evolve, and I'm sure she did too over time.

ONE DAY IN 1999, I mentioned to my local librarian that I was researching the White Panther underground newspapers.

"That's rings a bell," the librarian said. "Funny thing, I've just finished reading a book by Leslie Brody. Ever hear of her?"

Of course I had. After locating and reading her book, I was able to contact Leslie online in 1999. We hadn't communicated for 29 years, and I attempted to compare notes with her about our common experiences. She assured me, however, that she couldn't recall anything beyond the events that she described in her book. Viz. this E-mail she sent me Dec. 27th, 1999:

> Hi Ron,
>
> Your pictures came through this time. I'm sorry I can't be of any more help. As I told you before I included everything I remembered and some that I didn't in my book. Did I tell you that it won the PEN Center West award for Best nonfiction in 1999? The award was a great lift since its sales were pretty sluggish. Perhaps my best advice is to remind you of Hemingway's famous quote:
>
> "There's no such thing as nonfiction." Have a happy new year.
>
> Best, Leslie
>
> RED STAR SISTER: *Between Madness and Utopia*, by Leslie Brody, Hungry Mind Press, St. Paul MN. 1998.

Leslie's memories of events are at a slight variance to mine. She had her viewpoints and experiences that had no bearing on my own, even when we were in the same place at the same time. I put my full effort into portraying the events I'm describing here as accurately as I can. My memory is imperfect on certain points, and I welcome other perspectives. I've borrowed her name for Marvin, our undercover suspect, rather than invent another pseudonym for him, as his actual name and identity elude me.

Here are some follow ups to our other White Panther characters:

JOHN IN THE JOINT

White Panther Party Chairman John Sinclair, who is serving a 10-year sentence for having 2 joints, has been thrown into solitary confinement and had his personal belongings taken away. The prison officials charged John with "Typing subversive and inflammatory" material (the Black Panther Party Program) and called him a "threat to the security and good order of the institution"

John has been singled out for punishment ever since his

conviction a year and a half ago. At Marquette Prison he was accused of being the "ringleader" behind a black inmates organization demanded a course in black studies at the prison school—the warden's proof was that John was the only prisoner intelligent enough to be able to organize anything. As punishment he was transferred to Jackson State Prison, where he has now been charged with organizing a prisoners' strike for a minimum wage of $1 a day, although he had already been in the hole for a week when the strike started. White Panther Party lawyers are preparing a suit charging the corrections department with violations of John's civil rights and demanding damages and restoration of normal prison conditions.

Chicago Seed Vol. 6, number 4, page 13, 3rd col. Under "ROACHES"

FREE JOHN RALLY
JOHN'S FREE!

John Sinclair, White Panther Party founder, revolutionary and poet, is FREE on bond after spending 29 months in jail for handing two joints to a narc. John was sentenced to ten years for two joints in an obvious attempt to stop his political organizing.

The Rainbow People's Party has worked for two years to get John out of prison. (Rainbow People's Party was formerly the White Panther Party). Every legal avenue was exhausted...

Newspaper accounts of John being released from prison didn't make any mention of recent events in Michigan, however. In early December, plans began for a massive FREE JOHN BENEFIT to be held in Ann Arbor. By December 9th the day before the benefit was scheduled to take place, the Michigan legislature reduced the penalties for possession of marijuana.

Few people in Chicago even heard about the December 10th FREE JOHN BENEFIT until December 9th. John Lennon and Yoko Ono were scheduled to be there, as were Black Panther Party Chairman Bobby Seale, Jerry Rubin, Rennie Davis, David Dellinger, Stevie Wonder, Phil Ochs, Father James Gropi, The UP, David Peel and many others...

The benefit was like a small Woodstock... good vibrations were everywhere... At one point in the program a telephone call was put through to John Sinclair in prison. It was hooked up to the arena's speaker system and John talked to his wife, Leni, and to his four-year-old son, Sunny....

(A)bout 2:30 a.m. Co-MC's Anne LaVasseur and Bob Rudnick asked everyone not to rush the stage and to be cool, John and Yoko were coming on. They walked on stage to a thunderous cheer...

"If he'd been a soldier man
Shooting gooks in Viet Nam
If he was the CIA
Selling dope and making hay
He'd be free, they'd let him be
Breathing air like you and me
They gave him ten for two!
What else can judge Columbo do?
We gotta gotta gotta
gotta gotta gotta gotta
gotta gotta gotta gotta
gotta set him free!
Then they sang a song about English imperialism...

The Rainbow People's Party had printed thousands of posters which were given away. Yoko Ono had printed a huge poster which carried the inscription "To my Sisters..." these too, were free....

Lennon had said that flower power didn't work, so it's time to try something else. And there was talk that John and Yoko would do more political rallies in the coming months.

It wasn't the rally, however, that freed John, but the months of hard work by hundreds of sisters and brothers. But it was certainly ironic that the Michigan legislature changed marijuana laws a day before the rally...

...John Sinclair wrote... "...The repressive nature of the capitalist state has been exposed and nothing can cover it back up again. History cannot be turned back."

"Free John Rally John's Free!" Vol. 7, number 13, page 13 of the Seed.

Bob Rudnick's obituary, on July 28, 1995, By Marla Donato, Chicago Tribune Staff Writer:

"He was quite a personality. An original. He never did anything by standard operating procedure," said his friend, Chicago attorney Paul Karoll. "Everywhere he went there was a wave. So he had a lot of jobs. He was the Johnny Appleseed of radio."

Born in Pottsville, Pa., Mr. Rudnick, was a deejay at several radio stations on the West and East Coasts, as well as in the Detroit and Chicago areas.

"He was the inventor of free-form radio," said Mr. Rudnick's former roommate and "River Rats" poetry partner, Chris Chandler. "He would combine the music of the Sun Ra (avant-garde jazz) Orchestra, (jazz saxophonist) John Coltrane, (punk rock groups) MC5 and the Velvet Underground with the spoken words of Malcolm X and Lenny Bruce interspersed with a heavy up-the-wall political message. He was very politically committed. That grew out of the anti-war, civil rights movement."

Besides his work at numerous radio stations, Mr. Rudnick held other jobs, including a stint as a Playboy magazine editor.

A frequent face at rock concerts, he was often called on to be the master of ceremonies at local events, particularly those staged at Chicago's Metro nightclub.

Mr. Rudnick is credited with helping to revive the Chicago poetry scene in the 1980s, in part by persuading several area taverns to sponsor poetry nights, according to Northwestern University journalism professor Abe Peck.

Survivors include his mother, Theresa; and a brother. Services for Mr. Rudnick will be held at 1 p.m. Friday at Ridgelawn Cemetery, 5736 N. Pulaski Rd.

55

WRAPPING UP

Moving ahead to 1972, long after the White Panther Party had been transformed into the Rainbow People's Party and another election year held out new hope, they joined others in the political left who rallied support for George McGovern as the best alternative candidate to Dick Nixon. This was because McGovern endorsed the three-point Peace Pledge of:

1) Halting US military action in SE Asia within 24 hours of inauguration.

2) All US personnel to be withdrawn within 90 days and

3) All military aid to "puppet regimes" will be cut off within 30 days.

Sinclair And The Grassroots in Good Times, Vol. 5, number 10, page 6, May 5, 1972.

But this was long after I'd moved out of the city and onto a commune in the wilds of Wisconsin. I voted for McGovern there, and even though he lost, I felt the tide was turning in our favor, and working within the system seemed to be a better strategy than armed insurrection.

Although I lost my connection to former White Panthers, I kept in occasional touch with Rising Up Angry comrades and others, who remain active in Chicago politics and the progressive cultural scene. Michael James is still a strong voice on his HEARTLAND RADIO program and a valuable supporter of progressive candidates in Chicago and the national and international scene.

The only updates I got on the other Chicago White Panthers in the next few years were the rare and unreliable rumors picked up from freaks I met on the road. I heard that Fuzzy had gone back to his hillbilly roots to become a Bible thumping, Jesus freak, but who still exhibited his switch-hitting, bisexual orientation. Schmitty passed away. Jeff is on Facebook, Chris claims to have a poor memory, but after we share a few beers together, he brings up things that parallel what I recall.

I still hope to locate Bill Johnson some day. His parents lived just north of Fischer's Woods and I stopped in to visit soon after the breakup. He wasn't home, but Bill's folks received me with courtesy and whether they agreed with him or not, seemed not to be put off by his politics.

Kay returned from Cuba. We had a sweet reunion, and I almost had a chance to have more with her. By that time I had made my mind up to get back to nature on an organic farm, but she was a big city girl and didn't want to go check it out, so we parted ways.

Life in the Wisconsin countryside fulfilled me for years, but the wheel keeps on turning and I got spun off in several directions, including a trek across North Africa and on to the Himalayas, where I almost became a monk. That story will follow soon enough if time and my lifespan allows.

As for our old White Panther house on LaSalle Street, I understand that it was renovated, rather than torn down, which warms my heart. That house has a long history in which our occupation formed only a small part. It and the buildings on either side are still recognizable in their newly remodeled life, unlike most of the rest of us survivors of that time.

Time changes us all. My hair is shorn now, and I've made many other compromises under the demands of the times, although I've always tried to be true to my core convictions of what the glorious revolution really means.

If anyone recognizes themselves or the events as mentioned here, I'd love to hear from you and compare notes and perceptions of our experiences, no matter which side you chose in that turbulent era. We once young rebels are lost to history now, all but forgotten in a strange new world ruled by cyber robots. But I have faith in our successors, brothers and sisters, daughters, sons and grandkids, whose flame will continue to light up the world. Bet on it!

SEIZE THE TIME! RIGHT ON!

RONALD SCHULZ

 RONALD SCHULZ was born in the nineteen-fifties in Chicago. He dropped out to explore the Sixties radical counterculture before hitchhiking across Europe and Africa on a roundabout Buddhist pilgrimage to Nepal. Now a semi-retired hobo, and a new author writing his honest history of those tumultuous times, he hopes to honor the memory of departed friends before he too vanishes from this planet. He has taken advanced writing classes at the University of Washington and Hugo House. Ronald is a father of two, grandfather of three, who believes in living life to the fullest, regardless of circumstances.

ALSO BY RONALD SCHULZ

Chicago Rage

Home at the Edge

Teenage Runaway (Coming in 2025)

If you enjoyed this work, please leave a rating on Goodreads and the platform where you purchased it. Your feedback helps the author and encourages them to write more works for your enjoyment.

www.ingramcontent.com/pod-product-compliance
Lightning Source LLC
Chambersburg PA
CBHW070914120626
46546CB00001B/257